ABOUT THIS PUBLICATION

FOR SERVICE ASSISTANCE

Customer Service
1.704.898.0770

North Carolina General Statues is published by The Muliti-Media Group of Greater Charlotte in Charlotte, North Carolina. Copyright 2015 by the Multi-Media Group of Greater Charlotte. This book or parts thereof may not be reproduced in any form, stored in a retrieval system, or transmitted in any form by any means—electronic, mechanical, photocopy, recording or otherwise—without prior written permission of the publisher, except as provided by United States of America copyright law.

The records required by U.S. Code 2257(a) through (c) and the pertinent regulations 28 C.F.R. Cli. 1, Part 75 with respect to this publication and all materials associated with such records are maintained by The Multi-Media Group of Greater Charlotte, Publisher and available for review by Attorney General.

www.visionbooks.org

Copyright © 2015 by MMGGC
All rights reserved!

TID: 5071814
ISBN (10) digit: 150298833X
ISBN (13) digit: 978-1502988331

123-4-56789-01239-Paperback
123-4-56789-01239 Hardback

First Edition

090520140547

Printed in the United States of America

2015 EDITION

North Carolina Criminal Law And Procedure-Pamphlet # 58

Printed In conjunction with the Administration of the Courts

North Carolina Criminal Law and Procedure
Pamphlet Reference Guide

Chapters	Pamphlet
Chapter 1 Civil Procedure	1
Chapter 1 Civil Procedure (Continue)	2
Chapter 1A Rules of Civil Procedure	2
Chapter 1B Contribution.	2
Chapter 1C Enforcement of Judgments.	2
Chapter 1D Punitive Damages.	2
Chapter 1E Eastern Band of Cherokee Indians.	2
Chapter 1F North Carolina Uniform Interstate Depositions and Discovery Act.	2
Chapter 2 - Clerk of Superior Court [Repealed and Transferred.]	3
Chapter 3 - Commissioners of Affidavits and Deeds [Repealed.]	3
Chapter 4 - Common Law	3
Chapter 5 - Contempt [Repealed.]	3
Chapter 5A - Contempt	3
Chapter 6 - Liability for Court Costs	3
Chapter 7 - Courts [Repealed and Transferred.]	3
Chapter 7A – Judicial Department	3
Chapter 7A – Continuation (Judicial Department)	4
Chapter 7A – Continuation (Judicial Department)	5
Chapter 7B - Juvenile Code	5
Chapter 8 - Evidence	6
Chapter 8A - Interpreters for Deaf Persons [Recodified.]	6
Chapter 8B - Interpreters for Deaf Persons	6
Chapter 8C - Evidence Code	6
Chapter 9 - Jurors	6
Chapter 10 - Notaries [Repealed.]	6
Chapter 10A - Notaries [Recodified.]	6
Chapter 10B - Notaries	6
Chapter 11 - Oaths	6
Chapter 12 - Statutory Construction	6
Chapter 13 - Citizenship Restored	6
Chapter 14 - Criminal Law	7
Chapter 14 –Criminal Law (Continuation)	8
Chapter 15 - Criminal Procedure	9
Chapter 15A - Criminal Procedure Act (Continuation)	10
Chapter 15A - Criminal Procedure Act (Continuation)	11
Chapter 15B - Victims Compensation	11
Chapter 15C - Address Confidentiality Program	11
Chapter 16 - Gaming Contracts and Futures	11
Chapter 17 - Habeas Corpus	11

Chapter 17A - Law-Enforcement Officers [Recodified.]	11
Chapter 17B - North Carolina Criminal Justice Education and Training System [Recodified.] Chapter 17C - North Carolina Criminal Justice Education and Training Standards Commission	11
Chapter 17D - North Carolina Justice Academy	11
Chapter 17E - North Carolina Sheriffs' Education and Training Standards Commission	11
Chapter 18 - Regulation of Intoxicating Liquors [Repealed.]	12
Chapter 18A - Regulation of Intoxicating Liquors [Repealed.]	12
Chapter 18B - Regulation of Alcoholic Beverages	12
Chapter 18C - North Carolina State Lottery	12
Chapter 19 - Offenses against Public Morals	12
Chapter 19A - Protection of Animals	12
Chapter 20 - Motor Vehicles	13
Chapter 20 - Motor Vehicles (Continuation)	14
Chapter 20 - Motor Vehicles (Continuation)	15
Chapter 20 - Motor Vehicles (Continuation)	16
Chapter 21 - Bills of Lading	17
Chapter 22 - Contracts Requiring Writing	17
Chapter 22A - Signatures	17
Chapter 22B - Contracts Against Public Policy	17
Chapter 22C - Payments to Subcontractors	17
Chapter 23 - Debtor and Creditor	17
Chapter 24 – Interest	17
Chapter 25 – Uniform Commercial Code	18
Chapter 25 – Uniform Commercial Code (Continuation)	19
Chapter 25A – Retail Installment Sales Act	20
Chapter 25B - Credit	20
Chapter 25C - Sales of Artwork	20
Chapter 26 - Suretyship	20
Chapter 27 - Warehouse Receipts [Repealed.]	20
Chapter 28 - Administration [Repealed.]	20
Chapter 28A - Administration of Decedents' Estates	20
Chapter 28B - Estates of Absentees in Military Service	20
Chapter 28C - Estates of Missing Persons	20
Chapter 29 - Intestate Succession	21
Chapter 30 Surviving Spouses	21
Chapter 31 - Wills	21
Chapter 31A - Acts Barring Property Rights	21
Chapter 31B - Renunciation of Property and Renunciation of Fiduciary Powers Act	21
Chapter 31C - Uniform Disposition of Community Property Rights at Death Act	21
Chapter 32 - Fiduciaries	21
Chapter 32A - Powers of Attorney	21
Chapter 33 - Guardian and Ward [Repealed and Recodified.]	21

Chapter 33A - North Carolina Uniform Transfers to Minors Act	21
Chapter 33B - North Carolina Uniform Custodial Trust Act	21
Chapter 34 - Veterans' Guardianship Act	22
Chapter 35 - Sterilization Procedures	22
Chapter 35A - Incompetency and Guardianship	22
Chapter 36 - Trusts and Trustees [Repealed.]	22
Chapter 36A - Trusts and Trustees	22
Chapter 36B - Uniform Management of Institutional Funds Act [Repealed.]	22
Chapter 36C - North Carolina Uniform Trust Code	22
Chapter 36D - North Carolina Community Third Party Trusts, Pooled Trusts	23
Chapter 36E - Uniform Prudent Management of Institutional Funds Act	23
Chapter 37 - Allocation of Principal and Income [Repealed.]	23
Chapter 37A - Uniform Principal and Income Act	23
Chapter 38 - Boundaries	23
Chapter 38A - Landowner Liability	23
Chapter 39 - Conveyances	23
Chapter 39A - Transfer Fee Covenants Prohibited	23
Chapter 40 - Eminent Domain [Repealed.]	23
Chapter 40A - Eminent Domain	23
Chapter 41 - Estates	23
Chapter 41A - State Fair Housing Act	23
Chapter 42 - Landlord and Tenant	23
Chapter 42A - Vacation Rental Act	23
Chapter 43 - Land Registration	23
Chapter 44 - Liens	24
Chapter 44A - Statutory Liens and Charges	24
Chapter 45 - Mortgages and Deeds of Trust	24
Chapter 45A - Good Funds Settlement Act	24
Chapter 46 - Partition	24
Chapter 47 - Probate and Registration	25
Chapter 47A - Unit Ownership	25
Chapter 47B - Real Property Marketable Title Act	25
Chapter 47C - North Carolina Condominium Act	25
Chapter 47D - Notice of Settlement Act [Expired.]	25
Chapter 47E - Residential Property Disclosure Act	25
Chapter 47F - North Carolina Planned Community Act	25
Chapter 47G - Option to Purchase Contracts	25
Chapter 47H - Contracts for Deed	25
Chapter 48 - Adoptions +	26
Chapter 48A - Minors	26
Chapter 49 - Bastardy	26
Chapter 49A - Rights of Children	26
Chapter 50 - Divorce and Alimony	26
Chapter 50A - Uniform Child-Custody Jurisdiction and	

Enforcement Act	26
Chapter 50B - Domestic Violence	26
Chapter 50C - Civil No-Contact Orders	26
Chapter 51 - Marriage	26
Chapter 52 - Powers and Liabilities of Married Persons	27
Chapter 52A - Uniform Reciprocal Enforcement of Support Act [Repealed.]	27
Chapter 52B - Uniform Premarital Agreement Act	27
Chapter 52C - Uniform Interstate Family Support Act	27
Chapter 53 - Banks	27
Chapter 53A - Business Development Corporations and North Carolina Capital Resource Corporations	28
Chapter 53B - Financial Privacy Act	28
Chapter 54 - Cooperative Organizations	28
Chapter 54A - Capital Stock Savings and Loan Associations [Repealed.]	28
Chapter 54B - Savings and Loan Associations	29
Chapter 54C - Savings Banks	29
Chapter 55 - North Carolina Business Corporation Act	30
Chapter 55A - North Carolina Nonprofit Corporation Act	31
Chapter 55B - Professional Corporation Act	31
Chapter 55C - Foreign Trade Zones	31
Chapter 55D - Filings, Names, and Registered Agents for Corporations, Nonprofit Corporations, and Partnerships	31
Chapter 56 - Electric, Telegraph and Power Companies [Repealed.]	31
Chapter 57 - Hospital, Medical and Dental Service Corporations [Recodified.]	31
Chapter 57A - Health Maintenance Organization Act [Recodified.]	31
Chapter 57B - Health Maintenance Organization Act [Recodified.]	31
Chapter 57C - North Carolina Limited Liability Company Act.	31
Chapter 58 - Insurance.	32
Chapter 58 - Insurance (Continuation)	33
Chapter 58 - Insurance (Continuation)	34
Chapter 58 - Insurance (Continuation)	35
Chapter 58 - Insurance (Continuation)	36
Chapter 58 - Insurance (Continuation)	37
Chapter 58 - Insurance (Continuation)	38
Chapter 58A - North Carolina Health Insurance Trust Commission [Recodified.]	38
Chapter 59 - Partnership.	39
Chapter 59B - Uniform Unincorporated Nonprofit Association Act.	39
Chapter 60 - Railroads and Other Carriers [Repealed and Transferred.]	39
Chapter 61 - Religious Societies	39
Chapter 62 - Public Utilities	39

Chapter 62 - Public Utilities (Continuation)	40
Chapter 62A - Public Safety Telephone Service And Wireless Telephone Service	40
Chapter 63 - Aeronautics	40
Chapter 63A - North Carolina Global TransPark Authority	40
Chapter 64 - Aliens	40
Chapter 65 – Cemeteries	40
Chapter 66 - Commerce and Business	41
Chapter 67 - Dogs	41
Chapter 68 - Fences and Stock Law	41
Chapter 69 - Fire Protection	41
Chapter 70 - Indian Antiquities, Archaeological Resources and Unmarked Human Skeletal Remains Protection	42
Chapter 71 - Indians [Repealed.]	42
Chapter 71A - Indians	42
Chapter 72 - Inns, Hotels and Restaurants	42
Chapter 73 - Mills	42
Chapter 74 - Mines and Quarries	42
Chapter 74A - Company Police [Repealed.]	42
Chapter 74B - Private Protective Services Act [Repealed.]	42
Chapter 74C - Private Protective Services	42
Chapter 74D - Alarm Systems	42
Chapter 74E - Company Police Act	42
Chapter 74F - Locksmith Licensing Act	42
Chapter 74G - Campus Police Act	42
Chapter 75 - Monopolies, Trusts and Consumer Protection	42
Chapter 75A - Boating and Water Safety	43
Chapter 75B - Discrimination in Business	43
Chapter 75C - Motion Picture Fair Competition Act	43
Chapter 75D - Racketeer Influenced and Corrupt Organizations	43
Chapter 75E - Unlawful Activities in Connection With Certain Corporate Transactions	43
Chapter 76 - Navigation	43
Chapter 76A - Navigation and Pilotage Commissions	43
Chapter 77 - Rivers, Creeks, and Coastal Waters	43
Chapter 78 - Securities Law [Repealed.]	43
Chapter 78A - North Carolina Securities Act	43
Chapter 78B - Tender Offer Disclosure Act [Repealed.]	43
Chapter 78C - Investment Advisers	43
Chapter 78D - Commodities Act	43
Chapter 79 - Strays [Repealed.]	43
Chapter 80 - Trademarks, Brands, etc.	44
Chapter 81 - Weights and Measures [Recodified.]	44
Chapter 81A - Weights and Measures Act of 1975.	44
Chapter 82 - Wrecks [Repealed.]	44
Chapter 83 - Architects [Recodified.]	44

Chapter 83A - Architects	44
Chapter 84 - Attorneys-at-Law	44
Chapter 84A - Foreign Legal Consultants	44
Chapter 85 - Auctions and Auctioneers [Repealed.]	44
Chapter 85A - Bail Bondsmen and Runners [Recodified.]	44
Chapter 85B - Auctions and Auctioneers	44
Chapter 85C - Bail Bondsmen and Runners [Recodified.]	44
Chapter 86 - Barbers [Recodified.]	44
Chapter 86A - Barbers	44
Chapter 87 - Contractors	44
Chapter 88 - Cosmetic Art [Repealed.]	44
Chapter 88A - Electrolysis Practice Act	44
Chapter 88B - Cosmetic Art	45
Chapter 89 - Engineering and Land Surveying [Recodified.]	45
Chapter 89A - Landscape Architects	45
Chapter 89B - Foresters	45
Chapter 89C - Engineering and Land Surveying	45
Chapter 89D - Landscape Contractors	45
Chapter 89E - Geologists Licensing Act	45
Chapter 89F - North Carolina Soil Scientist Licensing Act	45
Chapter 89G - Irrigation Contractors	45
Chapter 90 - Medicine and Allied Occupations	45
Chapter 90 - Medicine and Allied Occupations (Continuation)	46
Chapter 90 - Medicine and Allied Occupations (Continuation)	47
Chapter 90 - Medicine and Allied Occupations (Continuation)	48
Chapter 90A - Sanitarians and Water and Wastewater Treatment Facility Operators	48
Chapter 90B - Social Worker Certification and Licensure Act	48
Chapter 90C - North Carolina Recreational Therapy Licensure Act	48
Chapter 90D - Interpreters and Transliterators	48
Chapter 91 - Pawnbrokers [Repealed.]	48
Chapter 91A - Pawnbrokers Modernization Act of 1989	48
Chapter 92 - Photographers [Deleted.]	48
Chapter 93 - Certified Public Accountants	48
Chapter 93A - Real Estate License Law	49
Chapter 93B - Occupational Licensing Boards	49
Chapter 93C - Watchmakers [Repealed.]	49
Chapter 93D - North Carolina State Hearing Aid Dealers and Fitters Board.	49
Chapter 93E - North Carolina Appraisers Act	49
Chapter 94 - Apprenticeship	49
Chapter 95 - Department of Labor and Labor Regulations	49
Chapter 95 - Department of Labor and Labor Regulations (Continuation)	50
Chapter 96 - Employment Security	50
Chapter 97 - Workers' Compensation Act	50
Chapter 97 - Workers' Compensation Act (Continuation)	51

Chapter 98 - Burnt and Lost Records	51
Chapter 99 - Libel and Slander	51
Chapter 99A - Civil Remedies for Criminal Actions	51
Chapter 99B - Products Liability	51
Chapter 99C - Actions Relating to Winter Sports Safety and Accidents	51
Chapter 99D - Civil Rights	51
Chapter 99E - Special Liability Provisions	51
Chapter 100 - Monuments, Memorials and Parks	51
Chapter 101 - Names of Persons	51
Chapter 102 - Official Survey Base	51
Chapter 103 - Sundays, Holidays and Special Days	51
Chapter 104 - United States Lands	51
Chapter 104A - Degrees of Kinship	51
Chapter 104B - Hurricanes or Other Acts of Nature	51
Chapter 104C - Atomic Energy, Radioactivity and Ionizing Radiation [Repealed and Recodified.]	51
Chapter 104D - Southern States Energy Compact	51
Chapter 104E - North Carolina Radiation Protection Act	51
Chapter 104F - Southeast Interstate Low-Level Radioactive Waste Management Compact [Repealed]	51
Chapter 104G - North Carolina Low-Level Radioactive Waste Management Authority Act of 1987 [Repealed]	51
Chapter 105 - Taxation	51
Chapter 105 - Taxation (Continuation)	52
Chapter 105 - Taxation (Continuation)	53
Chapter 105 - Taxation (Continuation)	54
Chapter 105A - Setoff Debt Collection Act	55
Chapter 105B - Defaulted Student Loan Recovery Act	55
Chapter 106 - Agriculture	55
Chapter 106 - Agriculture (Continue)	56
Chapter 106 - Agriculture (Continue)	57
Chapter 107 - Agricultural Development Districts [Repealed.]	57
Chapter 108 - Social Services [Repealed and Recodified.]	57
Chapter 108A - Social Services	57
Chapter 108B - Community Action Programs	58
Chapter 108C Medicaid and Health Choice Provider Requirements.	58
Chapter 108D Medicaid Managed Care for Behavioral Health Services.	58
Chapter 109 - Bonds [Recodified.]	58
Chapter 110 - Child Welfare	58
Chapter 111 - Aid to the Blind	58
Chapter 112 - Confederate Homes and Pensions [Repealed.]	58
Chapter 113 - Conservation and Development	58
Chapter 113 - Conservation and Development (Continuation)	59

Chapter 113A - Pollution Control and Environment	59
Chapter 113A - Pollution Control and Environment (Continuation)	60
Chapter 113B - North Carolina Energy Policy Act of 1975	60
Chapter 114 - Department of Justice	60
Chapter 115 - Elementary and Secondary Education [Repealed.]	60
Chapter 115A - Community Colleges, Technical Institutes, and Industrial Education Centers [Repealed.]	60
Chapter 115B - Tuition and Fee Waivers	60
Chapter 115C - Elementary and Secondary Education	60
Chapter 115C - Elementary and Secondary Education (Continuation)	61
Chapter 115C - Elementary and Secondary Education (Continuation)	62
Chapter 115C - Elementary and Secondary Education (Continuation)	63
Chapter 115D - Community Colleges	63
Chapter 115E - Private Educational Facilities Finance Act [Recodified]	63
Chapter 116 - Higher Education	63
Chapter 116 - Higher Education (Continuation)	63
Chapter 116A - Escheats and Abandoned Property [Repealed.]	64
Chapter 116B - Escheats and Abandoned Property	64
Chapter 116C - Continuum of Education Programs	64
Chapter 116D - Higher Education Bonds	64
Chapter 117 - Electrification	64
Chapter 118 - Firemen's and Rescue Squad Workers' Relief and Pension Funds [Recodified.]	64
Chapter 118A - Firemen's Death Benefit Act [Repealed.]	64
Chapter 118B - Members of a Rescue Squad Death Benefit Act [Repealed.]	64
Chapter 119 - Gasoline and Oil Inspection and Regulation	64
Chapter 120 - General Assembly	65
Chapter 120 - General Assembly (Continuation)	66
Chapter 120 - General Assembly (Continuation)	67
Chapter 120C - Lobbying	67
Chapter 121 - Archives and History	67
Chapter 122 - Hospitals for the Mentally Disordered [Repealed.]	67
Chapter 122A - North Carolina Housing Finance Agency	67
Chapter 122B - North Carolina Agricultural Facilities Finance Act [Repealed.]	67
Chapter 122C - Mental Health, Developmental Disabilities, and Substance Abuse Act of 1985	67
Chapter 122C - Mental Health, Developmental Disabilities, and Substance Abuse Act of 1985 (Continuation)	68
Chapter 122D - North Carolina Agricultural Finance Act	68

Chapter 122E - North Carolina Housing Trust and Oil Overcharge Act	68
Chapter 123 - Impeachment	69
Chapter 123A - Industrial Development [Repealed.]	69
Chapter 124 - Internal Improvements	69
Chapter 125 - Libraries	69
Chapter 126 - State Personnel System	69
Chapter 127 - Militia [Repealed.]	69
Chapter 127A - Militia	69
Chapter 127B - Military Affairs	69
Chapter 127C - Advisory Commission on Military Affairs	69
Chapter 128 - Offices and Public Officers	69
Chapter 128 - Offices and Public Officers (Continuation)	70
Chapter 129 - Public Buildings and Grounds	70
Chapter 130 - Public Health [Repealed.]	70
Chapter 130A - Public Health	70
Chapter 130A - Public Health (Continuation)	71
Chapter 130A - Public Health (Continuation)	72
Chapter 130B - Hazardous Waste Management Commission [Repealed.]	72
Chapter 131 - Public Hospitals [Repealed.]	72
Chapter 131A - Health Care Facilities Finance Act	72
Chapter 131B - Licensing of Ambulatory Surgical Facilities [Repealed.]	72
Chapter 131C - Charitable Solicitation Licensure Act [Repealed.]	72
Chapter 131D - Inspection and Licensing of Facilities	72
Chapter 131E - Health Care Facilities and Services	72
Chapter 131E - Health Care Facilities and Services (Continuation)	73
Chapter 131F - Solicitation of Contributions	73
Chapter 132 - Public Records	73
Chapter 133 - Public Works	74
Chapter 134 - Youth Development [Recodified.]	74
Chapter 134A - Youth Services [Repealed.]	74
Chapter 135 - Retirement System for Teachers and State Employees; Social Security; Health Insurance Program for Children	74
Chapter 135 - Retirement System for Teachers and State Employees; Social Security; Health Insurance Program for Children	75
Chapter 136 - Transportation	75
Chapter 136 - Transportation (Continuation)	76
Chapter 137 - Rural Rehabilitation [Repealed.]	76
Chapter 138 - Salaries, Fees and Allowances	76
Chapter 138A - State Government Ethics Act	76
Chapter 139 - Soil and Water Conservation Districts	76

Chapter 140 - State Art Museum; Symphony and Art Societies	76
Chapter 140A - State Awards System	76
Chapter 141 - State Boundaries	76
Chapter 142 - State Debt	76
Chapter 143 - State Departments, Institutions, and Commissions	77
Chapter 143 - State Departments, Institutions, and Commissions (Continuation)	78
Chapter 143 - State Departments, Institutions, and Commissions (Continuation)	79
Chapter 143 - State Departments, Institutions, and Commissions (Continuation)	80
Chapter 143A - State Government Reorganization	80
Chapter 143B - Executive Organization Act of 1973	80
Chapter 143B - Executive Organization Act of 1973 (Continuation)	81
Chapter 143B - Executive Organization Act of 1973 (Continuation)	82
Chapter 143C - State Budget Act	83
Chapter 143D - The State Governmental Accountability and Internal Control Act	83
Chapter 144 - State Flag, Official Governmental Flags, Motto, and Colors	83
Chapter 145 - State Symbols and Other Official Adoptions.	83
Chapter 146 - State Lands	83
Chapter 147 - State Officers	83
Chapter 148 - State Prison System	84
Chapter 149 - State Song and Toast	84
Chapter 150 - Uniform Revocation of Licenses [Repealed.]	84
Chapter 150A - Administrative Procedure Act [Recodified.]	84
Chapter 150B - Administrative Procedure Act	84
Chapter 151 - Constables [Repealed.]	84
Chapter 152 - Coroners	84
Chapter 152A - County Medical Examiner [Repealed.]	84
Chapter 152A - County Medical Examiner [Repealed.] (Continuation)	85
Chapter 153 - Counties and County Commissioners [Repealed.]	85
Chapter 153A - Counties	85
Chapter 153B - Mountain Resources Planning Act	85
Chapter 153C - Uwharrie Regional Resources Act	85
Chapter 154 - County Surveyor [Repealed.]	85
Chapter 155 - County Treasurer [Repealed.]	85
Chapter 156 - Drainage	85
Chapter 156 – Drainage (Continuation)	86

Chapter 157 - Housing Authorities and Projects	86
Chapter 157A - Historic Properties Commissions [Transferred.]	86
Chapter 158 - Local Development	86
Chapter 159 - Local Government Finance	86
Chapter 159 - Local Government Finance (Continuation)	87
Chapter 159A - Pollution Abatement and Industrial Facilities Financing Act [Unconstitutional.]	87
Chapter 159B - Joint Municipal Electric Power and Energy Act	87
Chapter 159C - Industrial and Pollution Control Facilities Financing Act	87
Chapter 159D - The North Carolina Capital Facilities Financing Act	87
Chapter 159E - Registered Public Obligations Act	87
Chapter 159F - North Carolina Energy Development Authority [Repealed.]	87
Chapter 159G - Water Infrastructure	87
Chapter 159H - [Reserved.]	87
Chapter 159I - Solid Waste Management Loan Program and Local Government Special Obligation Bonds	87
Chapter 160 - Municipal Corporations [Repealed And Transferred.]	87
Chapter 160A - Cities and Towns	88
Chapter 160A - Cities and Towns (Continuation)	89
Chapter 160B - Consolidated City-County Act	89
Chapter 160C - Baseball Park Districts [Repealed.]	90
Chapter 161 - Register of Deeds	90
Chapter 162 - Sheriff	90
Chapter 162A - Water and Sewer Systems	90
Chapter 162B Continuity of Local Government in Emergency.	90
Chapter 163 Elections and Election Laws.	90
Chapter 163 Elections and Election Laws. (Continuation)	91
Chapter 164 Concerning the General Statutes of North Carolina.	92
Chapter 165 Veterans.	92
Chapter 166 Civil Preparedness Agencies [Repealed.]	92
Chapter 166A North Carolina Emergency Management Act.	92
Chapter 167 State Civil Air Patrol [Repealed.]	92
Chapter 168 Persons with Disabilities.	92
Chapter 168A Persons With Disabilities Protection Act.	92

Article 1.

[Reserved.]

§§ 108B-1 through 108B-20. Reserved for future codification purposes.
Chapter 108B.

Community Action Programs.

Article 2.

Community Action Partnership Act.

§ 108B-21. Short title.

This Article may be cited as the Community Action Partnership Act. (1983 (Reg. Sess., 1984), c. 1034, s. 111.1.; 1989 (Reg. Sess., 1990), c. 1004, s. 34(c).)

§ 108B-22. Purpose.

It is the purpose of this Article to provide financial assistance to Community Action Agencies and Limited Purpose Agencies (hereinafter referred to as "agency" or "agencies") to enable those agencies to effectively mobilize public and private resources in order to promote economic self-sufficiency among the poor of the State and to expand those services to all political subdivisions of the State. (1983 (Reg. Sess., 1984), c. 1034, s. 111.1.; 1989 (Reg. Sess., 1990), c. 1004, s. 34(c).)

§ 108B-23. Designation of administering agency powers and responsibilities.

(a) For purposes of this Article, "Department" means the Department of Health and Human Services and "Secretary" means the Secretary of Health and Human Services.

(b) The Department is directed to carry out the purposes and provisions of this Article. In carrying out this directive, the Secretary shall promulgate rules consistent with the purposes and provisions of this Article. (1983 (Reg. Sess.,

1984), c. 1034, s. 111.1; 1989, c. 727, s. 48; c. 751, ss. 7(9), 8(11a); 1989 (Reg. Sess., 1990), c. 1004, ss. 34(c), 35; 1997-443, s. 11A.118(a).)

§ 108B-24. Designation of eligible agencies.

The Secretary shall designate agencies to fulfill the requirements of this Article in the service areas governed by one or more units of local government. An agency so designated may be one of the following:

(1) Agencies which have been officially designated as community action agencies or limited purpose agencies pursuant to Section 210 of the Economic Opportunity Act of 1964, Public Law 88-452, 78 Stat. 508 and which have not lost their designation as a result of a failure to comply with the provisions of that act.

(2) Private nonprofit agencies designated by the chief elected official of a political subdivision or one or more political subdivisions, in areas not served by agencies as defined in subdivision (1) of this section on July 1, 1984. Agencies eligible under this subdivision must apply to the Secretary for designation 60 days in advance of the beginning date of their fiscal year. Political subdivisions designated under this section are authorized to join existing community action agencies contiguous with their boundaries or to organize their own community action agency in order to provide services pursuant to this Article. (1983 (Reg. Sess., 1984), c. 1034, s. 111.1; 1989 (Reg. Sess., 1990), c. 1004, s. 34(c).)

§ 108B-25. Activities of Community Action Agency.

Agencies shall serve as the local catalyst for the reduction of the causes, conditions, and effects of poverty and shall provide social and economic opportunities that foster self-sufficiency for low-income persons. As such, agencies designated pursuant to G.S. 108B-24(1) shall be sponsors of the Community Services Block Grant and any successor program thereto. (1983 (Reg. Sess., 1984), c. 1034, s. 111.1; 1989 (Reg. Sess., 1990), c. 1004, s. 34(c).)

§ 108B-26. Organization and authority.

(a) Agencies, as provided in G.S. 108B-24 shall have or be required to establish a governing board of directors which shall consist of not less than 15 nor more than 51 members. One-third of the members shall be low-income, elderly, or handicapped consumers residing in the service area of the agency. Consumer representatives shall be selected through a democratic process pursuant to guidelines established by the Department. Not less than one-third of the members of the board shall be appointed by the chief elected officials in the service area. The remaining positions on the board, if any, shall be filled by officials or members of business, industry, labor, religious, welfare, education, or civic organizations located in the service area.

(b) The board of directors shall be responsible for all of the following:

(1) The appointment and dismissal of an executive director.

(2) The approval of contracts, budgets, requests, and major modifications of budgets and contracts.

(3) The performance of an annual audit by certified public accountants to include all assets, liabilities, revenue, and expenditures.

(4) The establishment of policies for the operation of the agency.

(5) Annually advising the chief elected officials of the units of local government within the service area of the nature and extent of poverty within the area. Included in this annual report will be an assessment of the community action agency policies and programs and their impact on the problems of poverty in the service area.

(6) The convening of public meetings to provide low-income and other persons the opportunity to comment upon public policies and programs to reduce poverty. (1983 (Reg. Sess., 1984), c. 1034, s. 111.1; 1989 (Reg. Sess., 1990), c. 1004, s. 34(c).)

Chapter 108C.

Medicaid and Health Choice Provider Requirements.

§ 108C-1. Scope; applicability of this Chapter.
This Chapter applies to providers enrolled in Medicaid or Health Choice. (2011-399, s. 1.)

§ 108C-2. Definitions.

The following definitions apply in this Chapter:

(1) Adverse determination. - A final decision by the Department to deny, terminate, suspend, reduce, or recoup a Medicaid payment or to deny, terminate, or suspend a provider's or applicant's participation in the Medical Assistance Program.

(2) Applicant. - An individual, partnership, group, association, corporation, institution, or entity that applies to the Department for enrollment as a provider in the North Carolina Medical Assistance Program or the North Carolina Health Insurance Program for Children.

(3) Department. - The North Carolina Department of Health and Human Services, its legally authorized agents, contractors, or vendors who acting within the scope of their authorized activities, assess, authorize, manage, review, audit, monitor, or provide services pursuant to Title XIX or XXI of the Social Security Act, the North Carolina State Plan of Medical Assistance, the North Carolina State Plan of the Health Insurance Program for Children, or any waivers of the federal Medicaid Act granted by the United States Department of Health and Human Services.

(4) Division. - The Division of Medical Assistance of the Department.

(5) Final overpayment, assessment, or fine. - The amount the provider owes after appeal rights have been exhausted, which shall not include any agency decision that is being contested at the Department or the Office of Administrative Hearings or in Superior Court, provided that the Superior Court has entered a stay pursuant to the provisions of G.S. 150B-48.

(6) Health Choice. - The Health Insurance Program for Children authorized by G.S. 108A-70.25 and as set forth in the North Carolina State Plan of the Health Insurance Program for Children.

(7) Managing employee. - As defined in 42 C.F.R. § 455.101.

(8) Medicaid. - The Medical Assistance program authorized by G.S. 108A-54 and as set forth in the North Carolina State Plan of Medical Assistance.

(9) Owner and/or operator. - As defined in 42 C.F.R. § 455.101.

(10) Provider. - An individual, partnership, group, association, corporation, institution, or entity required to enroll in the North Carolina Medical Assistance Program or the North Carolina Health Insurance Program for Children to provide services, goods, supplies, or merchandise to a Medicaid or Health Choice recipient.

(11) Revalidation. - The reenrollment of a provider in the Medicaid or Health Choice programs as required under federal law. (2011-399, s. 1.)

§ 108C-3. Medicaid and Health Choice provider screening.

(a) Provider Screening. - The Department shall conduct provider screening of Medicaid and Health Choice providers in accordance with applicable State or federal law or regulation.

(b) Enrollment Screening. - The Department must screen all initial provider applications for enrollment in Medicaid and Health Choice, including applications for a new practice location, and all revalidation requests based on Department assessment of risk and assignment of the provider to a categorical risk level of "limited," "moderate," or "high." If a provider could fit within more than one risk level described in this section, the highest level of screening is applicable.

(c) Limited Categorical Risk Provider Types. - The following provider types are hereby designated as "limited" categorical risk:

(1) Ambulatory surgical centers.

(2) End-stage renal disease facilities.

(3) Federally qualified health centers.

(4) Health programs operated by an Indian Health Program (as defined in section 4(12) of the Indian Health Care Improvement Act) or an urban Indian

organization (as defined in section 4(29) of the Indian Health Care Improvement Act) that receives funding from the Indian Health Service pursuant to Title V of the Indian Health Care Improvement Act.

(5)   Histocompatibility laboratories.

(6)   Hospitals, including critical access hospitals, Department of Veterans Affairs Hospitals, and other State or federally owned hospital facilities.

(7)   Local Education Agencies.

(8)   Mammography screening centers.

(9)   Mass immunization roster billers.

(10)   Nursing facilities, including Intermediate Care Facilities for the Mentally Retarded.

(11)   Organ procurement organizations.

(12)   Physician or nonphysician practitioners (including nurse practitioners, CRNAs, physician assistants, physician extenders, occupational therapists, speech/language pathologists, chiropractors, and audiologists), optometrists, dentists and orthodontists, and medical groups or clinics.

(13)   Radiation therapy centers.

(14)   Rural health clinics.

(15)   Hearing aid dealers.

(16)   Portable X-ray suppliers.

(17)   Religious nonmedical health care institutions.

(18)   Registered dieticians.

(19)   Clearinghouses, billing agents, and alternate payees.

(20)   Local health departments.

(d)   When the Department designates a provider as a "limited" categorical level of risk, the Department shall conduct such screening functions as required by federal law.

(e)   Moderate Categorical Risk Provider Types. - The following provider types are hereby designated as "moderate" categorical risk:

(1)   Ambulance services.

(2)   Comprehensive outpatient rehabilitation facilities.

(3)   Critical Access Behavioral Health Agencies.

(4)   Repealed by Session Laws 2013-378, s. 6, effective October 1, 2013.

(5)   Hospice organizations.

(6)   Independent clinical laboratories.

(7)   Independent diagnostic testing facilities.

(8)   Pharmacy Services.

(9)   Physical therapists enrolling as individuals or as group practices.

(10)   Revalidating adult care homes delivering Medicaid-reimbursed services.

(11)   Revalidating agencies providing durable medical equipment, including, but not limited to, orthotics and prosthetics.

(12)   Revalidating agencies providing home or community-based services pursuant to waivers authorized by the federal Centers for Medicare and Medicaid Services under 42 U.S.C. § 1396n(c).

(13)   Revalidating agencies providing private duty nursing, home health, personal care services or in-home care services, or home infusion.

(14)   Nonemergency medical transportation.

(f)   When the Department designates a provider as a "moderate"' categorical level of risk, the Department shall conduct such screening functions as required by federal law and regulation.

(g)   High Categorical Risk Provider Types. - The following provider types are hereby designated as "high" categorical risk:

(1)   Prospective (newly enrolling) adult care homes delivering Medicaid-reimbursed services.

(2)   Agencies providing behavioral health services, excluding Critical Access Behavioral Health Agencies.

(3)   Directly enrolled outpatient behavioral health services providers.

(4)   Prospective (newly enrolling) agencies providing durable medical equipment, including, but not limited to, orthotics and prosthetics.

(5)   Agencies providing HIV case management.

(6)   Prospective (newly enrolling) agencies providing home or community-based services pursuant to waivers authorized by the federal Centers for Medicare and Medicaid Services under 42 U.S.C. § 1396n(c).

(7)   Prospective (newly enrolling) agencies providing personal care services or in-home care services.

(8)   Prospective (newly enrolling) agencies providing private duty nursing, home health, or home infusion.

(9)   Providers against whom the Department has imposed a payment suspension based upon a credible allegation of fraud in accordance with 42 C.F.R. § 455.23 within the previous 12-month period. The Department shall return the provider to its original risk category not later than 12 months after the cessation of the payment suspension.

(10)   Providers that were excluded, or whose owners, operators, or managing employees were excluded, by the U.S. Department of Health and Human Services Office of Inspector General or another state's Medicaid program within the previous 10 years.

(11) Providers who have incurred a Medicaid or Health Choice final overpayment, assessment, or fine to the Department in excess of twenty percent (20%) of the provider's payments received from Medicaid and Health Choice in the previous 12-month period. The Department shall return the provider to its original risk category not later than 12 months after the completion of the provider's repayment of the final overpayment, assessment, or fine.

(12) Providers whose owners, operators, or managing employees were convicted of a disqualifying offense pursuant to G.S. 108C-4 but were granted an exemption by the Department within the previous 10 years.

(h) When the Department designates a provider as a "high" categorical level of risk, the Department shall conduct such screening functions as required by federal law and regulation.

(i) For providers dually enrolled in the federal Medicare program and Medicaid, the Department may rely on the results of the provider screening performed by Medicare contractors.

(j) For out-of-state providers, the Department may rely on the results of the provider screening performed by the Medicaid agencies or Health Insurance Program for Children agencies of other states. (2011-399, s. 1; 2013-378, s. 6.)

§ 108C-4. Criminal history record checks for certain providers.

(a) The Department shall conduct criminal history records checks of provider applicants and enrolled providers in accordance with federal law and regulation.

(b) The Division shall deny enrollment or terminate the enrollment of a provider where any person with a five percent (5%) or greater direct or indirect ownership interest in the provider has been convicted of a criminal offense related to that person's involvement with the Medicare, Medicaid, or Health Choice program in the last 10 years, unless the Division determines that denial or termination of enrollment is not in the best interests of Medicaid and the State Medicaid agency documents that determination in writing. The Department shall honor civil and criminal settlement agreements entered into with a provider or any person with a five percent (5%) or greater direct or indirect ownership interest in the provider within 10 years of the effective date of this act.

(c) The Division may deny enrollment or terminate the enrollment of a provider subject to G.S. 108C-3(g) for any of the following offenses of the provider, an owner and/or operator, or employee if, after review of the seriousness, age, and other circumstances involving the offense, the Division determines it is in the best interest of the integrity of Medicaid or Health Choice to do so: any criminal offenses as set forth in any of the following Articles of Chapter 14 of the General Statutes: Article 5, Counterfeiting and Issuing Monetary Substitutes; Article 5A, Endangering Executive, Legislative, and Court Officers; Article 6, Homicide; Article 7A, Rape and Other Sex Offenses; Article 8, Assaults; Article 10, Kidnapping and Abduction; Article 13, Malicious Injury or Damage by Use of Explosive or Incendiary Device or Material; Article 14, Burglary and Other Housebreakings; Article 15, Arson and Other Burnings; Article 16, Larceny; Article 17, Robbery; Article 18, Embezzlement; Article 19, False Pretenses and Cheats; Article 19A, Obtaining Property or Services by False or Fraudulent Use of Credit Device or Other Means; Article 19B, Financial Transaction Card Crime Act; Article 20, Frauds; Article 21, Forgery; Article 26, Offenses Against Public Morality and Decency; Article 26A, Adult Establishments; Article 27, Prostitution; Article 28, Perjury; Article 29, Bribery; Article 31, Misconduct in Public Office; Article 35, Offenses Against the Public Peace; Article 36A, Riots and Civil Disorders; Article 39, Protection of Minors; Article 40, Protection of the Family; Article 59, Public Intoxication; and Article 60, Computer-Related Crime. The crimes also include possession or sale of drugs in violation of the North Carolina Controlled Substances Act, Article 5 of Chapter 90 of the General Statutes, and alcohol-related offenses such as sale to underage persons in violation of G.S. 18B-302, or driving while impaired in violation of G.S. 20-138.1 through G.S. 20-138.5. (2011-399, s. 1.)

§ 108C-5. Payment suspension and audits utilizing extrapolation.

(a) The Department may suspend payments to a provider in accordance with the requirements and procedures set forth in 42 C.F.R. § 455.23.

(b) In addition to the procedures for suspending payment set forth at 42 C.F.R. § 455.23, the Department may also suspend payment to any provider that (i) owes a final overpayment, assessment, or fine to the Department and has not entered into an approved payment plan with the Department or (ii) has had its participation in the Medicaid or Health Choice programs suspended or terminated by the Department. For purposes of this section, a suspension or termination of participation does not become final until all administrative appeal rights have been exhausted and shall not include any agency decision that is being contested at the Department or the Office of Administrative Hearings or in Superior Court provided that the Superior Court has entered a stay pursuant to the provisions of G.S. 150B-48.

(c)   For providers who owe a final overpayment, assessment, or fine to the Department, the payment suspension shall begin the thirty-first day after the overpayment, assessment, or fine becomes final. The payment suspension shall not exceed the amount owed to the Department, including any applicable penalty and interest charges.

(d)   Providers whose participation in the Medicaid or Health Choice programs has been suspended or terminated shall have all payments suspended beginning on the thirty-first day after the suspension or termination becomes final.

(e)   The Department shall consult with the N.C. Departments of Treasury and Revenue and other State departments and agencies to determine if a provider owes debts or fines to the State. The Department may collect any of these debts owed to the State subsequent to consideration by the Department of the financial impact upon the provider and the impact upon access to the services provided by the provider.

(f)   When issuing payment suspensions in accordance with this Chapter, the Department may suspend payment to all providers which share the same IRS Employee Identification Number or corporate parent as the provider or provider site location which owes the final overpayment, assessment, or fine. The Department shall give 30 days advance written notice to all providers which share the same IRS Employee Identification Number or corporate parent as the provider or provider site location of the intention of the Department to implement a payment suspension.

(g)   The Department is authorized to approve a payment plan for a provider to pay a final overpayment, assessment, or fine including interest and any penalty. The payment plan can include a term of up to 24 months. The Department shall establish in rule the conditions of such provider payment plans. Nothing in this subsection shall prevent the provider and the Department from mutually agreeing to modifications of a payment plan.

(h) All payments suspended in accordance with this Chapter shall be applied toward any final overpayment, assessment, or fine owed to the Department.

(i) Prior to extrapolating the results of any audits, the Department shall demonstrate and inform the provider that (i) the provider failed to substantially comply with the requirements of State or federal law or regulation or (ii) the Department has credible allegation of fraud concerning the provider.

(j) Audits that result in the extrapolation of results must be performed and reviewed by individuals who shall be credentialed by the Department, as applicable, in the matters to be audited, including, but not limited to, coding or specific clinical issues.

(k) The Department, prior to conducting audits that result in the extrapolation of results shall identify to the provider the matters to be reviewed and specifically list the clinical, including, but not limited to, assessment of medical necessity, coding, authorization, or other matters reviewed and the time periods reviewed.

(l) For those matters and time periods identified in subsection (k) of this section, the provider shall not be subject to further audits by the Department, unless the Department receives a credible allegation of fraud concerning the same time period or the federal government initiates action based on allegations of fraud or other illegal activity for the same time period.

(m) The Department may specify in rules the means by which a provider may conduct voluntary self-audits upon matters subject to audit by the Department. The Department has the authority to review the self-audit for compliance with requirements of State or federal law and regulation and may reject any self-audit conducted by a provider found not in compliance. Upon the provider's payment or payment agreement for any final overpayment, assessment, or fine arising from the provider's self-audit, the provider shall not be subject to further audits by the Department of the matters and time periods subject to the provider's self-audit, except where the Department has received a credible allegation of fraud or the federal government initiates action based on allegations of fraud or other illegal activity for the same time period.

(n) The results of audits that result in the extrapolation of results may be challenged by a provider within the limited or moderate risk categories, pursuant to G.S. 108C-3.

(1) The provider shall notify the Department within 15 days of receipt of the tentative audit results of the provider's challenge of the Department's results under this subsection. The provider's notification shall select the means of challenging the error rate found by the Department.

(2) The provider may challenge the error rate found by the Department by doing one of the following:

a. Conducting a one hundred percent (100%) file review of those matters and time periods identified in subsection (k) of this section and providing the results to the Department within 60 days from the date of the receipt of the Department's notice of tentative audit results.

b. Conducting a second audit upon a sample identified and produced by the Department utilizing the same statistical and sampling methodology to produce a sample twice the size of the original sample to review those matters and time periods identified in subsection (k) of this section. The Department shall provide a new sample to the provider within 30 days from the date of receipt of a provider's request. The provider shall have 60 days from receipt of the new sample to conduct the audit and provide the results to the Department.

(3) The results of an audit conducted by the provider pursuant to this subsection shall be binding upon the provider. The Department has the authority to review the provider's audit for compliance with the requirements of State and federal law and regulation and may reject any audit conducted by a provider pursuant to this subsection found not in compliance.

(4) Nothing in this subsection shall limit a provider from challenging the accuracy of the Department's audit, the statistical methodology of the Department's original sample, or the credentials of the individuals who performed and reviewed the audit.

(o) The Department shall permit limited correction of clerical, typographical, scrivener's, and computer errors by the provider prior to final determination of any audit.

(p) The provider shall have no less than 30 days from the date of the receipt of the Department's notice of tentative audit results to provide additional documentation not provided to the Department during any audit.

(q)   Except as required by federal agency, law, or regulation, or instances of credible allegation of fraud, the provider shall be subject to audits which result in the extrapolation of results for a time period of up to 36 months from date of payment of a provider's claim.

(r)   At least annually, the Department shall publish notice of the intention to use audits that result in the extrapolation of results upon its Web site. Such notice shall include the services, provider types, audit elements, and the time periods subject to audit.

(s)   Nothing in this Chapter shall be construed to prevent the Department from conducting unannounced or targeted audits of providers. (2011-399, s. 1.)

§ 108C-5.1. Post-payment review and recovery audit contracts.

The Department shall not pay contingent fees pursuant to any contract with an entity conducting Medicaid post-payment reviews or Recovery Audit Contractor (RAC) audits before all appeal rights have been exhausted. Any contingent fee for Medicaid post-payment reviews or RAC audits shall be calculated as a percentage of the amount of the final overpayment, as defined in G.S. 108C-2(5). The State share of the contingent fee paid for Medicaid post-payment reviews or RAC audits shall not exceed the State share of the amount actually recovered by the Department and applied to the final overpayment. (2013-360, s. 12H.16(b).)

§ 108C-6. Agents, clearinghouses, and alternate payees; registration required.

The Department is authorized to establish a registry of billing agents, clearinghouses, and/or alternate payees that submit claims on behalf of providers and to charge a fee to recover the costs of maintaining the registry in accordance with 42 U.S.C. § 1396a(a)(79) and implementing regulations. All billing agents, clearinghouses, or alternate payees shall register with the Department before submitting claims on behalf of providers or within six months of enactment of this Chapter, whichever is later. Any billing agent, clearinghouse, or alternate payee that fails to register with the Department prior to submitting claims on behalf of providers shall be excluded from the registry for a period not to exceed one year. (2011-399, s. 1.)

§ 108C-7. Prepayment claims review.

(a) In order to ensure that claims presented by a provider for payment by the Department meet the requirements of federal and State laws and regulations and medical necessity criteria, a provider may be required to undergo prepayment claims review by the Department. Grounds for being placed on prepayment claims review shall include, but shall not be limited to, receipt by the Department of credible allegations of fraud, identification of aberrant billing practices as a result of investigations or data analysis performed by the Department or other grounds as defined by the Department in rule.

(b) Providers shall not be entitled to payment prior to claims review by the Department. The Department shall notify the provider in writing of the decision and the process for submitting claims for prepayment claims review no less than 20 calendar days prior to instituting prepayment claims review. The notice shall contain the following:

(1) An explanation of the Department's decision to place the provider on prepayment claims review.

(2) A description of the review process and claims processing times.

(3) A description of the claims subject to prepayment claims review.

(4) A specific list of all supporting documentation that the provider will need to submit contemporaneously with the claims that will be subject to the prepayment claims review.

(5) The process for submitting claims and supporting documentation.

(6) The standard of evaluation used by the Department to determine when a provider's claims will no longer be subject to prepayment claims review.

(c) For any claims in which the Department has given prior authorization, prepayment review shall not include review of the medical necessity for the approved services.

(d) The Department shall process all clean claims submitted for prepayment review within 20 calendar days of submission by the provider. If the provider failed to provide any of the specifically requested supporting documentation necessary to process a claim pursuant to this section, the Department shall send to the provider written notification of the lacking or deficient documentation within 15 calendar days of receipt of such claim. The Department shall have an additional 20 days to process a claim upon receipt of the documentation.

(e) The provider shall remain subject to the prepayment claims review process until the provider achieves three consecutive months with a minimum seventy percent (70%) clean claims rate. If the provider does not meet this standard within six months of being placed on prepayment claims review, the Department may implement sanctions, including termination of the applicable Medicaid Administrative Participation Agreement, or continuation of prepayment review for an additional six-month period. The Department shall give adequate advance notice of any modification, suspension, or termination of the Medicaid Administrative Participation Agreement. In no instance shall prepayment claims review continue longer than 12 months.

(f) The decision to place or maintain a provider on prepayment claims review does not constitute a contested case under Chapter 150B of the General Statutes. A provider may not appeal or otherwise contest a decision of the Department to place a provider on prepayment review. (2011-399, s. 1.)

§ 108C-8. Threshold recovery amount.

The Department shall not pursue recovery of Medicaid or Health Choice overpayments owed to the State for any total amount less than one hundred fifty dollars ($150.00) unless directed to do so by the Centers for Medicare and Medicaid Services or unless such recovery would be cost-effective and in the best interest of the State of North Carolina and Medicaid recipients. (2011-399, s. 1.)

§ 108C-9. Provider enrollment criteria.

(a) Applicants who submit an initial application for enrollment in North Carolina Medicaid or North Carolina Health Choice shall be required to submit an attestation and complete trainings prior to being enrolled.

(b) The applicant's attestation shall contain a statement that the applicant's organization has met the minimum business requirements necessary to comply with all federal and State requirements governing the Medicaid and Children's Health Insurance programs, does not owe any outstanding taxes or fines to the U.S. or North Carolina Departments of Revenue or Labor or the Division of Employment Security (DES) of the Department of Commerce, does not owe any final overpayment, assessment, or fine to the North Carolina Medicaid or North Carolina Health Choice programs or any other State Medicaid or Children's Health Insurance program, and has implemented a corporate compliance program as required under federal law. The Department shall set forth by rule the minimum business requirements necessary to comply with all federal and State requirements governing the Medicaid and Children's Health Insurance Program.

(c) Prior to being initially enrolled in the North Carolina Medicaid or Health Choice programs, an applicant's representative shall attend trainings as designated by the Department in rules, including, but not limited to, the following:

(1) The Basic Medicaid Billing Guide, common billing errors, and how to avoid them.

(2) Audit procedures, including explanation of the process by which the Department extrapolates audit results.

(3) How to identify Medicaid recipient fraud.

(4) How to report suspected fraud or abuse.

(5) Medicaid recipient due process and appeal rights.

Online training shall be available for completion through the Department's Web site. The Department may charge a fee to recover costs of such trainings.

(d) Making any materially false or misleading statement in an attestation or enrollment application shall be grounds for denial, termination of, or permanent exclusion from enrollment in the North Carolina Medicaid or North Carolina Health Choice programs. (2011-399, s. 1; 2011-401, s. 5.1.)

§ 108C-10. Change of ownership and successor liability.

(a) For providers subject to this Chapter, any of the following occurrences shall constitute a change of ownership:

(1) In the case of a partnership, the removal, addition, or substitution of a partner, unless the partners expressly agree otherwise, as permitted by Chapter 59 of the General Statutes.

(2) In the case of a Limited Liability Company (LLC), the withdrawal or removal of a member, or when a person acquires a membership interest from the LLC or when a business entity converts or merges into the LLC pursuant to Chapter 57A of the General Statutes.

(3) In the case of an unincorporated sole proprietorship, the transfer of title and property of the provider that constitute the provider's business of providing services, goods, supplies, or merchandise to a Medicaid or Health Choice recipient to another party.

(4) The merger of the provider corporation into another corporation, or the consolidation of two or more corporations, resulting in the creation of a new corporation. Transfer of corporate stock or the merger of another corporation into the provider corporation shall not constitute change of ownership. Merger of related provider corporations shall not constitute a change in ownership.

(5) The lease of all or part of a provider's facility that will continue to be utilized for the provision of services, goods, supplies, or merchandise to a Medicaid or Health Choice recipient shall constitute a change of ownership of the leased portion.

(b) A provider must notify the Department at least 30 calendar days prior to the effective date of any change of ownership.

(c) An assigned Medicaid administrative participation or enrollment agreement shall be subject to all applicable statutes and regulations and to the terms and conditions under which it was originally issued including, but not limited to, both of the following:

(1) Any existing plan of correction.

(2) Payment of any outstanding final overpayments, assessments, or fines owed to the Department.

(d) The Department shall not as a condition of enrollment require a provider to accept an assigned Medicaid administrative participation or enrollment agreement upon a change in ownership. (2011-399, s. 1.)

§ 108C-11. Cooperation with investigations and audits.

(a) Providers shall cooperate with all announced and unannounced site visits, audits, investigations, post-payment reviews, or other program integrity activities conducted by the Department. Providers who fail to grant prompt and reasonable access or who fail to timely provide specifically designated documentation to the Department may be terminated from the North Carolina Medicaid or North Carolina Health Choice programs.

(b) The Department shall make all attempts to examine documentation without interfering with the clinical activities of the provider while conducting activities on the provider's premises.

(c) Nothing in this Chapter shall be construed to limit the ability of the federal government, the Centers for Medicare and Medicaid Services, the U.S. Department of Health and Human Services Office of Inspector General, the U.S. Department of Justice, or any of the foregoing entities' contractors or agents, to enforce federal requirements for the submission of documentation in response to an audit or investigation. (2011-399, s. 1.)

§ 108C-12. Appeals by Medicaid providers and applicants.

(a) General Rule. - Notwithstanding any provision of State law or rules to the contrary, this section shall govern the process used by a Medicaid provider or applicant to appeal an adverse determination made by the Department.

(b) Appeals. - Except as provided by this section, a request for a hearing to appeal an adverse determination of the Department under this section is a contested case subject to the provisions of Article 3 of Chapter 150B of the General Statutes.

(c) Final Decision. - The Office of Administrative Hearings shall make a final decision within 180 days of the date of filing of the appeal with the Office of

Administrative Hearings. The time to make a final decision shall be extended in the event of delays caused or requested by the Department.

(d) Burden of Proof. - The Department shall have the burden of proof in appeals of Medicaid providers or applicants concerning an adverse determination. (2011-399, s. 1.)

§ 108C-13. Certain waivers of Medicaid and Health Choice co-payments prohibited.

(a) No provider that has obtained a permit pursuant to G.S. 90-85.21 or G.S. 90-85-21A shall waive the collection of co-payments owed by recipients of Medicaid and Health Choice, as required by the respective program, with the intent to induce recipients to purchase, lease, or order items or services from the permitted provider. For enforcement purposes, a permitted provider that waives a co-payment owed by a recipient of Medicaid or Health Choice is in violation of this subsection regardless of the monetary amount that is waived by the permitted provider. A permitted provider shall not be in violation of this subsection if the provider waives a co-payment owed by a recipient of Medicaid or Health Choice for any of the following reasons:

(1) The waiver is authorized under the Medical Assistance Program or the North Carolina Health Insurance Program for Children.

(2) The permitted provider determines on an individual basis that the collection of the co-payment amount would create a substantial financial hardship for the recipient, provided the waiver of co-payments is not a regular business practice of the provider. For the purposes of this subdivision, a provider shall be considered engaged in the regular business practice of waiving co-payments if the permitted provider holds himself or herself out to recipients as waiving required co-payments.

(3) The permitted provider has made a good-faith effort to collect the co-payment amount, but the permitted provider's reasonable collection efforts fail.

(4) The permitted provider is a health care facility regulated pursuant to Chapter 131E or Chapter 122C of the General Statutes or that is owned or operated by the State of North Carolina.

(b) A violation of this section shall result in suspension or termination by the Department of a permitted provider's participation in Medicaid and Health Choice in accordance with administrative sanctions and remedial measures established by the Department for violations of this section. (2013-145, s. 1.)

§ 108C-14. Provider performance bonds.

(a) Subject to the provisions of this section, the Department may require Medicaid-enrolled providers to purchase a performance bond in an amount not to exceed one hundred thousand dollars ($100,000) naming as beneficiary the Department of Health and Human Services, Division of Medical Assistance, or provide to the Department a validly executed letter of credit or other financial instrument issued by a financial institution or agency honoring a demand for payment in an equivalent amount. The Department may require the purchase of a performance bond or the submission of an executed letter of credit or financial instrument as a condition of initial enrollment, reenrollment, recredentialing, or reinstatement if any of the following are true:

(1) The provider fails to demonstrate financial viability.

(2) The Department determines there is significant potential for fraud and abuse.

(3) The Department otherwise finds it is in the best interest of the Medicaid program to do so.

The Department shall specify the circumstances under which a performance bond or executed letter of credit will be required.

(b) The Department may waive or limit the requirements of subsection (a) of this section for individual Medicaid-enrolled providers or for one or more classes of Medicaid-enrolled providers based on the following:

(1) The provider's or provider class's dollar amount of monthly billings to Medicaid.

(2) The length of time an individual provider has been licensed, endorsed, certified, or accredited in this State to provide services.

(3) The length of time an individual provider has been enrolled to provide Medicaid services in this State.

(4) The provider's demonstrated ability to ensure adequate record keeping, staffing, and services.

(5) The need to ensure adequate access to care.

In waiving or limiting requirements of this section, the Department shall take into consideration the potential fiscal impact of the waiver or limitation on the State Medicaid Program. The Department shall provide to the affected provider written notice of the findings upon which its action is based and shall include the performance bond requirements and the conditions under which a waiver or limitation apply. (2013-360, s. 12H.17(a).)

Chapter 108D.

Medicaid Managed Care for Behavioral Health Services.

Article 1.

General Provisions.

§ 108D-1. Definitions.

The following definitions apply in this Chapter, unless the context clearly requires otherwise:

(1) Applicant. - A provider of mental health, intellectual or developmental disabilities, and substance abuse services who is seeking to participate in the closed network of one or more local management entity/managed care organizations.

(2) Closed network. - The network of providers that have contracted with a local management entity/managed care organization to furnish mental health, intellectual or developmental disabilities, and substance abuse services to enrollees.

(3) Contested case hearing. - The hearing or hearings conducted at the Office of Administrative Hearings under G.S. 108D-15 to resolve a dispute

between an enrollee and a local management entity/managed care organization about a managed care action.

(4) Department. - The North Carolina Department of Health and Human Services.

(5) Emergency medical condition. - As defined in 42 C.F.R. § 438.114.

(6) Emergency services. - As defined in 42 C.F.R. § 438.114.

(7) Enrollee. - A Medicaid beneficiary who is currently enrolled with a local management entity/managed care organization.

(8) Local Management Entity or LME. - As defined in G.S. 122C-3(20b).

(9) Local Management Entity/Managed Care Organization or LME/MCO. - As defined in G.S. 122C-3(20c).

(10) Managed care action. - An action, as defined in 42 C.F.R. § 438.400(b).

(11) Managed Care Organization or MCO. - As defined in 42 C.F.R. § 438.2.

(12) Mental health, intellectual or developmental disabilities, and substance abuse services or MH/IDD/SA services. - Those mental health, intellectual or developmental disabilities, and substance abuse services covered under a contract in effect between the Department of Health and Human Services and a local management entity to operate a managed care organization or prepaid inpatient health plan (PIHP) under the 1915(b)/(c) Medicaid Waiver approved by the federal Centers for Medicare and Medicaid Services (CMS).

(13) Network provider. - An appropriately credentialed provider of mental health, intellectual or developmental disabilities, and substance abuse services that has entered into a contract for participation in the closed network of one or more local management entity/managed care organizations.

(14) Notice of managed care action. - The notice required by 42 C.F.R. § 438.404.

(15) Notice of resolution. - The notice described in 42 C.F.R. § 438.408(e).

(16) OAH. - The North Carolina Office of Administrative Hearings.

(17)   Prepaid Inpatient Health Plan or PIHP. - As defined in 42 C.F.R. § 438.2.

(18)   Provider of emergency services. - A provider that is qualified to furnish emergency services to evaluate or stabilize an enrollee's emergency medical condition. (2013-397, s. 1.)

§ 108D-2. Scope; applicability of this Chapter.

This Chapter applies to every LME/MCO and to every applicant, enrollee, provider of emergency services, and network provider of an LME/MCO. (2013-397, s. 1.)

§ 108D-3. Conflicts; severability.

(a)   To the extent that this Chapter conflicts with the Social Security Act or 42 C.F.R. Part 438, federal law prevails.

(b)   To the extent that this Chapter conflicts with any other provision of State law that is contrary to the principles of managed care that will ensure successful containment of costs for behavioral health care services, this Chapter prevails and applies.

(c)   If any section, term, or provision of this Chapter is adjudged invalid for any reason, these judgments shall not affect, impair, or invalidate any other section, term, or provision of this Chapter, but the remaining sections, terms, and provisions shall be and remain in full force and effect. (2013-397, s. 1.)

§ 108D-4: Reserved for future codification purposes.

§ 108D-5: Reserved for future codification purposes.

§ 108D-6: Reserved for future codification purposes.

§ 108D-7: Reserved for future codification purposes.

§ 108D-8: Reserved for future codification purposes.

§ 108D-9: Reserved for future codification purposes.

§ 108D-10: Reserved for future codification purposes.

Article 2.

Enrollee Grievances and Appeals.

§ 108D-11. LME/MCO grievance and appeal procedures, generally.

(a) Each LME/MCO shall establish and maintain internal grievance and appeal procedures that (i) comply with the Social Security Act and 42 C.F.R. Part 438, Subpart F, and (ii) afford enrollees, and network providers authorized in writing to act on behalf of enrollees, constitutional rights to due process and a fair hearing.

(b) Enrollees, or network providers authorized in writing to act on behalf of enrollees, may file requests for grievances and LME/MCO level appeals orally or in writing. However, unless the enrollee or network provider requests an expedited appeal, the oral filing must be followed by a written, signed grievance or appeal.

(c) An LME/MCO shall not attempt to influence, limit, or interfere with an enrollee's right or decision to file a grievance, request for an LME/MCO level appeal, or a contested case hearing. However, nothing in this Chapter shall be construed to prevent an LME/MCO from doing any of the following:

(1) Offering an enrollee alternative services.

(2) Engaging in clinical or educational discussions with enrollees or providers.

(3) Engaging in informal attempts to resolve enrollee concerns prior to the issuance of a notice of grievance disposition or notice of resolution.

(d) An LME/MCO shall not take punitive action against a provider for any of the following:

(1) Filing a grievance on behalf of an enrollee or supporting an enrollee's grievance.

(2) Requesting an LME/MCO level appeal on behalf of an enrollee or supporting an enrollee's request for an LME/MCO level appeal.

(3) Requesting an expedited LME/MCO level appeal on behalf of an enrollee or supporting an enrollee's request for an LME/MCO level expedited appeal.

(4) Requesting a contested case hearing on behalf of an enrollee or supporting an enrollee's request for a contested case hearing. (2013-397, s. 1.)

§ 108D-12. LME/MCO grievances.

(a) Filing of Grievance. - An enrollee, or a network provider authorized in writing to act on behalf of an enrollee, has the right to file a grievance with an LME/MCO at any time to express dissatisfaction about any matter other than a managed care action. Upon receipt of a grievance, an LME/MCO shall cause a written acknowledgment of receipt of the grievance to be sent by United States mail.

(b) Notice of Grievance Disposition. - The LME/MCO shall resolve the grievance and cause a notice of grievance disposition to be sent by United States mail to the enrollee and all other affected parties as expeditiously as the enrollee's health condition requires, but no later than 90 days after receipt of the grievance.

(c) Right to LME/MCO Level Appeal. - There is no right to appeal the resolution of a grievance to OAH or any other forum. (2013-397, s. 1.)

§ 108D-13. Standard LME/MCO level appeals.

(a) Notice of Managed Care Action. - An LME/MCO shall provide an enrollee with written notice of a managed care action by United States mail as required under 42 C.F.R. § 438.404. The notice of action will employ a standardized form included as a provision in the contracts between the LME/MCOs and the Department of Health and Human Services.

(b) Request for Appeal. - An enrollee, or a network provider authorized in writing to act on behalf of the enrollee, has the right to file a request for an LME/MCO level appeal of a notice of managed care action no later than 30 days after the mailing date of the grievance disposition or notice of managed care action. Upon receipt of a request for an LME/MCO level appeal, an LME/MCO shall acknowledge receipt of the request for appeal in writing by United States mail.

(c) Continuation of Benefits. - An LME/MCO shall continue the enrollee's benefits during the pendency of an LME/MCO level appeal to the same extent required under 42 C.F.R. § 438.420.

(d) Notice of Resolution. - The LME/MCO shall resolve the appeal as expeditiously as the enrollee's health condition requires, but no later than 45 days after receiving the request for appeal. The LME/MCO shall provide the enrollee and all other affected parties with a written notice of resolution by United States mail within this 45-day period.

(e) Right to Request Contested Case Hearing. - An enrollee, or a network provider authorized in writing to act on behalf of an enrollee, may file a request for a contested case hearing under G.S. 108D-15 as long as the enrollee or network provider has exhausted the appeal procedures described in this section or G.S. 108D-14.

(f) Request Form for Contested Case Hearing. - In the same mailing as the notice of resolution, the LME/MCO shall also provide the enrollee with an appeal request form for a contested case hearing that meets the requirements of G.S. 108D-15(f). (2013-397, s. 1.)

§ 108D-14. Expedited LME/MCO level appeals.

(a) Request for Expedited Appeal. - When the time limits for completing a standard appeal could seriously jeopardize the enrollee's life or health or ability to attain, maintain, or regain maximum function, an enrollee, or a network provider authorized in writing to act on behalf of an enrollee, has the right to file a request for an expedited appeal of a managed care action no later than 30 days after the mailing date of the notice of managed care action. For expedited appeal requests made by enrollees, the LME/MCO shall determine if the enrollee qualifies for an expedited appeal. For expedited appeal requests made by network providers on behalf of enrollees, the LME/MCO shall presume an expedited appeal is necessary.

(b)   Notice of Denial for Expedited Appeal. - If the LME/MCO denies a request for an expedited LME/MCO level appeal, the LME/MCO shall make reasonable efforts to give the enrollee and all other affected parties oral notice of the denial and follow up with written notice of denial by United States mail by no later than two calendar days after receiving the request for an expedited appeal. In addition, the LME/MCO shall resolve the appeal within the time limits established for standard LME/MCO level appeals in G.S. 108D-13.

(c)   Continuation of Benefits. - An LME/MCO shall continue the enrollee's benefits during the pendency of an expedited LME/MCO level appeal to the extent required under 42 C.F.R. § 438.420.

(d)   Notice of Resolution. - If the LME/MCO grants a request for an expedited LME/MCO level appeal, the LME/MCO shall resolve the appeal as expeditiously as the enrollee's health condition requires, and no later than three working days after receiving the request for an expedited appeal. The LME/MCO shall provide the enrollee and all other affected parties with a written notice of resolution by United States mail within this three-day period.

(e)   Right to Request Contested Case Hearing. - An enrollee, or a network provider authorized in writing to act on behalf of an enrollee, may file a request for a contested case hearing under G.S. 108D-15 as long as the enrollee or network provider has exhausted the appeal procedures described in G.S. 108D-13 or this section.

(f)   Reasonable Assistance. - An LME/MCO shall provide the enrollee with reasonable assistance in completing forms and taking other procedural steps necessary to file an appeal, including providing interpreter services and toll-free numbers that have adequate teletypewriter/telecommunications devices for the deaf (TTY/TDD) and interpreter capability.

(g) Request Form for Contested Case Hearing. - In the same mailing as the notice of resolution, the LME/MCO shall also provide the enrollee with an appeal request form for a contested case hearing that meets the requirements of G.S. 108D-15(f). (2013-397, s. 1.)

§ 108D-15. Contested case hearings on disputed managed care actions.

(a) Jurisdiction of the Office of Administrative Hearings. - The Office of Administrative Hearings does not have jurisdiction over a dispute concerning a managed care action, except as expressly set forth in this Chapter.

(b) Exclusive Administrative Remedy. - Notwithstanding any provision of State law or rules to the contrary, this section is the exclusive method for an enrollee to contest a notice of resolution issued by an LME/MCO. G.S. 108A-70.9A, 108A-70.9B, and 108A-70.9C do not apply to enrollees contesting a managed care action.

(c) Request for Contested Case Hearing. - A request for an administrative hearing to appeal a notice of resolution issued by an LME/MCO is a contested case subject to the provisions of Article 3 of Chapter 150B of the General Statutes. An enrollee, or a network provider authorized in writing to act on behalf of an enrollee, has the right to file a request for appeal to contest a notice of resolution as long as the enrollee or network provider has exhausted the appeal procedures described in G.S. 108D-13 or G.S. 108D-14.

(d) Filing Procedure. - An enrollee, or a network provider authorized in writing to act on behalf of an enrollee, may file a request for an appeal by sending an appeal request form that meets the requirements of subsection (e) of this section to OAH and the affected LME/MCO by no later than 30 days after the mailing date of the notice of resolution. A request for appeal is deemed filed when a completed and signed appeal request form has been both submitted into the care and custody of the chief hearings clerk of OAH and accepted by the chief hearings clerk. Upon receipt of a timely filed appeal request form, information contained in the notice of resolution is no longer confidential, and the LME/MCO shall immediately forward a copy of the notice of resolution to OAH electronically. OAH may dispose of these records after one year.

(e) Parties. - The LME/MCO shall be the respondent for purposes of this appeal. The LME/MCO or enrollee may move for the permissive joinder of the

Department under Rule 20 of the North Carolina Rules of Civil Procedure. The Department may move to intervene as a necessary party under Rules 19 and 24 of the North Carolina Rules of Civil Procedure.

(f) Appeal Request Form. - In the same mailing as the notice of resolution, the LME/MCO shall also provide the enrollee with an appeal request form for a contested case hearing which shall be no more than one side of one page. The form shall include at least all of the following:

(1) A statement that in order to request an appeal, the enrollee must file the form in accordance with OAH rules, by mail or fax to the address or fax number listed on the form, by no later than 30 days after the mailing date of the notice of resolution.

(2) The enrollee's name, address, telephone number, and Medicaid identification number.

(3) A preprinted statement that indicates that the enrollee would like to appeal a specific managed care action identified in the notice of resolution.

(4) A statement informing the enrollee of the right to be represented at the contested case hearing by a lawyer, a relative, a friend, or other spokesperson.

(5) A space for the enrollee's signature and date.

(g) Continuation of Benefits. - An LME/MCO shall continue the enrollee's benefits during the pendency of an appeal to the same extent required under 42 C.F.R. § 438.420. Notwithstanding any other provision of State law, the administrative law judge does not have the power to order and shall not order an LME/MCO to continue benefits in excess of what is required by 42 C.F.R. § 438.420.

(h) Simple Procedures. - Notwithstanding any other provision of Article 3 of Chapter 150B of the General Statutes, the chief administrative law judge of OAH may limit and simplify the administrative hearing procedures that apply to contested case hearings conducted under this section in order to complete these cases as expeditiously as possible. Any simplified hearing procedures approved by the chief administrative law judge under this subsection must comply with all of the following requirements:

(1)   OAH shall schedule and hear cases by no later than 55 days after receipt of a request for a contested case hearing.

(2)   OAH shall conduct all contested case hearings telephonically or by video technology with all parties, unless the enrollee requests that the hearing be conducted in person before the administrative law judge. An in-person hearing shall be conducted in the county that contains the headquarters of the LME/MCO unless the enrollee's impairments limit travel. For enrollees with impairments that limit travel, an in-person hearing shall be conducted in the enrollee's county of residence. OAH shall provide written notice to the enrollee of the use of telephonic hearings, hearings by video conference, and in-person hearings before the administrative law judge, as well as written instructions on how to request a hearing in the enrollee's county of residence.

(3)   The administrative law judge assigned to hear the case shall consider and rule on all prehearing motions prior to the scheduled date for a hearing on the merits.

(4)   The administrative law judge may allow brief extensions of the time limits imposed in this section only for good cause shown and to ensure that the record is complete. The administrative law judge shall only grant a continuance of a hearing in accordance with rules adopted by OAH for good cause shown and shall not grant a continuance on the day of a hearing, except for good cause shown. If an enrollee fails to make an appearance at a hearing that has been properly noticed by OAH by United States mail, OAH shall immediately dismiss the case, unless the enrollee moves to show good cause by no later than three business days after the date of dismissal. As used in this section, "good cause shown" includes delays resulting from untimely receipt of documentation needed to render a decision and other unavoidable and unforeseen circumstances.

(5)   OAH shall include information on at least all of the following in its notice of hearing to an enrollee:

a.   The enrollee's right to examine at a reasonable time before and during the hearing the contents of the enrollee's case file and any documents to be used by the LME/MCO in the hearing before the administrative law judge.

b.   The enrollee's right to an interpreter during the hearing process.

c. The circumstances in which a medical assessment may be obtained at the LME/MCO's expense and made part of the record, including all of the following:

1. A hearing involving medical issues, such as a diagnosis, an examining physician's report, or a decision by a medical review team.

2. A hearing in which the administrative law judge considers it necessary to have a medical assessment other than the medical assessment performed by an individual involved in any previous level of review or decision making.

(i) Mediation. - Upon receipt of an appeal request form as provided by G.S. 108D-15(f) or other clear request for a hearing by an enrollee, OAH shall immediately notify the Mediation Network of North Carolina, which shall contact the enrollee within five days to offer mediation in an attempt to resolve the dispute. If mediation is accepted, the mediation must be completed within 25 days of submission of the request for appeal. Upon completion of the mediation, the mediator shall inform OAH and the LME/MCO within 24 hours of the resolution by facsimile or electronic messaging. If the parties have resolved matters in the mediation, OAH shall dismiss the case. OAH shall not conduct a hearing of any contested case involving a dispute of a managed care action until it has received notice from the mediator assigned that either (i) the mediation was unsuccessful, (ii) the petitioner has rejected the offer of mediation, or (iii) the petitioner has failed to appear at a scheduled mediation. Nothing in this subsection shall restrict the right to a contested case hearing.

(j) Burden of Proof. - The enrollee has the burden of proof on all issues submitted to OAH for a contested case hearing under this section and has the burden of going forward. The administrative law judge shall not make any ruling on the preponderance of evidence until the close of all evidence in the case.

(k) New Evidence. - The enrollee shall be permitted to submit evidence regardless of whether it was obtained before or after the LME/MCO's managed care action and regardless of whether the LME/MCO had an opportunity to consider the evidence in resolving the LME/MCO level appeal. Upon the receipt of new evidence and at the request of the LME/MCO, the administrative law judge shall continue the hearing for a minimum of 15 days and a maximum of 30 days in order to allow the LME/MCO to review the evidence. Upon reviewing the evidence, if the LME/MCO decides to reverse the managed care action taken against the enrollee, it shall immediately inform the administrative law judge of its decision.

(l) Issue for Hearing. - For each managed care action, the administrative law judge shall determine whether the LME/MCO substantially prejudiced the rights of the enrollee and whether the LME/MCO, based upon evidence at the hearing:

(1) Exceeded its authority or jurisdiction.

(2) Acted erroneously.

(3) Failed to use proper procedure.

(4) Acted arbitrarily or capriciously.

(5) Failed to act as required by law or rule.

(m) To the extent that anything in this Part, Chapter 150B of the General Statutes, or any rules or policies adopted under these Chapters is inconsistent with the Social Security Act or 42 C.F.R. Part 438, Subpart F, federal law prevails and applies to the extent of the conflict. All rules, rights, and procedures for contested case hearings concerning managed care actions shall be construed so as to be consistent with federal law and shall provide the enrollee with no lesser and no greater rights than those provided under federal law. (2013-397, s. 1.)

§ 108D-16. Notice of final decision and right to seek judicial review.

The administrative law judge assigned to conduct a contested case hearing under G.S. 108D-15 shall hear and decide the case without unnecessary delay. The judge shall prepare a written decision that includes findings of fact and conclusions of law and send it to the parties in accordance with G.S. 150B-37. The written decision shall notify the parties of the final decision and of the right of the enrollee and the LME/MCO to seek judicial review of the decision under Article 4 of Chapter 150B of the General Statutes. (2013-397, s. 1.)

Chapter 109.

Bonds.

§§ 109-1 through 109-41: Recodified as Articles 72 to 77 of Chapter 58.

Chapter 110.

Child Welfare.

Article 1.

Child Labor Regulations.

§§ 110-1 through 110-20. Repealed by Session Laws 1979, c. 839, s. 2.

Article 1A.

Exhibition of Children.

§ 110-20.1. Exhibition of certain children prohibited.

(a)   Except to the extent otherwise provided in subsection (d) of this section, it is unlawful to exhibit publicly for any purpose, or to exhibit privately for the purpose of entertainment, or solely or primarily for the satisfaction of the curiosity of any observer, any child under the age of 18 years who is mentally ill or mentally retarded or who presents the appearance of having any deformity or unnatural physical formation or development, whether or not the exhibiting of the child is in return for a monetary or other consideration.

(b)   It is unlawful to employ, use, have custody of, or in any way be associated with any child described in subsection (a) for the purpose of an exhibition forbidden therein, or for one who has the care, custody or control of the child as a parent, relative, guardian, employer or otherwise, to neglect or refuse to restrain the child from participating in the exhibition.

(c)   It is unlawful to procure or arrange for, or participate in procuring or arranging for, anything made unlawful by subsections (a) and (b).

(d)   This section does not apply to the transmission of an image by television by a duly licensed television station, or to any exhibition by a federal, State, county or municipal government, or political subdivision or agency thereof, or to any exhibition by any corporation, unincorporated association, or other organization organized and operated exclusively for religious, charitable, or educational purposes, no part of the net earnings of which inures to the benefit of any private shareholder or individual.

(e)   Any violation of this Article shall be a Class 3 misdemeanor. Each day during which any violation of this Article continues after notice to the violator, from any county social services director, to cease and desist from any violation of this section shall constitute a separate and distinct offense. Any act or omission forbidden by this Article shall, with respect to each child described therein constitute a separate and distinct offense. (1969, c. 457, s. 1; c. 982; 1993, c. 539, s. 821; 1994, Ex. Sess., c. 24, s. 14(c).)

Article 2.

Juvenile Services.

§ 110-21: Repealed by Session Laws 1973, c. 1339, s. 2.

§ 110-21.1. Repealed by Session Laws 1969, c. 911, s. 1.

§ 110-22: Repealed by Session Laws 1979, c. 815, s. 2.

§ 110-22.1: Repealed by Session Laws 1969, c. 911, s. 1.

§ 110-23: Repealed by Session Laws 1998-202, s. 1(a).

§ 110-23.1. Repealed by Session Laws 1979, c. 815, s. 2.

§ 110-24: Repealed by Session Laws 1979, c. 815, s. 2.

§ 110-25. Repealed by Session Laws 1969, c. 911, s 1.

§ 110-25.1. Transferred to § 130-58.1 by Session Laws 1969, c. 911, s. 3.

§§ 110-26 through 110-38. Repealed by Session Laws 1969, c. 911, s. 1.

§110-39. Transferred to § 14-316.1 by Session Laws 1969, c. 911, s. 4.

§§ 110-40 through 110-44: Repealed by Session Laws 1969, c. 911, s. 1.

Article 2A.

Parental Control of Children.

§§ 110-44.1 through 110-44.4. Repealed by Session Laws 1998-202, s. 5, effective July 1, 1999.

Article 3.

Control over Child-Caring Facilities.

§ 110-45. Institution has authority of parent or guardian.

Every indigent child which may be placed in any orphanage, children's home, or child-placing institution in this State, which shall be an institution existing under and by virtue of the laws of this State, shall be under the control of the authorities of such institution so long as, under the rules and regulations of such institution, the child is entitled to remain in the same. The authority of the institution shall be the same as that of a parent or guardian before the child was placed in the institution; but such authority shall extend only to the person of the child. (1917, c. 133, s. 1; C.S., s. 5063.)

§ 110-46. Regulations of institution not abrogated.

Nothing in this Article shall be construed in any way to abrogate any of the rules and regulations of such institutions insofar as the rules and regulations have for their purpose the welfare and protection of the institutions. (1917, c. 133, s. 2; C.S., s. 5064.)

§ 110-47. Enticing a child from institution.

It is unlawful for any person to entice or attempt to entice, persuade, harbor, or conceal, or in any manner induce any indigent child to leave any of the institutions hereinbefore mentioned without the knowledge or consent of the authorities of such institutions. But this Article shall not interfere with a mother's right to her child in case she becomes able to sustain her child; and the county commissioners in the county in which she resides shall in case of doubt have authority to recommend to the institution concerning the child. (1917, c. 133, s. 3; C.S., s. 5065.)

§ 110-48. Violation a misdemeanor.

Any person violating any of the provisions of G.S. 110-45, 110-46 and 110-47 shall be guilty of a Class 1 misdemeanor. (1917, c. 133, s. 4; C.S., s. 5066; 1993, c. 539, s. 822; 1994, Ex. Sess., c. 24, s. 14(c).)

§ 110-49: Repealed by Session Laws 1983, c. 637, s. 3.

Article 4.

Placing or Adoption of Juvenile Delinquents or Dependents.

§§ 110-50 through 110-57: Repealed by Session Laws 1998, c. 202, s. 5.

Article 4A.

Interstate Compact on the Placement of Children.

§§ 110-57.1 through 110-57.7: Repealed by Session Laws 1998, c. 202, s. 5.

Article 5.

Interstate Compact on Juveniles.

§§ 110-58 through 110-64.5: Repealed by Session Laws 1979, c. 815, s. 2.

Article 5A.

Interstate Parole and Probation Hearing Procedures for Juveniles.

§§ 110-64.6 through 110-64.9: Repealed by Session Laws 1979, c. 815, s. 2.

Article 6.

Governor's Advocacy Council on Children and Youth.

§§ 110-65 through 110-66: Repealed by Session Laws 1977, c. 872, s. 7.

§§ 110-67 through 110-70. Repealed by Session Laws 1973, c. 476, s. 182.

§ 110-71. Repealed by Session Laws 1977, c. 872, s. 7.

§ 110-72. Repealed by Session Laws 1973, c. 476, s. 182.

§§ 110-73 through 110-84. Reserved for future codification purposes.

Article 7.

Child Care Facilities.

§ 110-85. Legislative intent and purpose.

Recognizing the importance of the early years of life to a child's development, the General Assembly hereby declares its intent with respect to the early care and education of children:

(1)   The State should protect children in child care facilities by ensuring that these facilities provide a physically safe and healthy environment where the developmental needs of these children are met and where these children are cared for by qualified persons of good moral character.

(2)   Repealed by Session Laws 1997-506, s. 2, effective September 16, 1997.

(3)   Achieving this level of protection and early education requires the following elements: mandatory licensing of child care facilities; promotion of higher quality child care through the development of enhanced standards which operators may comply with on a voluntary basis; and a program of education to help operators improve their programs and to deepen public understanding of child care needs and issues. (1971, c. 803, s. 1; 1987, c. 788, s. 1; 1997-506, ss. 1, 2.)

§ 110-86. Definitions.

Unless the context or subject matter otherwise requires, the terms or phrases used in this Article shall be defined as follows:

(1)   Commission. - The Child Care Commission created under this Article.

(2)   Child care. - A program or arrangement where three or more children less than 13 years old, who do not reside where the care is provided, receive care on a regular basis of at least once per week for more than four hours but less than 24 hours per day from persons other than their guardians or full-time custodians, or from persons not related to them by birth, marriage, or adoption. Child care does not include the following:

a.   Arrangements operated in the home of any child receiving care if all of the children in care are related to each other and no more than two additional children are in care;

b.   Recreational programs operated for less than four consecutive months in a year;

c. Specialized activities or instruction such as athletics, dance, art, music lessons, horseback riding, gymnastics, or organized clubs for children, such as Boy Scouts, Girl Scouts, 4-H groups, or boys and girls clubs;

d. Drop-in or short-term care provided while parents participate in activities that are not employment related and where the parents are on the premises or otherwise easily accessible, such as drop-in or short-term care provided in health spas, bowling alleys, shopping malls, resort hotels, or churches;

d1. Drop-in or short-term care provided by an employer for its part-time employees where (i) the child is provided care not to exceed two and one-half hours during that day, (ii) the parents are on the premises, and (iii) there are no more than 25 children in any one group in any one room;

e. Public schools;

f. Nonpublic schools described in Part 2 of Article 39 of Chapter 115C of the General Statutes that are accredited by national or regional accrediting agencies with early childhood standards and that operate a child care facility as defined in subdivision (3) of this section for less than six and one-half hours per day either on or off the school site;

g. Bible schools conducted during vacation periods;

h. Care provided by facilities licensed under Article 2 of Chapter 122C of the General Statutes;

i. Cooperative arrangements among parents to provide care for their own children as a convenience rather than for employment; and

j. Any child care program or arrangement consisting of two or more separate components, each of which operates for four hours or less per day with different children attending each component.

(2a) Child care administrator. - A person who is responsible for the operation of a child care facility and is on-site on a regular basis.

(3) Child care facility. - Includes child care centers, family child care homes, and any other child care arrangement not excluded by G.S. 110-86(2), that provides child care, regardless of the time of day, wherever operated, and whether or not operated for profit.

a. A child care center is an arrangement where, at any one time, there are three or more preschool-age children or nine or more school-age children receiving child care.

b. A family child care home is a child care arrangement located in a residence where, at any one time, more than two children, but less than nine children, receive child care.

(4) Repealed by Session Laws 1997-506, s. 3.

(4a) Department. - Department of Health and Human Services.

(5) Repealed by Session Laws 1975, c. 879, s. 15.

(5a) Lead teacher. - An individual who is responsible for planning and implementing the daily program of activities for a group of children in a child care facility.

(6) License. - A permit issued by the Secretary to any child care facility which meets the statutory standards established under this Article.

(7) Operator. - Includes the owner, director or other person having primary responsibility for operation of a child care facility subject to licensing.

(8) Secretary. - The Secretary of the Department of Health and Human Services. (1971, c. 803, s. 1; 1975, c. 879, s. 15; 1977, c. 4, ss. 1-3; 1983, c. 46, s. 1; c. 297, ss. 1, 2; 1983 (Reg. Sess., 1984), c. 1034, s. 78; 1985, c. 589, s. 36; c. 757, s. 155(c); 1987, c. 788, s. 2; 1989, c. 234; 1991, c. 273, s. 1; 1991 (Reg. Sess., 1992), c. 904, ss. 1, 2; c. 1024, s. 1; c. 1030, s. 51.12; 1997-443, ss. 11A.118(a), 11A.122; 1997-506, s. 3; 2005-416, s. 1; 2013-360, s. 8.29(b).)

§ 110-87. Repealed by Session Laws 1975, c. 879, s. 15.

§ 110-88. Powers and duties of the Commission.

The Commission shall have the following powers and duties:

(1)   To develop policies and procedures for the issuance of a license to any child care facility that meets all applicable standards established under this Article.

(1a)   To adopt applicable rules and standards based upon the capacity of a child care facility.

(2)   To require inspections by and satisfactory written reports from representatives of local or State health agencies, fire and building inspection agencies, and from representatives of the Department prior to the issuance of an initial license to any child care center.

(2a)   To require annually, inspections by and satisfactory written reports from representatives of local or State health agencies and fire inspection agencies after a license is issued.

(3)   Repealed by Session Laws 1997-506, s. 4.

(4)   Repealed by Session Laws 1975, c. 879, s. 15.

(5)   To adopt rules and develop policies for implementation of this Article, including procedures for application, approval, annual compliance visits for centers, and revocation of licenses.

(6)   To adopt rules for the issuance of a provisional license that shall be in effect for no more than 12 consecutive months to a child care facility that does not conform in every respect with the standards established in this Article and rules adopted by the Commission pursuant to this Article but that is making a reasonable effort to conform to the standards.

(6a)   To adopt rules for administrative action against a child care facility when the Secretary's investigations pursuant to G.S. 110-105(a)(3) substantiate that child abuse or neglect did occur in the facility. The rules shall provide for types of sanctions which shall depend upon the severity of the incident and the probability of reoccurrence. The rules shall also provide for written warnings and special provisional licenses.

(7)   To develop and adopt voluntary enhanced program standards which reflect higher quality child care than the mandatory standards established by this Article. These enhanced program standards must address, at a minimum, staff/child ratios, staff qualifications, parent involvement, operational and

personnel policies, developmentally appropriate curricula, and facility square footage.

(8) To develop a procedure by which the Department shall furnish those forms as may be required for implementation of this Article.

(9) Repealed by Session Laws 1985, c. 757, s. 156(66).

(10) To adopt rules for the issuance of a temporary license which shall expire in six months and which may be issued to the operator of a new center or to the operator of a previously licensed center when a change in ownership or location occurs.

(11) To adopt rules for child care facilities which provide care for children who are mildly sick.

(12) To adopt rules regulating the amount of time a child care administrator shall be on-site at a child care center.

(13) To adopt rules for child care facilities that provide care for medically fragile children.

(14) To adopt rules establishing standards for certification of child care centers providing Developmental Day programs.

The Division and the Commission shall permit individual facilities to make curriculum decisions and may not require the standards, policies, or curriculum of any single accrediting child care organization. If Division inquiries to providers include database fields or questions regarding accreditation, the inquiry shall permit daycare providers to fill in any accrediting organization from which they have received accreditation. (1971, c. 803, s. 1; 1975, c. 879, s. 15; 1985, c. 757, s. 155(d), (e), 156(a), (z), (aa), (bb); 1987, c. 543, s. 2; c. 788, s. 3; c. 827, s. 232; 1991, c. 273, s. 2; 1993, c. 185, s. 1; 1997-506, ss. 4(a), 28.3; 1999-130, ss. 1, 5; 2004-124, s. 10.35; 2009-187, s. 2.)

§ 110-88.1. Commission may not interfere with religious training offered in religious-sponsored child care facilities.

Nothing in this Article shall be interpreted to allow the State to determine the training or curriculum offered in any religious-sponsored child care facility as defined in G.S. 110-106(a). (1999-130, s. 6.)

§ 110-89. Repealed by Session Laws 1975, c. 879, s. 15.

§ 110-90. Powers and duties of Secretary of Health and Human Services.

The Secretary shall have the following powers and duties under the policies and rules of the Commission:

(1)   To administer the licensing program for child care facilities.

(1a)   To establish a fee for the licensing of child care facilities. The fee does not apply to a religious-sponsored child care facility operated pursuant to a letter of compliance. The amount of the fee may not exceed the amount listed in this subdivision.

Capacity of Facility	Maximum Fee
12 or fewer children	$ 52.00
13-50 children	$187.00
51-100 children	$375.00
101 or more children	$600.00

(2)   To obtain and coordinate the necessary services from other State departments and units of local government which are necessary to implement the provisions of this Article.

(3)   To employ the administrative personnel and staff as may be necessary to implement this Article where required services, inspections or reports are not available from existing State agencies and units of local government.

(4)   To issue a rated license to any child care facility which meets the standards established by this Article. The rating shall be based on the following:

a. Before January 1, 2008, for any child care facility currently holding a license of two to five stars, the rating shall be based on program standards, education levels of staff, and compliance history of the child care facility. By January 1, 2008, the rating shall be based on program standards and education levels of staff.

b. Effective January 1, 2006, for any new license issued to a child care facility with a rating of two to five stars, the rating shall be based on program standards and education levels of staff.

c. By January 1, 2008, for any child care facility to maintain a license or Notice of Compliance, the child care facility shall have a compliance history of at least seventy-five percent (75%), as assessed by the Department. When a child care facility fails to maintain a compliance history of at least seventy-five percent (75%) for the past 18 months or during the length of time the facility has operated, whichever is less, as assessed by the Department, the Department may issue a provisional license or Notice of Compliance.

d. Effective January 1, 2006, for any new license or Notice of Compliance issued to a child care facility, the facility shall maintain a compliance history of at least seventy-five percent (75%), as assessed by the Department. When a child care facility fails to maintain a compliance history of at least seventy-five percent (75%) for the past 18 months or during the length of time the facility has operated, whichever is less, as assessed by the Department, the Department may issue a provisional license or Notice of Compliance.

e. The Department shall provide additional opportunities for child care providers to earn points for program standards and education levels of staff.

(5) To revoke the license of any child care facility that ceases to meet the standards established by this Article and rules on these standards adopted by the Commission, or that demonstrates a pattern of noncompliance with this Article or the rules, or to deny a license to any applicant that fails to meet the standards or the rules. These revocations and denials shall be done in accordance with the procedures set out in G.S. 150B and this Article and rules adopted by the Commission.

(6) To prosecute or defend on behalf of the State, through the office of the Attorney General, any legal actions arising out of the administration or enforcement of this Article.

(7) To promote and coordinate educational programs and materials for operators of child care facilities which are designed to improve the quality of child care available in the State, using the resources of other State and local agencies and educational institutions where appropriate.

(8) Repealed by Session Laws 1997-506, s. 5.

(9) To levy a civil penalty pursuant to G.S. 110-103.1, or an administrative penalty pursuant to G.S. 110-102.2, or to order summary suspension of a license. These actions shall be done in accordance with the procedures set out in G.S. 150B and this Article and rules adopted by the Commission.

(10) To issue final agency decisions in all G.S. 150B contested cases proceedings filed as a result of actions taken under this Article including, but not limited to the denial, revocation, or suspension of a license or the levying of a civil or administrative penalty.

(11) To issue a license to any child care arrangement that does not meet the definition of child care facility in G.S. 110-86 whenever the operator of the arrangement chooses to comply with the requirements of this Article and the rules adopted by the Commission and voluntarily applies for a child care facility license. The Commission shall adopt rules for the issuance or removal of the licenses.

Notwithstanding any other provision of law, rules adopted by the Commission regarding a public school that voluntarily applies for a child care facility license shall provide that a classroom that meets the standards set out in G.S. 115C-521.1 shall satisfy child care facility licensure requirements as related to the physical classroom. (1971, c. 803, s. 1; 1975, c. 879, s. 15; 1985, c. 757, ss. 155(g), 156(cc), (dd); 1987, c. 788, s. 4; c. 827, s. 233; 1991, c. 273, s. 3; 1993, c. 185, s. 2; 1997-443, s. 11A.118(a); 1997-506, s. 5; 2003-284, s. 34.12(a); 2005-36, s. 1; 2009-123, s. 2; 2009-451, s. 10.11.)

§ 110-90.1: Repealed by Session Laws 1997-506, s. 6.

§ 110-90.2. Mandatory child care providers' criminal history checks.

(a) For purposes of this section:

(1) "Child care", notwithstanding the definition in G.S. 110-86, means any child care provided in child care facilities required to be licensed or regulated under this Article and nonlicensed child care homes approved to receive or receiving State or federal funds for providing child care.

(2) "Child care provider" means a person who:

a. Is employed by or seeks to be employed by a child care facility providing child care as defined in subdivision (1) of this subsection, whether in temporary or permanent capacity, including substitute providers;

b. Owns or operates or seeks to own or operate a child care facility or nonlicensed child care home providing child care as defined in subdivision (1) of this subsection; or

c. Is a member of the household in a family child care home, nonlicensed child care home, or child care center in a residence and who is over 15 years old, including family members and nonfamily members who use the home on a permanent or temporary basis as their place of residence.

(3) "Criminal history" means a county, state, or federal criminal history of conviction or pending indictment of a crime or criminal charge, whether a misdemeanor or a felony, that bears upon an individual's fitness to have responsibility for the safety and well-being of children. Such crimes include, but are not limited to, the following North Carolina crimes contained in any of the following Articles of Chapter 14 of the General Statutes: Article 6, Homicide; Article 7A, Rape and Kindred Offenses; Article 8, Assaults; Article 10, Kidnapping and Abduction; Article 13, Malicious Injury or Damage by Use of Explosive or Incendiary Device or Material; Article 14, Burglary; Article 16, Larceny; Article 17, Robbery; Article 19, False Pretenses and Cheats; Article 19A, Obtaining Property or Services by False or Fraudulent Use of Credit Device or Other Means; Article 19C, Identity Theft; Article 26, Offenses Against Public Morality and Decency; Article 27, Prostitution; Article 29, Bribery; Article 35, Offenses Against the Public Peace; Article 36A, Riots and Civil Disorders; Article 39, Protection of Minors; Article 40, Protection of the Family; Article 52, Miscellaneous Police Regulations; and Article 59, Public Intoxication. Such crimes also include cruelty to animals in violation of Article 3 of Chapter 19A of the General Statutes, possession or sale of drugs in violation of the North Carolina Controlled Substances Act, Article 5 of Chapter 90 of the General Statutes, and alcohol-related offenses such as sale to underage persons in violation of G.S. 18B-302 or driving while impaired in violation of G.S. 20-138.1

through G.S. 20-138.5. In addition to the North Carolina crimes listed in this subdivision, such crimes also include similar crimes under federal law or under the laws of other states.

(4) "Substitute provider" means a person who temporarily assumes the duties of a staff person for a time period not to exceed two consecutive months and may or may not be monetarily compensated by the facility.

(5) "Uncompensated provider" means a person who works in a child care facility and is counted in staff/child ratio or has unsupervised contact with children, but who is not monetarily compensated by the facility.

(a1) No person shall be a child care provider or uncompensated child care provider who has been any of the following:

(1) Convicted of a misdemeanor or a felony crime involving child neglect or child abuse.

(2) Adjudicated a "responsible individual" under G.S. 7B-807(a1).

(3) Convicted of a "reportable conviction" as defined under G.S. 14-208.6(4).

(b) Effective January 1, 1996, the Department shall ensure that, prior to employment and every three years thereafter, the criminal history of all child care providers is checked and a determination is made of the child care provider's fitness to have responsibility for the safety and well-being of children based on the criminal history. The Department shall ensure that all child care providers are checked for county, State, and federal criminal histories.

(b1) The Department may prevent an individual from being a child care provider if the Department determines that the individual is a habitually excessive user of alcohol, illegally uses narcotic or other impairing drugs, or is mentally or emotionally impaired to an extent that may be injurious to children.

(c) The Department of Justice shall provide to the Division of Child Development, Department of Health and Human Services, the criminal history from the State and National Repositories of Criminal Histories of any child care provider as requested by the Division.

The Division shall provide to the Department of Justice, along with the request, the fingerprints of the provider to be checked, any additional information required by the Department of Justice, and a form consenting to the check of the criminal record and to the use of fingerprints and other identifying information required by the repositories signed by the child care provider to be checked. The fingerprints of the provider shall be forwarded to the State Bureau of Investigation for a search of their criminal history record file and the State Bureau of Investigation shall forward a set of fingerprints to the Federal Bureau of Investigation for a federal criminal history record check.

At the time of application the child care provider whose criminal history is to be checked shall be furnished with a statement substantially similar to the following:

NOTICE

CHILD CARE PROVIDER

MANDATORY CRIMINAL HISTORY CHECK

NORTH CAROLINA LAW REQUIRES THAT A CRIMINAL HISTORY RECORD CHECK BE CONDUCTED ON ALL PERSONS WHO PROVIDE CHILD CARE IN A LICENSED CHILD CARE FACILITY, AND ALL PERSONS PROVIDING CHILD CARE IN NONLICENSED CHILD CARE HOMES THAT RECEIVE STATE OR FEDERAL FUNDS.

"Criminal history" means a county, state, or federal criminal history of conviction, pending indictment of a crime, or criminal charge, whether a misdemeanor or a felony, that bears on an individual's fitness to have responsibility for the safety and well-being of children. Such crimes include, but are not limited to, the following North Carolina crimes contained in any of the following Articles of Chapter 14 of the General Statutes: Article 6, Homicide; Article 7A, Rape and Kindred Offenses; Article 8, Assaults; Article 10, Kidnapping and Abduction; Article 13, Malicious Injury or Damage by Use of Explosive or Incendiary Device or Material; Article 14, Burglary; Article 16, Larceny; Article 17, Robbery; Article 19, False Pretenses and Cheats; Article 19A, Obtaining Property or Services by False or Fraudulent Use of Credit Device or Other Means; Article 19C, Identity Theft; Article 26, Offenses Against Public Morality and Decency; Article 27, Prostitution; Article 29, Bribery; Article 35, Offenses Against the Public Peace; Article 36A, Riots and Civil Disorders; Article 39, Protection of Minors; Article 40, Protection of the Family; and Article 59, Public Intoxication. Such crimes also include cruelty to animals in violation of Article 3 of Chapter 19A of the General Statutes, violation of the North Carolina Controlled Substances Act, Article 5 of Chapter 90 of the General Statutes, and alcohol-related offenses such as sale to underage persons in violation of G.S. 18B-302 or driving while impaired in violation of G.S. 20-138.1 through G.S. 20-138.5. In addition to the North Carolina crimes listed in this notice, such crimes also include similar crimes under federal law or under the laws of other states. Your fingerprints will be used to check the criminal history records of the State Bureau of Investigation (SBI) and the Federal Bureau of Investigation (FBI).

If it is determined, based on your criminal history, that you are unfit to have responsibility for the safety and well-being of children, you shall have the opportunity to complete, or challenge the accuracy of, the information contained in the SBI or FBI identification records.

If you disagree with the determination of the North Carolina Department of Health and Human Services on your fitness to provide child care, you may file a civil lawsuit within 60 days after receiving written notification of disqualification in the district court in the county where you live.

Any child care provider who intentionally falsifies any information required to be furnished to conduct the criminal history record check shall be guilty of a Class 2 misdemeanor.

Refusal to consent to a criminal history record check or intentional falsification of any information required to be furnished to conduct a criminal history record check is grounds for the Department to prohibit the child care provider from providing child care. Any child care provider who intentionally falsifies any information required to be furnished to conduct the criminal history shall be guilty of a Class 2 misdemeanor.

(d)   The Department shall notify in writing the child care provider, and the child care provider's employer, if any, or for nonlicensed child care homes the local purchasing agency, of the determination by the Department whether the child care provider is qualified to provide child care based on the child care provider's criminal history. In accordance with the law regulating the dissemination of the contents of the criminal history file furnished by the Federal Bureau of Investigation, the Department shall not release nor disclose any portion of the child care provider's criminal history to the child care provider or the child care provider's employer or local purchasing agency. The Department shall also notify the child care provider of the procedure for completing or challenging the accuracy of the criminal history and the child care provider's right to contest the Department's determination in court.

A child care provider who disagrees with the Department's decision may file a civil action in the district court of the county of residence of the child care provider within 60 days after receiving written notification of disqualification. Review of the Department's determination disqualifying a child care provider shall be de novo. No jury trial is available for appeals to district court under this section.

(e)   All the information that the Department receives through the checking of the criminal history is privileged information and is not a public record but is for the exclusive use of the Department and those persons authorized under this section to receive the information. The Department may destroy the information after it is used for the purposes authorized by this section after one calendar year.

(f)   There shall be no liability for negligence on the part of an employer of a child care provider, an owner or operator of a child care facility, a State or local agency, or the employees of a State or local agency, arising from any action taken or omission by any of them in carrying out the provisions of this section. The immunity established by this subsection shall not extend to gross negligence, wanton conduct, or intentional wrongdoing that would otherwise be actionable. The immunity established by this subsection is waived to the extent of indemnification by insurance, indemnification under Article 31A of Chapter 143 of the General Statutes, and to the extent sovereign immunity is waived under the Torts Claim Act, as set forth in Article 31 of Chapter 143 of the General Statutes.

(g)   The child care provider shall pay the cost of the fingerprinting and the federal criminal history record check in accordance with G.S. 114-19.5. The Department of Justice shall perform the State criminal history record check. The Department of Health and Human Services shall pay for and conduct the county criminal history record check. Child care providers who reside outside the State bear the cost of the county criminal history record check and shall provide the county criminal history record check to the Division of Child Development as required by this section.

(h)   Repealed by Session Laws 2013-410, s. 46, effective August 23, 2013. (1995, c. 507, s. 23.25(a); c. 542, s. 25.2; 1997-443, s. 11A.118(a); 1997-506, s. 7; 2012-160, s. 1; 2013-410, s. 46; 2013-413, s. 12.)

§ 110-91. Mandatory standards for a license.

All child care facilities shall comply with all State laws and federal laws and local ordinances that pertain to child health, safety, and welfare. Except as otherwise provided in this Article, the standards in this section shall be complied with by all child care facilities. However, none of the standards in this section apply to the school-age children of the operator of a child care facility but do apply to the preschool-age children of the operator. Children 13 years of age or older may receive child care on a voluntary basis provided all applicable required standards are met. The standards in this section, along with any other applicable State laws and federal laws or local ordinances, shall be the required standards for the issuance of a license by the Secretary under the policies and procedures of the Commission except that the Commission may, in its discretion, adopt less stringent standards for the licensing of facilities which provide care on a temporary, part-time, drop-in, seasonal, after-school or other than a full-time basis.

(1) Medical Care and Sanitation. - The Commission for Public Health shall adopt rules which establish minimum sanitation standards for child care centers and their personnel. The sanitation rules adopted by the Commission for Public Health shall cover such matters as the cleanliness of floors, walls, ceilings, storage spaces, utensils, and other facilities; adequacy of ventilation; sanitation of water supply, lavatory facilities, toilet facilities, sewage disposal, food protection facilities, bactericidal treatment of eating and drinking utensils, and solid-waste storage and disposal; methods of food preparation and serving; infectious disease control; sleeping facilities; and other items and facilities as are necessary in the interest of the public health. The Commission for Public Health shall allow child care centers to use domestic kitchen equipment, provided appropriate temperature levels for heating, cooling, and storing are maintained. Child care centers that fry foods shall use commercial hoods. These rules shall be developed in consultation with the Department.

The Commission shall adopt rules for child care facilities to establish minimum requirements for child and staff health assessments and medical care procedures. These rules shall be developed in consultation with the Department. Each child shall have a health assessment before being admitted or within 30 days following admission to a child care facility. The assessment shall be done by: (i) a licensed physician, (ii) the physician's authorized agent who is currently approved by the North Carolina Medical Board, or comparable certifying board in any state contiguous to North Carolina, (iii) a certified nurse practitioner, or (iv) a public health nurse meeting the Departments Standards for

Early Periodic Screening, Diagnosis, and Treatment Program. However, no health assessment shall be required of any staff or child who is and has been in normal health when the staff, or the child's parent, guardian, or full-time custodian objects in writing to a health assessment on religious grounds which conform to the teachings and practice of any recognized church or religious denomination.

Organizations that provide prepared meals to child care centers only are considered child care centers for purposes of compliance with appropriate sanitation standards.

(2) Health-Related Activities. -

a. through f. Repealed by Session Laws 2012-142, s. 10.1(c1), effective July 1, 2012.

g. Nutrition standards. - The Commission shall adopt rules for child care facilities to ensure that food and beverages provided by a child care facility are nutritious and align with children's developmental needs. The Commission shall consult with the Division of Child Development and Early Education of the Department of Health and Human Services to develop nutrition standards to provide for requirements appropriate for children of different ages. In developing nutrition standards, the Commission shall consider the following recommendations:

1. Limiting or prohibiting the serving of sweetened beverages, other than one hundred percent (100%) fruit juice to children of any age.

2. Limiting or prohibiting the serving of whole milk to children two years of age or older or flavored milk to children of any age.

3. Limiting or prohibiting the serving of more than six ounces of juice per day to children of any age.

4. Limiting or prohibiting the serving of juice from a bottle.

h. Parental exceptions. -

1. Parents or guardians of a child enrolled in a child care facility may (i) provide food and beverages to their child that may not meet the nutrition standards adopted by the Commission and (ii) opt out of any supplemental food

program provided by the child care facility. The child care facility shall not provide food or beverages to a child whose parent or guardian has opted out of any supplemental food program provided by the child care facility and whose parent or guardian is providing food and beverages for the child.

2. The Commission, the Division of Child Development and Early Education of the Department of Health and Human Services, or any State agency or contracting entity with a State agency shall not evaluate the nutritional value or adequacy of the components of food and beverages provided by a parent or guardian to his or her child enrolled in a child care facility as an indicator of environmental quality ratings.

i. Rest time. - Each child care facility shall have a rest period for each child in care after lunch or at some other appropriate time and arrange for each child in care to be out-of-doors each day if weather conditions permit.

(3) Location. - Each child care facility shall be located in an area which is free from conditions which are considered hazardous to the physical and moral welfare of the children in care in the opinion of the Secretary.

(4) Building. - Each child care facility shall be located in a building which meets the appropriate requirements of the North Carolina Building Code under standards which shall be developed by the Building Code Council, subject to adoption by the Commission specifically for child care facilities, including facilities operated in a private residence. These standards shall be consistent with the provisions of this Article. A local building code enforcement officer shall approve any proposed alternate material, design, or method of construction, provided the building code enforcement officer finds that the alternate, for the purpose intended, is at least the equivalent of that prescribed in the technical building codes in quality, strength, effectiveness, fire resistance, durability, or safety. A local building code enforcement officer shall require that sufficient evidence or proof be submitted to substantiate any claim made regarding the alternate. The Child Care Commission may request changes to the Building Code to suit the special needs of preschool children. Satisfactorily written reports from representatives of building inspection agencies shall be required prior to the issuance of a license and whenever renovations are made to a child care center, or when the operator requests licensure of space not previously approved for child care.

(5) Fire Prevention. - Each child care facility shall be located in a building that meets appropriate requirements for fire prevention and safe evacuation that

apply to child care facilities as established by the Department of Insurance in consultation with the Department. Except for child care centers located on State property, each child care center shall be inspected at least annually by a local fire department or volunteer fire department for compliance with these requirements. Child care centers located on State property shall be inspected at least annually by an official designated by the Department of Insurance.

(6) Space and Equipment Requirements. - There shall be no less than 25 square feet of indoor space for each child for which a child care center is licensed, exclusive of closets, passageways, kitchens, and bathrooms, and this floor space shall provide during rest periods 200 cubic feet of airspace per child for which the center is licensed. There shall be adequate outdoor play area for each child under rules adopted by the Commission which shall be related to the size of center and the availability and location of outside land area. In no event shall the minimum required exceed 75 square feet per child. The outdoor area shall be protected to assure the safety of the children receiving child care by an adequate fence or other protection. A center operated in a public school shall be deemed to have adequate fencing protection. A center operating exclusively during the evening and early morning hours, between 6:00 P.M. and 6:00 A.M., need not meet the outdoor play area requirements mandated by this subdivision.

Each child care facility shall provide indoor area equipment and furnishings that are child size, sturdy, safe, and in good repair. Each child care facility that provides outdoor area equipment and furnishings shall provide outdoor area equipment and furnishings that are child size, sturdy, free of hazards that pose a threat of serious injury to children while engaged in normal play activities, and in good repair. The Commission shall adopt standards to establish minimum requirements for equipment appropriate for the size of child care facility. Space shall be available for proper storage of beds, cribs, mats, cots, sleeping garments, and linens as well as designated space for each child's personal belongings.

The Division of Child Development of the Department of Health and Human Services shall establish and implement a policy that defines any building which is currently approved for school occupancy and which houses a public or private elementary school to include the playgrounds and athletic fields as part of the school building when that building is used to serve school-age children in after-school child care programs. Playgrounds and athletic fields referenced in this section that do not meet licensure standards promulgated by the North

Carolina Child Care Commission shall be noted on the program's licensure and rating information.

(7) Staff-Child Ratio and Capacity for Child Care Facilities. - In determining the staff-child ratio in child care facilities, all children younger than 13 years old shall be counted.

a. The Commission shall adopt rules for child care centers regarding staff-child ratios, group sizes and multi-age groupings other than for infants and toddlers, provided that these rules shall be no less stringent than those currently required for staff-child ratios as enacted in Section 156(e) of Chapter 757 of the 1985 Session Laws.

1. Except as otherwise provided in this subdivision, the staff-child ratios and group sizes for infants and toddlers in child care centers shall be no less stringent than as follows:

Age	Ratio Staff/Children	Group Size
0 to 12 months	1/5	10
12 to 24 months	1/6	12
2 to 3 years	1/10	20.

No child care center shall care for more than 25 children in one group. Child care centers providing care for 26 or more children shall provide for two or more groups according to the ages of children and shall provide separate supervisory personnel and separate identifiable space for each group.

2. When any preschool-aged child is enrolled in a child care center and the licensed capacity of the center is six through 12 children, the staff-child ratios shall be no less stringent than as follows:

Age	Ratio Staff/Children
0 to 12 months	1/5 preschool children plus 3 additional school-aged children

12 to 24 months   1/6 preschool children plus 2 additional school-aged children.

The following shall also apply:

I.   There is no specific group size.

II.   When only one caregiver is required to meet the staff-child ratio, the operator shall make available to parents the name, address, and phone number of an adult who is nearby and available for emergency relief.

III.   Children shall be supervised at all times. All children who are not asleep or resting shall be visually supervised. Children may sleep or rest in another room as long as a caregiver can hear them and respond immediately.

b.   Family Child Care Home Capacity. - Of the children present at any one time in a family child care home, no more than five children shall be preschool-aged, including the operator's own preschool-age children.

(8)   Qualifications for Staff. - All child care center administrators shall be at least 21 years of age. All child care center administrators shall have the North Carolina Early Childhood Administration Credential or its equivalent as determined by the Department. All child care administrators performing administrative duties as of the date this act becomes law and child care administrators who assume administrative duties at any time after this act becomes law and until September 1, 1998, shall obtain the required credential by September 1, 2000. Child care administrators who assume administrative duties after September 1, 1998, shall begin working toward the completion of the North Carolina Early Childhood Administration Credential or its equivalent within six months after assuming administrative duties and shall complete the credential or its equivalent within two years after beginning work to complete the credential. Each child care center shall be under the direction or supervision of a person meeting these requirements. All staff counted toward meeting the required staff-child ratio shall be at least 16 years of age, provided that persons younger than 18 years of age work under the direct supervision of a credentialed staff person who is at least 21 years of age. All lead teachers in a child care center shall have at least a North Carolina Early Childhood Credential or its equivalent as determined by the Department. Lead teachers shall be enrolled in the North Carolina Early Childhood Credential coursework or its equivalent as determined by the Department within six months after becoming employed as a lead teacher or within six months after this act becomes law,

whichever is later, and shall complete the credential or its equivalent within 18 months after enrollment.

For child care centers licensed to care for 200 or more children, the Department, in collaboration with the North Carolina Institute for Early Childhood Professional Development, shall establish categories to recognize the levels of education achieved by child care center administrators and teachers who perform administrative functions. The Department shall use these categories to establish appropriate staffing based on the size of the center and the individual staff responsibilities.

Effective January 1, 1998, an operator of a licensed family child care home shall be at least 21 years old and have a high school diploma or its equivalent. Operators of a family child care home licensed prior to January 1, 1998, shall be at least 18 years of age and literate. Literate is defined as understanding licensing requirements and having the ability to communicate with the family and relevant emergency personnel. Any operator of a licensed family child care home shall be the person on-site providing child care.

The Commission shall adopt standards to establish appropriate qualifications for all staff in child care centers. These standards shall reflect training, experience, education and credentialing and shall be appropriate for the size center and the level of individual staff responsibilities. It is the intent of this provision to guarantee that all children in child care are cared for by qualified people. Pursuant to G.S. 110-106, no requirements may interfere with the teachings or doctrine of any established religious organization. The staff qualification requirements of this subdivision do not apply to religious-sponsored child care facilities pursuant to G.S. 110-106.

(8a) Expired pursuant to Session Laws 2010-178, s. 2, as amended by Session Laws 2011-145, s. 10.4A, effective July 1, 2011.

(9) Records. - Each child care facility shall keep accurate records on each child receiving care in the child care facility and on each staff member or other person delegated responsibility for the care of children in accordance with a form furnished or approved by the Commission, and shall submit records as required by the Department.

All records of any child care facility, except financial records, shall be available for review by the Secretary or by duly authorized representatives of the Department or a cooperating agency who shall be designated by the Secretary and shall be submitted as required by the Department.

(10)   Each operator or staff member shall attend to any child in a nurturing and appropriate manner, and in keeping with the child's developmental needs.

Each child care facility shall have a written policy on discipline, describing the methods and practices used to discipline children enrolled in that facility. This written policy shall be discussed with, and a copy given to, each child's parent prior to the first time the child attends the facility. Subsequently, any change in discipline methods or practices shall be communicated in writing to the parents prior to the effective date of the change.

The use of corporal punishment as a form of discipline is prohibited in child care facilities and may not be used by any operator or staff member of any child care facility, except that corporal punishment may be used in religious sponsored child care facilities as defined in G.S. 110-106, only if (i) the religious sponsored child care facility files with the Department a notice stating that corporal punishment is part of the religious training of its program, and (ii) the religious sponsored child care facility clearly states in its written policy of discipline that corporal punishment is part of the religious training of its program. The written policy on discipline of nonreligious sponsored child care facilities shall clearly state the prohibition on corporal punishment.

(11)   Staff Development. - The Commission shall adopt minimum standards for ongoing staff development for facilities but limited to the following topic areas:

a.   Planning a safe, healthy learning environment;

b.   Steps to advance children's physical and intellectual development;

c.   Positive ways to support children's social and emotional development;

d.   Strategies to establish productive relationships with families;

e.   Strategies to manage an effective program operation;

f.   Maintaining a commitment to professionalism;

g.   Observing and recording children's behavior;

h. Principles of child growth and development; and

i. Learning activities that promote inclusion of children with special needs.

These standards shall include annual requirements for ongoing staff development appropriate to job responsibilities. A person may carry forward in-service training hours that are in excess of the previous year's requirement to meet up to one-half of the current year's required in-service training hours.

(12) Developmentally Appropriate Activities. - Each facility shall have developmentally appropriate activities and play materials. The Commission shall establish minimum standards for developmentally appropriate activities for child care facilities. Each child care facility shall have a planned schedule of developmentally appropriate activities displayed in a prominent place for parents to review and the appropriate materials and equipment available to implement the scheduled activities. Each child care center shall make four of the following activity areas available daily: art and other creative play, children's books, blocks and block building, manipulatives, and family living and dramatic play.

(13) Transportation. - When a child care facility staff person or a volunteer of a child care facility transports children in a vehicle, each adult and child shall be restrained by an appropriate seat safety belt or restraint device when the vehicle is in motion. Children may never be left unattended in a vehicle.

The ratio of adults to children in child care vehicles may not be less than the staff/child ratios prescribed by G.S. 110-91(7). The Commission shall adopt standards for transporting children under the age of two, including standards addressing this particular age's staff/child ratio during transportation.

(14) Any effort to falsify information provided to the Department shall be considered by the Secretary to be evidence of violation of this Article on the part of the operator or sponsor of the child care facility and shall constitute a cause for revoking or denying a license to such child care facility.

(15) Safe Sleep Policy. - Operators of child care facilities that care for children ages 12 months or younger shall develop and maintain a written safe sleep policy, in accordance with rules adopted by the Commission. The safe sleep policy shall address maintaining a safe sleep environment and shall include the following requirements:

a. A caregiver in a child care facility shall place a child age 12 months or younger on the child's back for sleeping, unless: (i) for a child age 6 months or younger, the operator of the child care facility obtains a written waiver of this requirement from a health care professional, as defined in rules adopted by the Commission; or (ii) for a child older than 6 months, the operator of the child care facility obtains a written waiver of this requirement from a health care professional, as defined in rules adopted by the Commission, a parent, or a legal guardian.

b. The operator of the child care facility shall discuss the safe sleep policy with the child's parent or guardian before the child is enrolled in the child care facility. The child's parent or guardian shall sign a statement attesting that the parent or guardian received a copy of the safe sleep policy and that the policy was discussed with the parent or guardian before the child's enrollment.

c. Any caregiver responsible for the care of children ages 12 months or younger shall receive training in safe sleep practices. (1971, c. 803, s. 1; 1973, c. 476, s. 128; 1975, c. 879, s. 15; 1977, c. 1011, s. 4; c. 1104; 1979, c. 9, ss. 1, 2; 1981 (Reg. Sess., 1982), c. 1382, ss. 1, 2; 1983, c. 46, s. 2; cc. 62, 277, 612; 1985, c. 757, ss. 155(h), (i), 156(c)-(h); 1987, c. 543, s. 3; c. 788, s. 6; c. 827, s. 234; 1989 (Reg. Sess., 1990), c. 1004, s. 56; 1991, c. 273, s. 5; c. 640, s. 1; 1993, c. 185, s. 3; c. 321, s. 254(c); c. 513, s. 9; c. 553, s. 32; 1995, c. 94, s. 32; 1997-443, s. 11A.44; 1997-456, s. 43.1(a); 1997-506, s. 8(a); 1998-217, s. 11; 1999-130, s. 2; 2003-407, s. 1; 2007-182, s. 2; 2009-64, s. 1; 2009-244, s. 1; 2010-117, s. 1; 2010-178, s. 1; 2011-145, s. 10.4A; 2012-142, 10.1(c1); 2012-160, s. 2.)

§ 110-92. Duties of State and local agencies.

When requested by an operator of a child care center or by the Secretary, it shall be the duty of local and district health departments to visit and inspect a child care center to determine whether the center complies with the health and sanitation standards required by this Article and with the minimum sanitation standards adopted as rules by the Commission for Public Health as authorized by G.S. 110-91(1), and to submit written reports on these visits or inspections to the Department on forms approved and provided by the Department of Environment and Natural Resources.

When requested by an operator of a child care center or by the Secretary, it shall be the duty of the building inspector, fire prevention inspector, or fireman employed by local government, or any fireman having jurisdiction, or other officials or personnel of local government to visit and inspect a child care center for the purposes specified in this Article, including plans for evacuation of the premises and protection of children in case of fire, and to report on these visits or inspections in writing to the Secretary so that these reports may serve as the basis for action or decisions by the Secretary or Department as authorized by this Article. (1971, c. 803, s. 1; 1973, c. 476, ss. 128, 138; 1975, c. 879, s. 15; 1985, c. 757, s. 155(j); 1987, c. 543, s. 4; 1989, c. 727, s. 31; 1989 (Reg. Sess., 1990), c. 1024, s. 21; 1991, c. 273, s. 6; 1997-443, s. 11A.45; 1997-506, s. 9; 2007-182, s. 2.)

§ 110-93. Application for a license.

(a) Each person who seeks to operate a child care facility shall apply to the Department for a license. The application shall be in the form required by the Department. Each applicant seeking a license shall be responsible for supplying with the application the necessary supporting data and reports to show conformity with rules adopted by the Commission for Public Health pursuant to G.S. 110-91(1) and with the standards established or authorized by this Article, including any required reports from the local and district health departments, local building inspectors, local firemen, voluntary firemen, and others, on forms which shall be provided by the Department.

(b) If an applicant conforms to the rules adopted by the Commission for Public Health pursuant to G.S. 110-91(1) and with the standards established or authorized by this Article as shown in the application and other supporting data, the Secretary shall issue a license that shall remain valid until the Secretary notifies the licensee otherwise pursuant to G.S. 150B-3 or other provisions of this Article, subject to suspension or revocation for cause as provided in this Article. If the applicant fails to conform to the required rules and standards, the Secretary may issue a provisional license under the policies of the Commission. The Department shall notify the applicant in writing by registered or certified mail the reasons the Department issued a provisional license.

(c) Repealed by Session Laws 1997-506, s. 10, effective September 16, 1997.

(d) Repealed by Session Laws 1977, c. 929, s. 1. (1971, c. 803, s. 1; 1975, c. 879, s. 15; 1977, c. 4, s. 4; c. 929, s. 1; 1985, c. 757, s. 155(k), (l); 1987, c. 543, ss. 5, 6; c. 788, s. 7; 1991, c. 273, s. 7; 1997-443, s. 11A.118(a); 1997-506, s. 10; 1999-130, s. 3; 2007-182, s. 2.)

§ 110-93.1: Repealed by Session Laws 2006-66, s. 10.2(a), (b), effective July 1, 2006.

§ 110-94. Administrative Procedure Act.

The provisions of Chapter 150B of the General Statutes shall be applicable to the Commission, to the rules the Commission adopts, and to child care contested cases. However, a child care operator shall have 30 days to file a petition for a contested case pursuant to G.S. 150B-23. The contested case hearing shall be scheduled to be held within 120 days of the date the petition for a hearing is received, pursuant to G.S. 150B-23(a), in any contested case resulting from administrative action taken by the Secretary to revoke a license or Letter of Compliance or from administrative action taken in a situation in which child abuse or neglect in a child care facility has been substantiated. A request for continuance of a hearing shall be granted upon a showing of good cause by either party. (1971, c. 803, s. 1; 1975, c. 879, s. 15; 1977, c. 929, s. 2; 1985, c. 757, s. 155(m); 1987, c. 788, s. 8; 1989, c. 429; 1991, c. 273, s. 8; 1997-506, s. 11.)

§§ 110-95 through 110-97. Repealed by Session Laws 1977, c. 929, s. 1.

§ 110-98. Mandatory compliance.

It shall be unlawful for any person to:

(1) Offer or provide child care without complying with the provisions of this Article; or

(2) Advertise without disclosing the child care facility's identifying number that is on the license or the letter of compliance. (1971, c. 803, s. 1; 1985, c. 757, s. 156(ee); 1987, c. 788, s. 9; 1997-506, s. 12.)

§ 110-98.1. Prima facie evidence of existence of child care.

A child care arrangement providing child care for more than two children for more than four hours per day on two or more consecutive days shall be prima facie evidence of the existence of a child care facility. (1977, c. 4, s. 6; 1987, c. 788, s. 10; 1997-506, s. 13.)

§ 110-99. Possession and display of license.

(a) It shall be unlawful for a child care facility to operate without a current license authorized for issuance under G.S. 110-88.

(a1) Each child care facility shall display its current license in a prominent place at all times so that the public may be on notice that the facility is licensed and may observe any rating which may appear on the license. Any license issued to a child care facility under this Article shall remain the property of the State and may be removed by persons employed or designated by the Secretary in the event that the license is revoked or suspended, or in the event that the rating is changed.

(b) A person who provides only drop-in or short-term child care as described in G.S. 110-86(2)d. and G.S. 110-86(2)d1., excluding drop-in or short-term child care provided in churches, shall register with the Department that the person is providing only drop-in or short-term child care. Any person providing only drop-in or short-term child care as described in G.S. 110-86(2)d. and G.S. 110-86(2)d1., excluding drop-in or short-term child care provided in churches, shall display in a prominent place at all times a notice that the child care arrangement is not required to be licensed and regulated by the Department and is not licensed and regulated by the Department. (1971, c. 803, s. 1; 1997-506, s. 14; 1999-130, s. 4; 2003-192, s. 2; 2005-416, s. 2.)

§ 110-100: Repealed by Session Laws 1997-506, s. 15.

§ 110-101: Repealed by Session Laws 1997-506, s. 16.

§ 110-101.1. Corporal punishment banned in certain "nonlicensed" homes.

The use of corporal punishment as a form of discipline is prohibited in those child care homes that are not required to be licensed under this Article but that receive State or federal subsidies for child care unless this care is provided to children by their parents, stepparents, grandparents, aunts, uncles, step-grandparents, or great-grandparents. Care provided children by their parents, stepparents, grandparents, aunts, uncles, step-grandparents, or great-grandparents is not subject to this section. Religious sponsored nonlicensed homes are also exempt from this section. (1993, c. 268, s. 1; 1997-506, s. 17.)

§ 110-102. Information for parents.

The Secretary shall provide to each operator of a child care facility a summary of this Article for the parents, guardian, or full-time custodian of each child receiving child care in the facility to be distributed by the operator. Operators of child care facilities shall provide a copy of the summary to each child's parent, guardian, or full-time custodian before the child is enrolled in the child care facility. The child's parent, guardian, or full-time custodian shall sign a statement attesting that he or she received a copy of the summary before the child's enrollment. The summary shall include the name and address of the Secretary and the address of the Commission. The summary shall explain how parents may obtain information on individual child care facilities maintained in public files by the Division of Child Development. The summary shall also include a statement regarding the mandatory duty prescribed in G.S. 7B-301 of any person suspecting child abuse or neglect has taken place in child care, or elsewhere, to report to the county Department of Social Services. The statement shall include the definitions of child abuse and neglect described in the Juvenile Code in G.S. 7B-101 and of child abuse described in the Criminal Code in G.S. 14-318.2 and G.S. 14-318.4. The statement shall stress that this reporting law does not require that the person reporting reveal the person's identity.

The summary of this Article shall be posted with the facility's license in accordance with G.S. 110-99. Religious-sponsored programs operating pursuant to G.S. 110-106 shall post the summary in a prominent place at all times so that it is easily reviewed by parents. (1971, c. 803, s. 1; 1975, c. 879, s. 15; 1977, c. 1011, s. 3; 1985, c. 757, ss. 155(o), 156(v); 1997-443, s. 11A.118(a); 1997-506, s. 18; 1998-202, s. 13(w); 2003-196, s. 1.)

§ 110-102.1. Reporting of missing or deceased children.

(a)   Notwithstanding G.S. 14-318.5, operators and staff, as defined in G.S. 110-86(7), and G.S. 110-91(8), or any adult present with the approval of the care provider in a child care facility as defined in G.S. 110-86(3) and G.S. 110-106, upon learning that a child which has been placed in their care or presence is missing, shall immediately report the missing child to law enforcement. For purposes of this Article, a child is anyone under the age of 16.

(b)   If a child dies while in child care, or of injuries sustained in child care, a report of the death must be made by the child care operator to the Secretary within 24 hours of the child's death or on the next working day. (1985, c. 392; 1987, c. 788, s. 12; 1997-506, s. 19; 2013-52, s. 4.)

§ 110-102.1A. Unauthorized administration of medication.

(a)   It is unlawful for an employee, owner, household member, volunteer, or operator of a licensed or unlicensed child care facility as defined in G.S. 110-86, including child care facilities operated by public schools and nonpublic schools as defined in G.S. 110-86(2)(f), to willfully administer, without written authorization, prescription or over-the-counter medication to a child attending the child care facility. For the purposes of this section, written authorization shall include the child's name, date or dates for which the authorization is applicable, dosage instructions, and signature of the child's parent or guardian. For the purposes of this section, a child care facility operated by a public school does not include kindergarten through twelfth grade classes.

(b)   In the event of an emergency medical condition and the child's parent or guardian is unavailable, it shall not be unlawful to administer medication to a child attending the child care facility without written authorization as required under subsection (a) of this section if the medication is administered with the authorization and in accordance with instructions from a bona fide medical care provider. For purposes of this subsection, the following definitions apply:

(1)   A bona fide medical care provider means an individual who is licensed, certified, or otherwise authorized to prescribe the medication.

(2)   An emergency medical condition means circumstances where a prudent layperson acting reasonably would have believed that an emergency medical condition existed.

(c)   A violation of this section that results in serious injury to the child shall be punished as a Class F felony.

(d)   Any other violation of this section where medication is administered willfully shall be punished as a Class A1 misdemeanor. (2003-406, s. 2.)

§ 110-102.2. Administrative penalties.

For failure to comply with this Article, the Secretary may:

(1)   Issue a written warning and a request for compliance;

(2)   Issue an official written reprimand;

(3)   Place a licensee upon probation until his compliance with this Article has been verified by the Commission or its agent;

(4)   Order suspension of a license for a specified length of time not to exceed one year;

(5)   Permanently revoke a license issued under this Article.

The issuance of an administrative penalty may be appealed as provided in G.S. 110-90(5) and G.S. 110-90(9). (1985, c. 757, s. 156(ff); 1987, c. 788, s. 13; c. 827, s. 235.)

§ 110-103. Criminal penalty.

(a)   Any person who violates the provisions of G.S. 110-98 shall be guilty of a Class 1 misdemeanor. Violations of G.S. 110-98(2), 110-99(b), 110-99(c), and 110-102 are exempted from the provisions of this subsection.

(b)   It shall be a Class I felony for any person who operates a child care facility to:

(1)   Willfully violate the provisions of G.S. 110-99(a), or

(2)   Willfully violate the provisions of this Article while providing child care for three or more children, for more than four hours per day on two consecutive days.

(c)   Any person who violates the provisions of this Article and, as a result of the violation, causes serious injury to a child attending the child care facility, shall be guilty of a Class H felony.

(d)   Any person who violates subsection (a) of this section, and has a prior conviction for violating subsection (a), shall be guilty of a Class H felony. (1971, c. 803, s. 1; 1983, c. 297, s. 3; 1985, c. 757, s. 156(gg); 1987, c. 788, s. 14; 1993, c. 539, s. 824; 1994, Ex. Sess., c. 24, s. 14(c); 1997-506, s. 20; 2003-192, s. 1.)

§ 110-103.1. Civil penalty.

(a)   A civil penalty may be levied against any operator of any child care facility who violates any provision of this Article. The penalty shall not exceed one thousand dollars ($1,000) for each violation documented on any given date. Every operator shall be provided a schedule of the civil penalties established by the Commission pursuant to this Article.

(b)   In determining the amount of the penalty, the threat of or extent of harm to children in care as well as consistency of violations shall be considered, and no penalty shall be imposed under this section unless there is a specific finding that this action is reasonably necessary to enforce the provisions of this Article or its rules.

(c)   A person who is assessed a penalty shall be notified of the penalty by registered or certified mail. The notice shall state the reasons for the penalty. If a person fails to pay a penalty, the Secretary shall refer the matter to the Attorney General for collection.

(d) The clear proceeds of penalties provided for in this section shall be remitted to the Civil Penalty and Forfeiture Fund in accordance with G.S. 115C-457.2. (1985, c. 757, s. 156(gg); 1987, c. 788, s. 15; c. 827, s. 236; 1991, c. 273, s. 9; 1997-506, s. 21; 1998-215, s. 75.)

§ 110-104. Injunctive relief.

The Secretary or the Secretary's designee may seek injunctive relief in the district court of the county in which a child care facility is located against the continuing operation of that child care facility at any time, whether or not any administrative proceedings are pending. The district court may grant injunctive relief, temporary, preliminary, or permanent, when there is any violation of this Article or of the rules promulgated by the Commission or the Commission for Public Health that threatens serious harm to children in the child care facility, or when a final order to deny or revoke a license has been violated, or when a child care facility is operating without a license, or when a child care facility repeatedly violates the provisions of this Article or rules adopted pursuant to it after having been notified of the violation. (1977, c. 4, s. 5; c. 929, s. 3; c. 1011, s. 1; 1985, c. 757, s. 156(hh); 1987, c. 543, s. 7; c. 788, s. 16; c. 827, s. 237; 1997-506, s. 22; 2007-182, s. 2.)

§ 110-105. Authority to inspect facilities.

(a) The Commission shall adopt standards and rules under this subsection which provide for the following types of inspections:

(1) An initial licensing inspection, which shall not occur until the administrator of the facility receives prior notice of the initial inspection visit;

(2) A plan for visits to all facilities, including announced and unannounced visits, which shall be confidential unless a court orders its disclosure;

(3) An inspection that may be conducted without notice, if there is probable cause to believe that an emergency situation exists or there is a complaint

alleging a violation of licensure law. When the Department is notified by the county director of social services that the director has received a report of child abuse or neglect in a child care facility, or when the Department is notified by any other person that alleged abuse or neglect has occurred in a facility, the Commission's rules shall provide for an inspection conducted without notice to the child care facility to determine whether the alleged abuse or neglect has occurred. This inspection shall be conducted within seven calendar days of receipt of the report, and when circumstances warrant, additional visits shall be conducted.

The Secretary or the Secretary's designee, upon presenting appropriate credentials to the operator of the child care facility, may perform inspections in accordance with the standards and rules promulgated under this subsection. The Secretary or the Secretary's designee may inspect any area of a building in which there is reasonable evidence that children are in care.

(b)   If an operator refuses to allow the Secretary or the Secretary's designee to inspect the child care facility, the Secretary shall seek an administrative warrant in accordance with G.S. 15-27.2. (1983, c. 261, s. 1; 1985, c. 757, s. 156(ii); 1987, c. 788, s. 17; c. 827, s. 238; 1991, c. 273, s. 10; 1997-506, s. 23.)

§ 110-105.1: Repealed by Session Laws 1997-506, s. 24.

§ 110-105.2. Abuse and neglect violations.

(a)   For purposes of this Article, child abuse and neglect, as defined in G.S. 7B-101 and in G.S. 14-318.2 and G.S. 14-318.4, occurring in child care facilities, are violations of the licensure standards and of the licensure law. The Department, local departments of social services, and local law enforcement personnel shall cooperate with the medical community to ensure that reports of child abuse or neglect in child care facilities are properly investigated.

(b)   When an investigation pursuant to G.S. 110-105(a)(3) substantiates that child abuse or neglect did occur in a child care facility, the Department may issue a written warning which shall specify any corrective action to be taken by the operator. The Department shall make an unannounced visit within one month after issuance of the written warning to determine whether the corrective action has occurred. If the corrective action has not occurred, then the Department may issue a special provisional license.

(c)   When the Department issues a special provisional license pursuant to this section, the Department shall send a letter which states the reasons for the special provisional status, and the license shall specify corrective action that shall be taken by the operator. A special provisional license issued pursuant to this section shall be in effect for no more than six months from issuance. The operator shall post, where parents can see them, the letter stating the reasons for the special provisional status and the special provisional license. Under the terms of the special provisional license, the Secretary may limit enrollment of new children until satisfied the abusive or neglectful situation no longer exists. The Department shall make unannounced visits as often as the Department believes it is necessary during the period the special provisional license is in effect.

(d)   Specific corrective action required by a written warning, special provisional license, or any other administrative penalty authorized by this Article may include the permanent removal of the substantiated abuser or neglecter from child care.

(e)   Nothing in this section shall restrict the Secretary from using any other statutory or administrative remedies available. (1985, c. 757, s. 156(w); 1987, c. 788, s. 19; 1997-506, s. 25; 1998-202, s. 13(x); 2003-407, s. 2.)

§ 110-106. Religious sponsored child care facilities.

(a)   The term "religious sponsored child care facility" as used in this section shall include any child care facility or summer day camp operated by a church, synagogue or school of religious charter.

(b)   Procedure Regarding Religious Sponsored Child Care Facilities. -

(1)   Religious sponsored child care facilities shall file with the Department a notice of intent to operate a child care facility and the date it will begin operation at least 30 days prior to that date. Within 30 days after beginning operation, the facility shall provide to the Department written reports and supporting data which show the facility is in compliance with applicable provisions of G.S. 110-91. After the religious sponsored child care facility has filed this information with the

Department, the facility shall be visited by a representative of the Department to ensure compliance with the applicable provisions of G.S. 110-91.

(2) Each religious sponsored child care facility shall file with the Department a report indicating that it meets the minimum standards for facilities as provided in the applicable provisions of G.S. 110-91 as required by the Department. The reports shall be in accordance with rules adopted by the Commission. Each religious sponsored child care facility shall be responsible for supplying with its report the necessary supporting data to show conformity with those minimum standards, including reports from the local and district health departments, local building inspectors, local firemen, volunteer firemen, and other, on forms which shall be provided by the Department.

(3) It shall be the responsibility of the Department to notify the facility if it fails to meet the minimum requirements. The Secretary shall be responsible for carrying out the enforcement provisions provided by the General Assembly in Article 7 of Chapter 110 including inspection to ensure compliance. The Secretary may issue an order requiring a religious sponsored child care facility which fails to meet the standards established pursuant to this Article to cease operating. A religious sponsored child care facility may request a hearing to determine if it is in compliance with the applicable provisions of G.S. 110-91. If the Secretary determines that it is not, the Secretary may order the facility to cease operation until it is in compliance.

(4) Religious sponsored child care facilities including summer day camps shall be exempt from the requirement that they obtain a license and that the license be displayed and shall be exempt from any subsequent rule or regulatory program not dealing specifically with the minimum standards as provided in the applicable provisions of G.S. 110-91. Nothing in this Article shall be interpreted to allow the State to regulate or otherwise interfere with the religious training offered as a part of any religious sponsored child care program. Nothing in this Article shall prohibit any religious sponsored child care facility from becoming licensed by the State if it so chooses.

(5) Religious sponsored child care facilities found to be in violation of the applicable provisions of G.S. 110-91 shall be subject to the injunctive provisions of G.S. 110-104, except that they may not be enjoined for operating without a license. The Secretary may seek an injunction against any religious sponsored child care facility under the conditions specified in G.S. 110-104 with the above exception and when any religious sponsored child care facility operates without

submitting the required forms and following the procedures required by this Article.

(c)   G.S. 110-91(8), 110-91(11), 110-91(12) do not apply to religious sponsored child care facilities, and these facilities are exempt from any requirements prescribed by subsection (b) of this section that arise out of these provisions.

(d)   No person shall be an operator of nor be employed in a religious sponsored child care facility who has been convicted of a crime involving child neglect, child abuse, or moral turpitude, or who is a habitually excessive user of alcohol or who illegally uses narcotic or other impairing drugs, or who is mentally or emotionally impaired to an extent that may be injurious to children.

(e)   Each religious sponsored child care facility shall be under the direction or supervision of a literate person at least 21 years of age. All staff counted toward meeting the required staff/child ratio shall be at least 16 years old, provided that persons younger than 18 years old work under the direct supervision of a literate staff person at least 21 years old. Effective January 1, 1998, a person operating a religious sponsored child care home must be at least 21 years old and literate. Persons operating religious sponsored child care homes prior to January 1, 1998, shall be at least 18 years old and literate. The definition of literate in G.S. 110-91(8) shall apply to this subsection. (1983, c. 283, ss. 1, 2; 1985, c. 757, ss. 155(p), 156(k); 1987, c. 788, s. 20; 1997-506, s. 26.)

§ 110-106.1: Repealed by Session Laws 1997-506, s. 27.

§ 110-107. Fraudulent misrepresentation.

(a)   A person, whether a provider or recipient of child care subsidies or someone claiming to be a provider or recipient of child care subsidies, commits the offense of fraudulent misrepresentation when both of the following occur:

(1)   With the intent to deceive, that person makes a false statement or representation regarding a material fact, or fails to disclose a material fact.

(2) As a result of the false statement or representation or the omission, that person obtains, attempts to obtain, or continues to receive a child care subsidy for himself or herself or for another person.

(b) If the child care subsidy is not more than one thousand dollars ($1,000), the person is guilty of a Class 1 misdemeanor. If the child care subsidy is more than one thousand dollars ($1,000), the person is guilty of a Class I felony.

(c) As used in this section:

(1) "Child care subsidy" means the use of public funds to pay for day care services for children.

(2) "Person" means an individual, association, consortium, corporation, body politic, partnership, or other group, entity, or organization. (1999-279, s. 1.)

§ 110-108: Repealed by Session Laws 2002-126, s. 10.58, effective July 1, 2002.

§ 110-109: Repealed by Session Laws 2001-424, s. 21.73(a).

§§ 110-110 through 110-114. Reserved for future codification purposes.

Article 8.

Child Abuse and Neglect.

§§ 110-115 through 110-123: Repealed by Session Laws 1979, c. 815, s. 2.

§§ 110-124 through 110-127. Reserved for future codification purposes.

Article 9.

Child Support.

§ 110-128. Purposes.

The purposes of this Article are to provide for the financial support of dependent children; to enforce spousal support when a child support order is being enforced; to provide that public assistance paid to dependent children is a supplement to the support required to be provided by the responsible parent; to provide that the payment of public assistance creates a debt to the State; to provide that the acceptance of public assistance operates as an assignment of the right to child support; to provide for the location of absent parents; to provide for a determination that a responsible parent is able to support his children; and to provide for enforcement of the responsible parent's obligation to furnish support and to provide for the establishment and administration of a program of child support enforcement in North Carolina. (1975, c. 827, s. 1; 1977, 2nd Sess., c. 1186, s. 1; 1985, c. 506, s. 2.)

§ 110-129. Definitions.

As used in this Article:

(1) "Court order" means any judgment or order of the courts of this State or of another state.

(2) "Dependent child" means any person under the age of 18 who is not otherwise emancipated, married or a member of the Armed Forces of the United States, or any person over the age of 18 for whom a court orders that support payments continue as provided in G.S. 50-13.4(c).

(3) "Responsible parent" means the natural or adoptive parent of a dependent child who has the legal duty to support said child and includes the father of a child born out-of-wedlock and the parents of a dependent child who is the custodial or noncustodial parent of the dependent child requiring support. If

both the parents of the child requiring support were unemancipated minors at the time of the child's conception, the parents of both minor parents share primary liability for their grandchild's support until both minor parents reach the age of 18 or become emancipated. If only one parent of the child requiring support was an unemancipated minor at the time of the child's conception, the parents of both parents are liable for any arrearages in child support owed by the adult or emancipated parent until the other parent reaches the age of 18 or becomes emancipated.

(4)   "Program" means the Child Support Enforcement Program established and administered pursuant to the provisions of this Article and Title IV-D of the Social Security Act.

(5)   "Designated representative" means any person or agency designated by a board of county commissioners or the Department of Health and Human Services to administer a program of child support enforcement for a county or region of the State.

(6)   "Disposable income" means any form of periodic payment to an individual, regardless of sources, including but not limited to wages, salary, commission, self-employment income, bonus pay, severance pay, sick pay, incentive pay, vacation pay, compensation as an independent contractor, worker's compensation, unemployment compensation benefits, disability, annuity, survivor's benefits, pension and retirement benefits, interest, dividends, rents, royalties, trust income and other similar payments, which remain after the deduction of amounts for federal, State, and local taxes, Social Security, and involuntary retirement contributions. However, Supplemental Security Income, Work First Family Assistance, and other public assistance payments shall be excluded from disposable income. For employers, disposable income means "wage" as it is defined by G.S. 95-25.2(16). Unemployment compensation benefits shall be treated as disposable income only for the purposes of income withholding under the provisions of G.S. 110-136.4, and the amount withheld shall not exceed twenty-five percent (25%) of the unemployment compensation benefits.

(7)   "IV-D case" means a case in which services have been applied for or are being provided by a child support enforcement agency established pursuant to Title IV-D of the Social Security Act as amended and this Article.

(8)   "Non-IV-D case" means any case, other than a IV-D case, in which child support is legally obligated to be paid.

(9) "Initiating party" means the party, the attorney for a party, a child support enforcement agency who initiates an action, proceeding, or procedure as allowed or required by law for the establishment or enforcement of a child support obligation.

(10) "Mistake of fact" means that the obligor:

a. Is not in arrears in an amount equal to the support payable for one month; or

b. Did not request that withholding begin, if withholding is pursuant to a purported request by the obligor for withholding; or

c. Is not the person subject to the court order of support for the child named in the advance notice of withholding; or

d. Does not owe the amount of current support or arrearages specified in the advance notice or motion of withholding; or

e. Has a rate of withholding which exceeds the amount of support specified in the court order.

(11) "Obligee", in a IV-D case, means the child support enforcement agency, and in a non-IV-D case means the individual to whom a duty of support, whether child support, alimony, or postseparation support, is owed or the individual's legal representative.

(12) "Obligor" means the individual who owes a duty to make child support payments or payments of alimony or postseparation support under a court order.

(13) "Payor" means any payor, including any federal, State, or local governmental unit, of disposable income to an obligor. When the payor is an employer, payor means employer as is defined at 29 USC § 203(d) in the Fair Labor Standards Act. (1975, c. 827, s. 1; 1977, 2nd Sess., c. 1186, ss. 2, 3; 1985, c. 592; 1985 (Reg. Sess., 1986), c. 949, s. 1; 1987, c. 764, s. 3; 1989, c. 601, s. 1; 1991, c. 541, s. 3; 1995, c. 518, s. 2; 1997-443, ss. 11A.118(a), 12.27; 1997-465, s. 27; 1998-176, ss. 9, 10; 2010-96, s. 30; 2011-183, s. 75.)

§ 110-129.1. Additional powers and duties of the Department.

(a) In addition to other powers and duties conferred upon the Department of Health and Human Services, Child Support Enforcement Program, by this Chapter or other State law, the Department shall have the following powers and duties:

(1) Upon authorization of the Secretary, to issue a subpoena for the production of books, papers, correspondence, memoranda, agreements, or other information, documents, or records relevant to a child support establishment or enforcement proceeding or paternity establishment proceeding. The subpoena shall be signed by the Secretary and shall state the name of the person or entity required to produce the information authorized under this section, and a description of the information compelled to be produced. The subpoena may be served in the manner provided for service of subpoenas under the North Carolina Rules of Civil Procedure. The form of subpoena shall generally follow the practice in the General Court of Justice in North Carolina. Return of the subpoena shall be to the person who issued the subpoena. Upon the refusal of any person to comply with the subpoena, it shall be the duty of any judge of the district court, upon application by the person who issued the subpoena, to order the person subpoenaed to show cause why he should not comply with the requirements, if in the discretion of the judge the requirements are reasonable and proper. Refusal to comply with the subpoena or with the order shall be dealt with as for contempt of court and as otherwise provided by law. Information obtained as a result of a subpoena issued pursuant to this subdivision is confidential and may be used only by the Child Support Enforcement Program in conjunction with a child support establishment or enforcement proceeding or paternity establishment proceeding.

(2) For the purposes of locating persons, establishing paternity, or enforcing child support orders, the Program shall have access to any information or data storage and retrieval system maintained and used by the Department of Transportation for drivers license issuance or motor vehicle registration, or by a law enforcement agency in this State for law enforcement purposes, as permitted pursuant to G.S. 132-1.4, except that the Program shall have access to information available to the law enforcement agency pertaining to drivers licenses and motor vehicle registrations issued in other states.

(3) Establish and implement procedures under which in IV-D cases either parent or, in the case of an assignment of support, the State may request that a child support order enforced under this Chapter be reviewed and, if appropriate,

adjusted in accordance with the most recently adopted uniform statewide child support guidelines prescribed by the Conference of Chief District Court Judges.

(4) Develop procedures for entering into agreements with financial institutions to develop and operate a data match system as provided under G.S. 110-139.2.

(5) Develop procedures for ensuring that when a noncustodial parent providing health care coverage pursuant to a court order changes employers and is eligible for health care coverage from the new employer, the new employer, upon receipt of notice of the order from the Department, enrolls the child in the employer's health care plan.

(6) Develop and implement an administrative process for paternity establishment in accordance with G.S. 110-132.2.

(7) Establish and implement administrative procedures to change the child support payee to ensure that child support payments are made to the appropriate caretaker when custody of the child has changed, in accordance with G.S. 50-13.4(d).

(8) Establish and implement expedited procedures to take the following actions relating to the establishment of paternity or to establishment of support orders, without obtaining an order from a judicial tribunal:

a. Subpoena the parties to undergo genetic testing as provided under G.S. 110-132.2;

b. Implement income withholding in accordance with this Chapter;

c. For the purpose of securing overdue support, increase the amount of monthly support payments by implementation of income withholding procedures established under G.S. 110-136.4, or by notice and opportunity to contest to an obligor who is not subject to income withholding. Increases under this subdivision are subject to the limitations of G.S. 110-136.6;

d. For purposes of exerting and retaining jurisdiction in IV-D cases, transfer cases between jurisdictions in this State without the necessity for additional filing by the petitioner or service of process upon the respondent.

(9)	Implement and maintain performance standards for each of the State and county child support enforcement offices across the State. The performance standards shall include the following:

a.	Cost per collections.

b.	Consumer satisfaction.

c.	Paternity establishments.

d.	Administrative costs.

e.	Orders established.

f.	Collections on arrearages.

g.	Location of absent parents.

h.	Other related performance measures.

The Department shall monitor the performance of each office and shall implement a system of reporting that allows each local office to review its performance as well as the performance of other local offices. The Department shall publish an annual performance report that includes the statewide and local office performance of each child support office.

(b)	As used in this section, the term "Secretary" means the Secretary of Health and Human Services, the Secretary's designee, or a designated representative as defined under G.S. 110-129(5). (1997-433, s. 2; 1997-443, s. 11A.122; 1998-17, s. 1; 2009-451, s. 10.46.)

§ 110-129.2. State Directory of New Hires established; employers required to report; civil penalties for noncompliance; definitions.

(a)	Directory Established. - There is established the State Directory of New Hires. The Directory shall be developed and maintained by the Department. The Directory shall be a central repository for employment information to assist in the location of persons owing child support, and in the establishment and enforcement of child support orders.

(b) Employer Reporting. - Every employer in this State shall report to the Directory the hiring of every employee for whom a federal W-4 form is required to be completed by the employee at the time of hiring. The employer shall report the information required under this section not later than 20 days from the date of hire, or, in the case of an employer who transmits new hire reports magnetically or electronically by two monthly transmissions, not less than 12 nor more than 16 days apart. The Department shall notify employers of the information they must report under this section and of the penalties for not reporting the required information. The required forms must be provided by the Department to employers.

(c) Report Contents. - Each report required by this section shall contain the name, address, social security number of the newly hired employee, the date services for remuneration were first performed by the newly hired employee, and the name and address of the employer and the employer's identifying number assigned under section 6109 of the Internal Revenue Code of 1986 and the employer's State employer identification number. Reports shall be made on the W-4 form or, at the option of the employer, an equivalent form, and may be transmitted magnetically, electronically, or by first-class mail.

(d) Penalties for Failure to Report. - Upon a finding that an employer has failed to comply with the reporting requirements of this section, the district court shall impose a civil penalty in an amount not to exceed twenty-five dollars ($25.00). If the court finds that an employer's failure to comply with the reporting requirements is the result of a conspiracy between the employer and the employee to not supply the required report or to supply a false or incomplete report, then the court shall impose upon the employer a civil penalty in an amount not to exceed five hundred dollars ($500.00). Penalties collected under this subsection shall be deposited to the General Fund.

(e) Entry of Report Data Into Directory. - Within five business days of receipt of the report from the employer, the Department shall enter the information from the report into the Directory.

(f) Notice to Employer to Withhold. - Within two business days of the date the information was entered into the Directory, the Department or its designated representative as defined under G.S. 110-129(5) shall transmit notice to the employer of the newly hired employee directing the employer to withhold from the income of the employee an amount equal to the monthly or other periodic child support obligation, including any past-due support obligation of the employee and subject to the limitations of G.S. 110-136.6, unless the employee's income is not subject to withholding.

(g) Other Uses of Directory Information. - The following agencies may access information entered into the Directory from employer reports for the purposes stated:

(1) The Division of Employment Security for the purpose of administering employment security programs.

(2) The North Carolina Industrial Commission for the purpose of administering workers' compensation programs.

(3) The Department of Revenue for the purpose of administering the taxes it has a duty to collect under Chapter 105 of the General Statutes.

(h) Department May Contract for Services. - The Department may contract with other State or private entities to perform the services necessary to implement this section.

(i) Information Confidential. - Except as otherwise provided in this section, information contained in the Directory is confidential and may be used only by the State Child Support Enforcement Program.

(j) Definitions. - As used in this section, unless the context clearly requires otherwise, the term:

(1) "Business day" means a day on which State offices are open for business.

(2) "Department" means the Department of Health and Human Services.

(3) "Employee" means an individual who is an employee within the meaning of Chapter 24 of the Internal Revenue Code of 1986. The term "employee" does not include an employee of a federal or State agency performing intelligence or counterintelligence functions, if the head of the agency has determined that reporting information as required under this section could endanger the safety of the employee or compromise an ongoing investigation or intelligence mission.

(4) "Employer" has the meaning given the term in section 3401(d) of the Internal Revenue Code of 1986 and includes persons who are governmental

entities and labor organizations. The term "labor organization" shall have the meaning given that term in section 2(5) of the National Labor Relations Act, and includes any entity which is used by the organization and an employer to carry out requirements described in section 8(f)(3) of the National Labor Relations Act of an agreement between the organization and the employer.

(5) "Newly hired employee" means (i) an employee who has not previously been employed by the employer and (ii) an employee who was previously employed by the employer but has been separated from such prior employment for at least 60 consecutive days. (1997-433, s. 1; 1997-443, s. 11A.122; 1998-17, s. 1; 1999-438, s. 30; 2011-401, s. 3.13; 2012-134, s. 3(a), (b).)

§ 110-130. Action by the designated representatives of the county commissioners.

Any county interested in the paternity and/or support of a dependent child may institute civil or criminal proceedings against the responsible parent of the child, or may take up and pursue any paternity and/or support action commenced by the mother, custodian or guardian of the child. Such action shall be undertaken by the designated representative in the county where the mother of the child resides or is found, in the county where the father resides or is found, or in the county where the child resides or is found. Any legal proceeding instituted under this section may be based upon information or belief. The parent of the child may be subpoenaed for testimony at the trial of the action to establish the paternity of and/or to obtain support for the child either instituted or taken up by the designated representative of the county commissioners. The husband-wife privilege shall not be grounds for excusing the mother or father from testifying at the trial nor shall said privilege be grounds for the exclusion of confidential communications between husband and wife. If a parent called for examination declines to answer upon the grounds that his testimony may tend to incriminate him, the court may require him to answer in which event he shall not thereafter be prosecuted for any criminal act involved in the conception of the child whose paternity is in issue and/or for whom support is sought, except for perjury committed in this testimony. (1975, c. 827, s. 1; 1977, 2nd Sess., c. 1186, s. 4; 1985, c. 410.)

§ 110-130.1. Non-Work First services.

(a) All child support collection and paternity determination services provided under this Article to recipients of public assistance shall be made available to any individual not receiving public assistance in accordance with federal law and as contractually authorized by the nonrecipient, upon proper application and payment of a nonrefundable application fee of twenty-five dollars ($25.00). The fee shall be reduced to ten dollars ($10.00) if the individual applying for the services is indigent. An indigent individual is an individual whose gross income does not exceed one hundred percent (100%) of the federal poverty guidelines issued each year in the Federal Register by the U.S. Department of Health and Human Services. For the purposes of this subsection, the term "gross income" has the same meaning as defined in G.S. 105-134.1.

In the case of an individual who has never received assistance under a State program funded pursuant to Title IV-A of the Social Security Act and for whom the State has collected and disbursed to the family in a federal fiscal year at least five hundred dollars ($500.00) of support, the State shall impose an annual fee of twenty-five dollars ($25.00) for each case in which services are furnished. The child support agency shall retain the fee from support collected on behalf of the individual. However, the child support agency shall not retain the fee from the first five hundred dollars ($500.00) collected. The child support agency shall use the fee to support the ongoing operation of the program.

(b) Repealed by Session Laws 1989, c. 490.

(b1) In cases in which a public assistance debt which accrued pursuant to G.S. 110-135 remains unrecovered, support payments shall be transmitted to the Department of Health and Human Services for appropriate distribution. When services are terminated and all costs and any public assistance debts have been satisfied, the support payment shall be redirected to the client.

(c) Actions or proceedings to establish, enforce, or modify a duty of support or establish paternity as initiated under this Article shall be brought in the name of the county or State agency on behalf of the public assistance recipient or nonrecipient client. Collateral disputes between a custodial parent and noncustodial parent, involving visitation, custody and similar issues, shall be considered only in separate proceedings from actions initiated under this Article. The attorney representing the designated representative of programs under Title IV-D of the Social Security Act shall be deemed attorney of record only for proceedings under this Article, and not for the separate proceedings. No attorney/client relationship shall be considered to have been created between the attorney who represents the child support enforcement agency and any person by virtue of the action of the attorney in providing the services required.

(c1) The Department is hereby authorized to use the electronic and print media in attempting to locate absent and deserting parents. Due diligence must be taken to ensure that the information used is accurate or has been verified. Print media shall be under no obligation or duty, except that of good faith, to anyone to verify the correctness of any information furnished to it by the Department or county departments of social services.

(d) Any fee imposed by the North Carolina Department of Revenue or the Secretary of the Treasury to cover their costs of withholding for non-Work First arrearages certified for the collection of past due support from State or federal income tax refunds shall be borne by the client by deducting the fee from the amount collected.

Any income tax refund offset amounts which are subsequently determined to have been incorrectly withheld and distributed to a client, and which must be refunded by the State to a responsible parent or the nondebtor spouse, shall constitute a debt to the State owed by the client. (1983, c. 527, s. 1; 1985, c. 781, ss. 1-5; 1985 (Reg. Sess., 1986), c. 931, ss. 1-3; 1989, c. 490; 1995, c. 538, s. 3; 1997-223, s. 2; 1997-443, ss. 11A.118(a), 12.28; 2007-460, s. 1.)

§ 110-130.2. Collection of spousal support.

Spousal support shall be collected for a spouse or former spouse with whom the absent parent's child is living when a child support order is being enforced under this Article. However, the spousal support shall be collected: (i) only if there is an order establishing the support obligation with respect to such spouse; and (ii) only if an order establishing the support obligation with respect to the child is being enforced under this Article. The Child Support Enforcement Program is not authorized to assist in the establishment of a spousal support obligation. (1985, c. 506, s. 1.)

§ 110-131. Compelling disclosure of information respecting the nonsupporting responsible parent of a child receiving public assistance.

(a) If a parent of any dependent child receiving public assistance fails or refuses to cooperate with the county in locating and securing support from a nonsupporting responsible parent, this parent may be cited to appear before any judge of the district court and compelled to disclose such information under oath and/or may be declared ineligible for public assistance by the county department of social services for as long as he fails to cooperate.

(b) Any parent who, having been cited to appear before a judge of the district court pursuant to subsection (a), fails or refuses to appear or fails or refuses to provide the information requested may be found to be in contempt of said court and may be fined not more than one hundred dollars ($100.00) or imprisoned not more than six months or both.

(c) Any parent who is declared ineligible for public assistance by the county department of social services shall have his needs excluded from consideration in determining the amount of the grant, and the needs of the remaining family members shall be met in the form of a protective payment in accordance with G.S. 108-50. (1975, c. 827, s. 1.)

§ 110-131.1. Notice; due process requirements met.

In any child support enforcement proceeding the trial court may deem State due process requirements for notice and service of process to be met with respect to the nonmoving party, upon delivery of written notice in accordance with the notice requirements of Chapter 1A-1, Rule 5(b) of the Rules of Civil Procedure with respect to all pleadings subsequent to the original complaint. (1997-433, s. 2.3; 1998-17, s. 1.)

§ 110-132. Affidavit of parentage and agreement to motion to set aside affidavit of parentage.

(a) In lieu of or in conclusion of any legal proceeding instituted to establish paternity, the written affidavits of parentage executed by the putative father and the mother of the dependent child shall constitute an admission of paternity and shall have the same legal effect as a judgment of paternity for the purpose of establishing a child support obligation, subject to the right of either signatory to rescind within the earlier of:

(1) 60 days of the date the document is executed, or

(2) The date of entry of an order establishing paternity or an order for the payment of child support.

In order to rescind, a challenger must request the district court to order the rescission and to include in the order specific findings of fact that the request for rescission was filed with the clerk of court within 60 days of the signing of the document. The court must also find that all parties, including the child support enforcement agency, if appropriate, have been served in accordance with Rule 4 of the North Carolina Rules of Civil Procedure. In the event the court orders rescission and the putative father is thereafter found not to be the father of the child, then the clerk of court shall send a copy of the order of rescission to the State Registrar of Vital Statistics. Upon receipt of an order of rescission, the State Registrar shall remove the putative father's name from the birth certificate. In the event that the putative father defaults or fails to present or prosecute the issue of paternity, the trial court shall find the putative father to be the biological father as a matter of law.

(a1) Paternity established under subsection (a) of this section may be set aside in accordance with subsection (a2) of this section or in accordance with G.S. 50-13.13.

(a2) Notwithstanding the time limitations of G.S. 1A-1, Rule 60 of the North Carolina Rules of Civil Procedure, or any other provision of law, an affidavit of parentage may be set aside by a trial court after 60 days have elapsed if each of the following applies:

(1) The affidavit of parentage was entered as the result of fraud, duress, mutual mistake, or excusable neglect.

(2) Genetic tests establish that the putative father is not the biological father of the child.

The burden of proof in any motion to set aside an affidavit of parentage after 60 days allowed for rescission shall be on the moving party. Upon proper motion alleging fraud, duress, mutual mistake, or excusable neglect, the court shall order the child's mother, the child whose parentage is at issue, and the putative father to submit to genetic paternity testing pursuant to G.S. 8-50.1(b1). If the court determines, as a result of genetic testing, the putative father is not the biological father of the child and the affidavit of parentage was entered as a result of fraud, duress, mutual mistake, or excusable neglect, the court may set aside the affidavit of parentage. Nothing in this subsection shall be construed to affect the presumption of legitimacy where a child is born to a mother and the putative father during the course of a marriage.

(a3) A written agreement to support the child by periodic payments, which may include provision for reimbursement for medical expenses incident to the pregnancy and the birth of the child, accrued maintenance and reasonable expense of prosecution of the paternity action, when acknowledged as provided herein, filed with, and approved by a judge of the district court at any time, shall have the same force and effect as an order of support entered by that court, and shall be enforceable and subject to modification in the same manner as is provided by law for orders of the court in such cases. The written affidavit shall contain the social security number of the person executing the affidavit. Voluntary agreements to support shall contain the social security number of each of the parties to the agreement. The written affidavits and agreements to support shall be sworn to before a certifying officer or notary public or the equivalent or corresponding person of the state, territory, or foreign country where the affirmation, acknowledgment, or agreement is made, and shall be binding on the person executing the same whether the person is an adult or a minor. The child support enforcement agency shall ensure that the mother and putative father are given oral and written notice of the legal consequences and responsibilities arising from the signing of an affidavit of parentage and of any alternatives to the execution of an affidavit of parentage. The mother shall not be excused from making the affidavit on the grounds that it may tend to disgrace or incriminate her; nor shall she thereafter be prosecuted for any criminal act involved in the conception of the child as to whose paternity she attests.

(b) At any time after the filing with the district court of an affidavit of parentage, upon the application of any interested party, the court or any judge thereof shall cause a summons signed by him or by the clerk or assistant clerk of superior court, to be issued, requiring the putative father to appear in court at a time and place named therein, to show cause, if any he has, why the court should not enter an order for the support of the child by periodic payments, which order may include provision for reimbursement for medical expenses incident to the pregnancy and the birth of the child, accrued maintenance and reasonable expense of the action under this subsection on the affidavit of parentage previously filed with said court. The court may order the responsible parents in a IV-D establishment case to perform a job search, if the responsible parent is not incapacitated. This includes IV-D cases in which the responsible parent is a noncustodial mother or a noncustodial father whose affidavit of parentage has been filed with the court or when paternity is not at issue for the child. The court may further order the responsible parent to participate in the work activities, as defined in 42 U.S.C. § 607, as the court deems appropriate. The amount of child support payments so ordered shall be determined as provided in G.S. 50-13.4(c). The prior judgment as to paternity shall be res judicata as to that issue and shall not be reconsidered by the court. (1975, c. 827, s. 1; 1977, 2nd Sess., c. 1186, ss. 5, 6; 1981, c. 275, s. 8; 1989, c. 529, s. 8; 1997-433, s. 4.7; 1998-17, s. 1; 1999-293, s. 1; 2001-237, s. 2; 2011-328, s. 2.)

§ 110-132.1. Paternity determination by another state entitled to full faith and credit.

A paternity determination made by another state:

(1)   In accordance with the laws of that state, and

(2)   By any means that is recognized in that state as establishing paternity

shall be entitled to full faith and credit in this State. (1993 (Reg. Sess., 1994), c. 733, s. 2.)

§ 110-132.2. Expedited procedures to establish paternity in IV-D cases.

(a)   In a IV-D court action, a local child support enforcement office may, without obtaining a court order, subpoena a minor child, the minor child's mother, and the putative father of the minor child (including the mother's husband, if different from the putative father) to appear for the purpose of undergoing blood or genetic testing to establish paternity. A subpoena issued pursuant to this section must be served in accordance with Rule 4 of the North Carolina Rules of Civil Procedure. Refusal to comply with a subpoena may be dealt with as for contempt of court, and as otherwise provided under law. A party may contest the results of the genetic or blood test. If the results are contested, the agency shall, upon request and advance payment by the contestant, obtain additional testing.

(b) A person subpoenaed to submit to testing pursuant to subsection (a) of this section may contest the subpoena. To contest the subpoena, a person must, within 15 days of receipt of the subpoena, request a hearing in the county where the local child support enforcement office that issued the subpoena is located. The hearing shall be before the district court and notice of the hearing must be served by the petitioner on all parties to the proceeding. Service shall be in accordance with Rule 4 of the North Carolina Rules of Civil Procedure. The hearing shall be held and a determination made within 30 days of the petitioner's request for hearing as to whether the petitioner must comply with the subpoena to undergo testing. If the trial court determines that the petitioner must comply with the subpoena, the determination shall not prejudice any defenses the petitioner may present at any future paternity litigation. (1997-433, s. 4.11; 1998-17, s. 1.)

§ 110-133. Agreements of support.

In lieu of or in conclusion of any legal proceeding instituted to obtain support from a responsible parent for a dependent child born of the marriage, a written agreement to support the child by periodic payments executed by the responsible parent when acknowledged before a certifying officer or notary public or the equivalent or corresponding person of the state, territory, or foreign country where the acknowledgment is made and filed with and approved by a judge of the district court in the county where the custodial parent of the child resides or is found, or in the county where the noncustodial parent resides or is found, or in the county where the child resides or is found shall have the same force and effect, retroactively and prospectively, in accordance with the terms of the agreement, as an order of support entered by the court, and shall be enforceable and subject to modification in the same manner as is provided by law for orders of the court in such cases. A responsible parent executing a written agreement under this section shall provide on the agreement the responsible parent's social security number. (1975, c. 827, s. 1; 1977, 2nd Sess., c. 1186, s. 7; 1995, c. 538, s. 5; 1997-433, s. 4.8; 1998-17, s. 1.)

§ 110-134. Filing of affidavits, agreements, and orders; fees.

All affidavits, agreements, and resulting orders entered into under the provisions of G.S. 110-132 and G.S. 110-133 shall be filed by the clerk of superior court in the county in which they are entered. The filing fee for the institution of an action through the entry of an order under either of these provisions shall be in an amount equal to that provided in G.S. 7A-308(a)(18). (1975, c. 827, s. 1; 1977, 2nd Sess., c. 1186, s. 8; 2001-237, s. 3; 2010-31, s. 15.6.)

§ 110-135. Debt to State created.

Acceptance of public assistance by or on behalf of a dependent child creates a debt, in the amount of public assistance paid, due and owing the State by the responsible parent or parents of the child. Provided, however, that in those cases in which child support was required to be paid incident to a court order during the time of receipt of public assistance, the debt shall be limited to the amount specified in such court order. This liability shall attach only to public assistance granted subsequent to June 30, 1975, and only with respect to the period of time during which public assistance is granted, and only if the responsible parent or parents were financially able to furnish support during this period.

The United States, the State of North Carolina, and any county within the State which has provided public assistance to or on behalf of a dependent child shall be entitled to share in any sum collected under this section, and their proportionate parts of such sum shall be determined in accordance with the matching formulas in use during the period for which assistance was paid.

No action to collect such debt shall be commenced after the expiration of five years subsequent to the receipt of the last grant of public assistance. The county attorney or an attorney retained by the county and/or State shall represent the State in all proceedings brought under this section.

A past-due public assistance debt as described in this section may be deemed negotiable and subject to reduction if the public assistance debt is not less than fifteen thousand dollars ($15,000) and the responsible parent continues to be obligated to pay current child support. Upon agreement between the State and the responsible parent, and upon approval of the court upon an inquiry into the financial status of the obligor, the responsible parent shall pay all child support payments, including payments due on child support arrears, entered by a valid court order for a 24-month period of time. Upon the timely payment of each court-ordered child support obligation during the full 24-month period, including payments due on child support arrears, the State shall reduce the responsible parent's public assistance debt by two-thirds. If the responsible parent is late or defaults on any single payment during the 24-month period, no portion of the public assistance debt shall be reduced. The responsible parent may attempt to achieve 24 consecutive months of child support payments as often as possible in order to reduce his or her public assistance debt. However, once the responsible parent's public assistance debt has been reduced by two-thirds because of the successful completion of this agreement, the responsible parent shall no longer be eligible for this program. The reduction of public assistance debt as set forth in this section shall be in addition to all other remedies available to the State for the retirement of the debt. This program shall not prevent the State from taking any and all other measures available by law.

Upon the termination of a child support obligation due to the death of the obligor, the Department shall determine whether the obligor's estate contains sufficient assets to satisfy any child support arrearages. If sufficient assets are available, the Department shall attempt to collect the arrearage. (1975, c. 827, s. 1; 1977, 2nd Sess., c. 1186, ss. 9, 10; 2003-288, s. 1.1; 2005-389, s. 2.)

§ 110-136. Garnishment for enforcement of child-support obligation.

(a) Notwithstanding any other provision of the law, in any case in which a responsible parent is under a court order or has entered into a written agreement pursuant to G.S. 110-132 or 110-133 to provide child support, a judge of the district court in the county where the mother of the child resides or is found, or in the county where the father resides or is found, or in the county where the child resides or is found may enter an order of garnishment whereby no more than forty percent (40%) of the responsible parent's monthly disposable earnings shall be garnished for the support of his minor child. For purposes of this section, "disposable earnings" is defined as that part of the compensation paid or payable to the responsible parent for personal services, whether denominated as wages, salary, commission, bonus, or otherwise (including periodic payments pursuant to a pension, retirement, or other deferred compensation program) which remains after the deduction of any amounts required by law to be withheld. The garnishee is the person, firm, association, or corporation by whom the responsible parent is employed.

(b) The mother, father, custodian, or guardian of the child or any designated representative interested in the support of a dependent child may move the court for an order of garnishment. The motion shall be verified and shall state that the responsible parent is under court order or has entered into a written agreement pursuant to G.S. 110-132 or 110-133 to provide child support, that said parent is delinquent in such child support or has been erratic in making child-support payments, the name and address of the employer of the responsible parent, the responsible parent's monthly disposable earnings from said employer (which may be based upon information and belief), and the amount sought to be garnished, not to exceed forty percent (40%) of the responsible parent's monthly disposable earnings. The motion for the wage garnishment order along with a motion to join the alleged employer as a third-party garnishee defendant shall be served on both the responsible parent and the alleged employer in accordance with the provisions of G.S. 1A-1, Rules of Civil Procedure. The time period for answering or otherwise responding to pleadings, motions and other papers issued pursuant to this section shall be in accordance with the time periods set forth in G.S. 1A-1, Rules of Civil Procedure, except that the alleged employer third-party garnishee shall have 10 days from the date of service of process to answer both the motion to join him as a defendant garnishee and the motion for the wage garnishment order.

(b1)   In addition to the foregoing method for instituting a continuing wage garnishment proceeding for child support through motion, the mother, father, custodian, or guardian of the child or any designated representative interested in the support of a dependent child may in an independent proceeding petition the court for an order of continuing wage garnishment. The petition shall be verified and shall state that the responsible parent is under court order or has entered into a written agreement pursuant to G.S. 110-132 or 110-133 to provide child support, that said parent is delinquent in such child support or has been erratic in making child-support payments, the name and address of the alleged-employer garnishee of the responsible parent, the responsible parent's monthly disposable earnings from said employer (which may be based on information and belief), and the amount sought to be garnished, not to exceed forty percent (40%) of the responsible parent's monthly disposable earnings. The petition shall be served on both the responsible parent and his alleged employer in accordance with the provisions for service of process set forth in G.S. 1A-1, Rule 4. The time period for answering or otherwise responding to process issued pursuant to this section shall be in accordance with the time periods set forth in G.S. 1A-1, Rules of Civil Procedure.

(c)   Following the hearing held pursuant to this section, the court may enter an order of garnishment not to exceed forty percent (40%) of the responsible parent's monthly disposable earnings. If an order of garnishment is entered, a copy of same shall be served on the responsible parent and the garnishee either personally or by certified or registered mail, return receipt requested. The order shall set forth sufficient findings of fact to support the action by the court and the amount to be garnished for each pay period. The amount garnished shall be increased by an additional one dollar ($1.00) processing fee to be assessed and retained by the employer for each payment under the order. The order shall be subject to review for modification and dissolution upon the filing of a motion in the cause.

(d)   Upon receipt of an order of garnishment, the garnishee shall transmit without delay to the State Child Support Collection and Disbursement Unit the amount ordered by the court to be garnished. These funds shall be disbursed to the party designated by the court which in those cases of dependent children receiving public assistance shall be the North Carolina Department of Health and Human Services.

(e)   Any garnishee violating the terms of an order of garnishment shall be subject to punishment as for contempt. (1975, c. 827, s. 1; 1977, 2nd Sess., c. 1186, ss. 11, 12; 1979, c. 386, ss. 1-8; 1983 (Reg. Sess., 1984), c. 1047, s. 1; 1985, c. 660, s. 2; 1997-443, s. 11A.118(a); 1999-293, s. 17.)

§ 110-136.1. Assignment of wages for child support.

Pursuant to G.S. 50-13.4(f)(1), the court may require the responsible parent to execute an assignment of wages, salary, or other income due or to become due whenever his employer's voluntary written acceptance of the wage assignment under G.S. 95-31 is filed with the court. Such acceptance remains effective until the employer files an express written revocation with the court. The amount assigned shall be increased by an additional one dollar ($1.00) processing fee to be assessed and retained by the employer for each payment under the order. (1981, c. 275, s. 7; 1983 (Reg. Sess., 1984), c. 1047, s. 2.)

§ 110-136.2. Use of unemployment compensation benefits for child support.

(a)   A responsible parent may voluntarily assign unemployment compensation benefits to a child support agency to satisfy a child support obligation or a child support enforcement agency may request a responsible parent to voluntarily assign unemployment benefits to satisfy a child support obligation. An assignment of less than the full amount of the support obligation shall not relieve the responsible parent of liability for the remaining amount.

(b) Upon notification of a voluntary assignment by the Department of Health and Human Services, the Division of Employment Security shall deduct and withhold the amount assigned by the responsible parent as provided in G.S. 96-17.

(c) Any amount deducted and withheld shall be paid by the Division of Employment Security to the Department of Health and Human Services for distribution as required by federal law.

(d) Voluntary assignment of unemployment compensation benefits shall remain effective until the Division of Employment Security receives notification from the Department of Health and Human Services of an express written revocation by the responsible parent.

(e) The Department of Health and Human Services shall ensure that payments received under this section are properly credited against the responsible parent's child support obligation.

(f) In the absence of a voluntary assignment of unemployment compensation benefits, the Department of Health and Human Services shall implement income withholding as provided in this Article for IV-D cases. The amount withheld shall not exceed twenty-five percent (25%) of the unemployment compensation benefits. Notice of the requirement to withhold shall be served upon the Division and payment shall be made by the Division directly to the Department of Health and Human Services pursuant to G.S. 96-17 or to another state under G.S. 52C-5-501. Except for the requirement to withhold from unemployment compensation benefits and the forwarding of withheld funds to the Department of Health and Human Services or to another state under G.S. 52C-5-501, the Division is exempt from the provisions of G.S. 110-136.8. (1983, c. 33, s. 1; 1987, c. 764, ss. 1, 2; 1997-443, s. 11A.118(a); 1999-293, s. 6; 2011-401, s. 3.14.)

§ 110-136.3. Income withholding procedures; applicability.

(a) Required Contents of Support Orders. All child support orders, civil or criminal, entered or modified in the State in IV-D cases shall include a provision ordering income withholding to take effect immediately. All child support orders, civil or criminal, initially entered in the State in non-IV-D cases on or after January 1, 1994, shall include a provision ordering income withholding to take effect immediately as provided in G.S. 110-136.5(c1), unless one of the exceptions specified in G.S. 110-136.5(c1) applies. A non-IV-D child support order that contains an income withholding requirement and a IV-D child support order shall:

(1)   Require the obligor to keep the clerk of court or IV-D agency informed of the obligor's current residence and mailing address;

(2),(2a) Repealed by Session Laws 1993, c. 517, s. 1.

(3)   Require the obligor to cooperate fully with the initiating party in the verification of the amount of the obligor's disposable income;

(4)   Require the custodial party to keep the obligor informed of (i) the custodial party's disposable income and the amount and effective date of any substantial change in this disposable income and (ii) the current residence and mailing address of the child, unless the court has determined that notice to the obligor is inappropriate because the obligor has made verbal or physical threats that constitute domestic violence under Chapter 50B of the General Statutes; and

(5)   Require the obligor to keep the initiating party informed of the name and address of any payor of the obligor's disposable income and of the amount and effective date of any substantial change in this disposable income.

(a1)   Payment Plan/Work Requirement for Past-Due Support. In any IV-D case in which an obligor owes past-due support and income withholding has been ordered but cannot be implemented against the obligor, the court may order the obligor to pay the support in accordance with a payment plan approved by the court and, if the obligor is subject to the payment plan and is not incapacitated, the court may order the obligor to participate in such work activities, as defined under 42 U.S.C. § 607, as the court deems appropriate.

(b)   When obligor subject to withholding.

(1)   In IV-D cases in which a new or modified child support order is entered on or after October 1, 1989, an obligor is subject to income withholding immediately upon entry of the order. In IV-D cases in which the child support order was entered prior to October 1, 1989, an obligor shall become subject to income withholding on the date on which the obligor fails to make legally

obligated child support payments in an amount equal to the support payable for one month, or the date on which the obligor or obligee requests withholding.

(2)   In non-IV-D cases in which the child support order was entered prior to January 1, 1994, an obligor shall be subject to income withholding on the earliest of:

a.   The date on which the obligor fails to make legally obligated child support payments in an amount equal to the support payable for one month;

b.   The date on which the obligor requests withholding; or

c.   The date on which the court determines, pursuant to a motion or independent action filed by the obligee under G.S. 110-136.5(a), that the obligor is or has been delinquent in making child support payments or has been erratic in making child support payments.

(3)   In IV-D child support cases in which an order was issued or modified in this State prior to October 1, 1996, and in which the obligor is not otherwise subject to withholding, the obligor shall become subject to withholding if the obligor fails to make legally obligated child support payments in an amount equal to the support payable for one month.

(4)   In the enforcement of alimony or postseparation support orders pursuant to G.S. 110-130.2, an obligor shall become subject to income withholding on the earlier of:

a.   The date on which the obligor fails to make legally obligated alimony or postseparation payments; or

b.   The date on which the obligor or obligee requests withholding.

(c)   Repealed by Session Laws 1993, c. 517, s. 1.

(d)   Interstate cases. An interstate case is one in which a child support order of one state is to be enforced in another state.

(1)   In interstate cases withholding provisions shall apply to a child support order of this or any other state. A petition addressed to this State to enforce a child support order of another state or a petition from an initiating party in this

State addressed to another state to enforce a child support order entered in this State shall include:

a. A certified copy of the support order with all modifications, including any income withholding notice or order still in effect;

b. A copy of the income withholding law of the jurisdiction which issued the support order, provided that this jurisdiction has a withholding law;

c. A sworn statement of arrearages;

d. The name, address, and social security number of the obligor, if known;

e. The name and address of the obligor's employer or of any other source of income of the obligor derived in the state in which withholding is sought; and

f. The name and address of the agency or person to whom support payments collected by income withholding shall be transmitted.

(2) The law of the state in which the support order was entered shall apply in determining when withholding shall be implemented and interpreting the child support order. The law and procedures of the state where the obligor is employed shall apply in all other respects.

(3) Except as otherwise provided by subdivision (2), income withholding initiated under this subsection is subject to all of the notice, hearing and other provisions of Chapter 110.

(4) In all interstate cases notices and orders to withhold shall be served upon the payor by a North Carolina agency or judicial officer. In all interstate non-IV-D cases, the advance notice to the obligor shall be served pursuant to G.S. 1A-1, Rule 4, Rules of Civil Procedure.

(5) For purposes of enforcing a petition under this subsection, jurisdiction is limited to the purposes of income withholding and Chapter 52A of the General Statutes shall not apply. Nothing in this subsection precludes any remedy otherwise available in a proceeding under Chapter 52A of the General Statutes.

(d1) Recodified as § 110-139(c1) by Session Laws 2001-237, s. 5.

(e) Procedures and regulations. Procedures, rules, regulations, forms, and instructions necessary to effect the income withholding provisions of this Article shall be established by the Secretary of the Department of Health and Human Services or the Secretary's designee and the Administrative Office of the Courts. Forms and instructions shall be sent with each order or notice of withholding. (1985 (Reg. Sess., 1986), c. 949, s. 2; 1987, c. 589, s. 1; 1989, c. 601, s. 2; 1993, c. 517, s. 1; 1997-433, ss. 3, 6.1; 1997-443, s. 11A.118(a); 1998-17, s. 1; 1998-176, s. 4; 2000-140, s. 20(b); 2001-237, s. 5.)

§ 110-136.4. Implementation of withholding in IV-D cases.

(a) Withholding based on arrearages or obligor's request.

(1) Advance notice of withholding. When an obligor in a IV-D case becomes subject to income withholding, the obligee shall, after verifying the obligor's current employer or other payor, wages or other disposable income, and mailing address, serve the obligor with advance notice of withholding in accordance with G.S. 1A-1, Rule 4, Rules of Civil Procedure.

(2) Contents of advance notice. The advance notice to the obligor shall contain, at a minimum, the following information:

a. Whether the proposed withholding is based on the obligor's failure to make legally obligated child support, alimony or postseparation support payments on the obligor's request for withholding, on the obligee's request for withholding, or on the obligor's eligibility for withholding under G.S. 110-136.3(b)(3);

b. The amount of overdue child support, overdue alimony or postseparation support payments, the total amount to be withheld, and when the withholding will occur;

c. The name of each child or person for whose benefit the child support, alimony or postseparation support payments are due and information sufficient to identify the court order under which the obligor has a duty to support the child, spouse, or former spouse;

d. The amount and sources of disposable income;

e. That the withholding will apply to the obligor's wages or other sources of disposable income from current payors and all subsequent payors once the procedures under this section are invoked;

f. An explanation of the obligor's rights and responsibilities pursuant to this section;

g. That withholding will be continued until terminated pursuant to G.S. 110-136.10.

(3) Contested withholding. The obligor may contest the withholding only on the basis of a mistake of fact, except that G.S. 110-129(10)(a) is not applicable if withholding is based on the obligor's or obligee's request for withholding. To contest the withholding, the obligor must, within 10 days of receipt of the advance notice of withholding, request a hearing in the county where the support order was entered before the district court and give notice to the obligee specifying the mistake of fact upon which the hearing request is based. If the asserted mistake of fact can be resolved by agreement between the obligee and the obligor, no hearing shall occur. Otherwise, a hearing shall be held and a determination made, within 30 days of the obligor's receipt of the advance notice of withholding, as to whether the asserted mistake of fact is valid. No withholding shall occur pending the hearing decision. The failure to hold a hearing within 30 days shall not invalidate an otherwise properly entered order. If it is determined that a mistake of fact exists, no withholding shall occur. Otherwise, within 45 days of the obligor's receipt of the advance notice of withholding, the obligee shall serve the payor, pursuant to G.S. 1A-1, Rule 5, Rules of Civil Procedure, with notice of his obligation to withhold, and shall mail a copy of such notice to the obligor and file a copy with the clerk. In the event of appeal, withholding shall not be stayed. If the appeal is concluded in favor of the obligor, the obligee shall promptly repay sums wrongfully withheld and notify the payor to cease withholding.

(4) Uncontested withholding. If the obligor does not contest the withholding within the 10-day response period, the obligee shall serve the payor, pursuant to G.S. 1A-1, Rule 5, Rules of Civil Procedure, with notice of his obligation to withhold, and shall mail a copy of such notice to the obligor and file a copy with the clerk.

(5) Payment not a defense to withholding. The payment of overdue support shall not be a basis for terminating or not implementing withholding.

(6) Inability to implement withholding. When an obligor is subject to withholding, but withholding under this section cannot be implemented because the obligor's location is unknown, because the extent and source of his disposable income cannot be determined, or for any other reason, the obligee shall either request the clerk of superior court to initiate enforcement proceedings under G.S. 15A-1344.1(d) or G.S. 50-13.9(d) or take other appropriate available measures to enforce the support obligation.

(b) Immediate income withholding. When a new or modified child support order is entered, the district court judge shall, after hearing evidence regarding the obligor's disposable income, place the obligor under an order for immediate income withholding. The IV-D agency shall serve the payor pursuant to G.S. 1A-1, Rule 5, Rules of Civil Procedure, with a notice of his obligation to withhold, and shall mail a copy of such notice to the obligor and file a copy with the clerk. If information is unavailable regarding an obligor's disposable income, or the obligor is unemployed, or an agreement is reached between both parties which provides for an alternative arrangement, immediate income withholding shall not apply. The obligor, however, is subject to income withholding pursuant to G.S. 110-136.4(a).

(c) Subsequent payors. If the obligor changes employment or source of disposable income, notice to subsequent payors of their obligation to withhold shall be served as required by G.S. 1A-1, Rule 5, Rules of Civil Procedure. Copies of such notice shall be filed with the clerk of court and served upon the obligor by first class mail.

(d) Multiple withholdings. The obligor must notify the obligee if the obligor is currently subject to another withholding for child support. In the case of two or more withholdings against one obligor, the obligee or obligees shall attempt to resolve any conflict between the orders in a manner that is fair and equitable to all parties and within the limits specified by G.S. 110-136.6. If the conflict cannot be so resolved, an injured party, upon request, shall be granted a hearing in accordance with the procedure specified in G.S. 110-136.4(c). The conflict between the withholding orders shall be resolved in accordance with G.S. 110-136.7.

(e) Modification of withholding. When an order for withholding has been entered under this section, the obligee may modify the withholding based on changed circumstances. The obligee shall proceed as is provided in this section.

(f) Applicability of section. The provisions of this section apply to IV-D cases only. (1985 (Reg. Sess., 1986), c. 949, s. 2; 1989, c. 601, s. 3; 1997-433, s. 6.2; 1998-17, s. 1; 1998-176, s. 5; 2001-237, s. 4.)

§ 110-136.5. Implementation of withholding in non-IV-D cases.

(a) Withholding based on delinquent or erratic payments. Notwithstanding any other provision of law, when an obligor is delinquent in making child support payments or has been erratic in making child support payments, the obligee may apply to the court, by motion or in an independent action, for an order for income withholding.

(1) The motion or complaint shall be verified and state, to the extent known:

a. Whether the obligor is under a court order to provide child support and, if so, information sufficient to identify the order;

b. Either:

1. That the obligor is currently delinquent in making child support payments; or

2. That the obligor has been erratic in making child support payments;

c. The amount of overdue support and the total amount sought to be withheld;

d. The name of each child for whose benefit support is payable; and

e. The name, location, and mailing address of the payor or payors from whom withholding is sought and the amount of the obligor's monthly disposable income from each payor.

(2) The motion or complaint shall include or be accompanied by a notice to the obligor, stating:

a. That withholding, if implemented, will apply to the obligor's current payors and all subsequent payors; and

b. That withholding, if implemented, will be continued until terminated pursuant to G.S. 110-136.10.

At any time the parties may agree to income withholding by consent order.

(b) Withholding Based on Obligor's Request. The obligor may request at any time that income withholding be implemented. The request may be made either verbally in open court or by written request.

(1) A written request for withholding shall state:

a. That the obligor is under a court order to provide child support, and information sufficient to identify the order;

b. Whether the obligor is delinquent and the amount of any overdue support;

c. The name of each child for whose benefit support is payable;

d. The name, location, and mailing address of the payor or payors from whom the obligor receives disposable income and the amount of the obligor's monthly disposable income from each payor;

e. That the obligor understands that withholding, if implemented, will apply to the obligor's current payors and all subsequent payors and will be continued until terminated pursuant to G.S. 110-136.10; and

f. That the obligor understands that the amount withheld will include an amount sufficient to pay current child support, an additional amount toward liquidation of any arrearages, and a two dollar ($2.00) processing fee to be retained by the employer for each withholding, but that the total amount withheld may not exceed the following percent of disposable income:

1. Forty percent (40%) if there is only one order for withholding;

2. Forty-five percent (45%) if there is more than one order for withholding and the obligor is supporting other dependent children or his or her spouse; or

3. Fifty percent (50%) if there is more than one order for withholding and the obligor is not supporting other dependent children or a spouse.

(2) A written request for withholding shall be filed in the office of the clerk of superior court of the court that entered the order for child support. If the request states and the clerk verifies that the obligor is not delinquent, the court may enter an order for withholding without further notice or hearing. If the request states or the clerk finds that the obligor is delinquent, the matter shall be scheduled for hearing unless the obligor in writing waives his right to a hearing and consents to the entry of an order for withholding of an amount the court determines to be appropriate. The court may require a hearing in any case. Notice of any hearing under this subdivision shall be sent to the obligee.

(c) Order for withholding. If the district court judge finds after hearing evidence that the obligor, at the time of the filing of the motion or complaint was, or at the time of the hearing is, delinquent in child support payments or that the obligor has been erratic in making child support payments in accordance with G.S. 110-136.5(a), or that the obligor has requested that income withholding begin in accordance with G.S. 110-136.5(b), the court shall enter an order for income withholding, unless:

(1) The obligor proves a mistake of fact, except that G.S. 110-129(10)(a) is not applicable if withholding is based on the obligee's motion or independent action alleging that the obligor is delinquent or has been erratic in making child support payments; or

(2) The court finds that the child support obligation can be enforced and the child's right to receive support can be ensured without entry of an order for income withholding; or

(3) The court finds that the obligor has no disposable income subject to withholding or that withholding is not feasible for any other reason.

If the obligor fails to respond or appear, the court shall hear evidence and enter an order as provided herein.

(c1) Immediate income withholding. In non-IV-D cases in which a child support order is initially entered on or after January 1, 1994, an obligor is subject to income withholding immediately upon entry of the order, unless either of the following applies:

a. One of the parties demonstrates, and the court finds, that there is good cause not to require immediate income withholding.

b. A written agreement is reached between the parties that provides for an alternative arrangement.

The term "good cause" as used in this subsection includes a reasonable and workable plan for consistent and timely payments by some means other than income withholding. In considering whether a plan is reasonable, the court may consider the obligor's employment history and record of meeting financial obligations in a timely manner.

In entering an order for immediate income withholding under this subsection, the court shall follow the requirements and procedures as specified in other sections of this Article, including amount to be withheld, multiple withholdings, notice to payor, and termination of withholding.

(d) Notice to payor and obligor. If an order for income withholding is entered, a notice of obligation to withhold shall be served on the payor as required by G.S. 1A-1, Rule 5, Rules of Civil Procedure. Copies of such notice shall be filed with the clerk of court and served upon the obligor by first class mail.

(e) Modification of withholding. When an order for withholding has been entered under this section, any party may file a motion seeking modification of the withholding based on changed circumstances. The clerk or the court on its own motion may initiate a hearing for modification when it appears that modification of the withholding is required or appropriate. (1985 (Reg. Sess., 1986), c. 949, s. 2; 1987, c. 60; 1989, c. 601, s. 4; 1993, c. 517, s. 2; 1999-293, s. 18; 2001-487, s. 72.)

§ 110-136.6. Amount to be withheld.

(a) Computation of amount. When income withholding is implemented pursuant to this Article, the amount to be withheld shall include:

(1) An amount sufficient to pay current child support; and

(2) An additional amount toward liquidation of arrearages; and

(3) A processing fee of two dollars ($2.00) to cover the cost of withholding, to be retained by the payor for each withholding unless waived by the payor.

The amount withheld may also include court costs and attorneys fees as may be awarded by the court in non-IV-D cases and as may be awarded by the court in IV-D cases pursuant to G.S. 110-130.1.

(b) Limits on amount withheld. Withholding for current support, arrearages, processing fees, court costs, and attorneys fees shall not exceed forty percent (40%) of the obligor's disposable income for one pay period from the payor when there is one order of withholding. The sum of multiple withholdings, for current support, arrearages, processing fees, court costs, and attorneys fees shall not exceed:

(1) Forty-five percent (45%) of disposable income for one pay period from the payor in the case of an obligor who is supporting his spouse or other dependent children; or

(2) Fifty percent (50%) of disposable income for one pay period from the payor in the case of an obligor who is not supporting a spouse or other dependent children.

(b1) When there is an order of income withholding for current or delinquent payments of alimony or postseparation support or for any portion of the payments, the total amount withheld under this Article and under G.S. 50-16.7 shall not exceed the amounts allowed under section 303(b) of the Consumer Credit Protection Act, 15 U.S.C. § 1673(b).

(c) Contents of order and notice. An order or advance notice for withholding and any notice to a payor of his obligation to withhold shall state a specific monetary amount to be withheld and the amount of disposable income from the applicable payor on which the amount to be withheld was determined. The notice shall clearly indicate that in no event shall the amount withheld exceed the appropriate percentage of disposable income paid by a payor as provided in subsection (b). (1985 (Reg. Sess., 1986), c. 949, s. 2; 1998-176, s. 6.)

§ 110-136.7. Multiple withholding.

When an obligor is subject to more than one withholding for child support, withholding for current child support shall have priority over past-due support. Where two or more orders for current support exist, each family shall receive a pro rata share of the total amount withheld based on the respective child support orders being enforced. (1985 (Reg. Sess., 1986), c. 949, s. 2.)

§ 110-136.8. Notice to payor; payor's responsibilities.

(a) Contents of notice. Notice to a payor of his obligation to withhold shall include information regarding the payor's rights and responsibilities, the amount of disposable income attributable to that payor on which that withholding is based, the penalties under this section, and the maximum percentages of disposable income that may be withheld as provided in G.S. 110-136.6.

(b) Payor's responsibilities. A payor who has been properly served with a notice to withhold is required to:

(1) Withhold from the obligor's disposable income and, within 7 business days of the date the obligor is paid, send to the State Child Support Collection and Disbursement Unit the amount specified in the notice and the date the amount was withheld, but in no event more than the amount allowed by G.S. 110-136.6; however, if a lesser amount of disposable income is available for any pay period, the payor shall either:

a. Compute, and send the appropriate amount to the State Child Support Collection and Disbursement Unit, using the percentages as provided in G.S. 110-136.6; or

b. Request the initiating party to inform the payor of the proper amount to be withheld for that period;

(2) Continue withholding until further notice from the IV-D agency, the clerk of superior court, or the State Child Support Collection and Disbursement Unit;

(3) Withhold for child support before withholding pursuant to any other legal process under State law against the same disposable income;

(4) Begin withholding from the first payment due the obligor in the first pay period that occurs 14 days following the date the notice of the obligation to withhold was served on the payor;

(5) Promptly notify the obligee in a IV-D case, or the clerk of superior court or the State Child Support Collection and Disbursement Unit in a non-IV-D case, in writing:

a. If there are one or more orders of child support withholding for the obligor;

a1. If there are one or more orders of alimony or postseparation support withholding for the obligor;

b. When the obligor terminates employment or otherwise ceases to be entitled to disposable income from the payor, and provide the obligor's last known address, and the name and address of his new employer, if known;

c. Of the payor's inability to comply with the withholding for any reason; and

(6) Cooperate fully with the initiating party in the verification of the amount of the obligor's disposable income.

(c) Change in obligor's employment. If the obligor changes employment within the State when withholding is in effect, the requirement for withholding shall continue, and

(1) In a IV-D case, the IV-D obligee shall make any necessary adjustments to the withholding, notify the obligor and his new employer in accordance with this section, and file a copy of the adjusted withholding with the clerk of superior court;

(2) In a non-IV-D case, the clerk shall serve a notice of obligation to withhold according to the terms of the withholding order on the new employer and on the obligor; if the obligor or payor gives notice that an adjustment to the withholding order, other than the change in payor, is needed, the matter shall be scheduled for hearing before a child support hearing officer or district court judge who shall make any necessary adjustments to the withholding.

(d) The payor may combine amounts withheld from obligors' disposable incomes in a single payment to the State Child Support Collection and Disbursement Unit if the payor separately identifies by name and case number the portion of the single payment attributable to each individual obligor and the date that each payment was withheld from the obligor's disposable income.

(e) Prohibited conduct by payor; civil penalty. Notwithstanding any other provision of law, when a court finds, pursuant to a motion in the cause filed by the initiating party joining the payor as a third party defendant, with 30 days notice to answer the motion, that a payor has willfully refused to comply with the provisions of this section, such payor shall be ordered to commence withholding and shall be held liable to the initiating party for any amount which such payor should have withheld, except that such payor shall not be required to vary the normal pay or disbursement cycles in order to comply with these provisions.

A payor shall not discharge from employment, refuse to employ, or otherwise take disciplinary action against any obligor solely because of the withholding. When a court finds that a payor has taken any of these actions, the payor shall be liable for a civil penalty. For a first offense, the civil penalty shall be one hundred dollars ($100.00). For second and third offenses, the civil penalty shall be five hundred dollars ($500.00) and one thousand dollars ($1,000), respectively. Any payor who violates any provision of this paragraph shall be liable in a civil action for reasonable damages suffered by an obligor as a result of the violation, and an obligor discharged or demoted in violation of this paragraph shall be entitled to be reinstated to his former position. The statute of limitations for actions under this subsection shall be one year pursuant to G.S. 1-54.

The clear proceeds of civil penalties provided for in this subsection shall be remitted to the Civil Penalty and Forfeiture Fund in accordance with G.S. 115C-457.2.

(f) Any payor who withholds the sum provided in any notice or order to the payor shall not be liable for any penalties under this section. (1985 (Reg. Sess., 1986), c. 949, s. 2; 1987, c. 589, s. 2; 1991, c. 541, ss. 1, 2; 1997-433, s. 6; 1997-465, s. 27; 1998-17, s. 1; 1998-176, s. 7; 1998-215, s. 76; 1999-293, ss. 19, 20.)

§ 110-136.9. Payment of withheld funds.

In all cases, the State Child Support Collection and Disbursement Unit shall distribute payments received from payors to the appropriate recipient. (1985 (Reg. Sess., 1986), c. 949, s. 2; 1997-443, s. 11A.118(a); 1999-293, s. 21.)

§ 110-136.10. Termination of withholding.

A requirement that income be withheld for child support shall promptly terminate as to prospective payments when the payor receives notice from the court or IV-D agency that:

(1) The child support order has expired or become invalid; or

(2) The initiating party, the obligor, and the district court judge agree to termination because there is another adequate means to collect child support or arrearages; or

(3) The whereabouts of the child and obligee are unknown, except that withholding shall not be terminated until all valid arrearages to the State are paid in full. (1985 (Reg. Sess., 1986), c. 949, s. 2.)

§ 110-136.11. National Medical Support Notice required.

(a) Notice Required. - The National Medical Support Notice shall be used to notify employers and health insurers or health care plan administrators of an order entered pursuant to G.S. 50-13.11 for dependent health benefit plan coverage in a IV-D case. For purposes of this section and G.S. 110-136.12 through G.S. 110-136.14, the terms "health benefit plan" and "health insurer" are as defined in G.S. 108A-69(a).

(b) Exception. - The National Medical Support Notice shall not be used in cases where the court has ordered nonemployment-based health benefit plan coverage or where the parties have stipulated to nonemployment-based health benefit plan coverage. (2001-237, s. 8.)

§ 110-136.12. IV-D agency responsibilities.

(a) Within five business days after the order for dependent health benefit plan coverage has been filed in a IV-D case, the IV-D agency shall serve, pursuant to G.S. 1A-1, Rule 5, Rules of Civil Procedure, the National Medical Support Notice on the employer, if known to the agency, of the noncustodial parent.

(b)   In cases where the obligor is a newly hired employee, the agency shall serve, pursuant to G.S. 1A-1, Rule 5, Rules of Civil Procedure, the National Medical Support Notice, along with the income withholding notice pursuant to G.S. 110-136.8, on the employer within two business days after the date of entry of an obligor in the State Directory of New Hires.

(c)   The IV-D agency shall notify the employer within 10 business days when there is no longer a current order for medical support for which the agency is responsible.

(d)   In cases where the health insurer or health care plan administrator reports that there is more than one health care option available under the health benefit plan, the IV-D agency, in consultation with the custodian, may within 20 business days of the date the insurer or administrator informed the agency of the option, select an option and inform the health insurer or health care plan administrator of the option selected. (2001-237, s. 9.)

§ 110-136.13. Employer responsibilities.

(a)   For purposes of this section, G.S. 110-136.11, 110-136.12, and 110-136.14, the term "employer" means employer as is defined at 29 U.S.C. § 203(d) in the Fair Labor Standards Act.

(b)   Within 20 business days after the date of the National Medical Support Notice, the employer shall transfer the Notice to the health insurer or health care plan administrator that provides health benefit plan coverage for which the child is eligible unless one of following applies:

(1)   The employer does not maintain or contribute to plans providing dependent or family health insurance.

(2)   The employee is among a class of employees that are not eligible for family health benefit plan coverage under any group health plan maintained by the employer or to which the employer contributes.

(3)   Health benefit plan coverage is not available because the employee is no longer employed by this employer.

(4) State or federal withholding limitations prevent the withholding from the obligor's income of the amount required to obtain insurance under the terms of the plan.

(c) If the employer is not required to transfer the Notice under subsection (b) of this section, then the employer shall, within the 20 business days after the date of the Notice, inform the agency in writing of the reason or reasons the Notice was not transferred.

(d) Upon receipt from the health insurer or health care plan administrator of the cost of dependent coverage, the employer shall withhold this amount from the obligor's wages and transfer this amount directly to the insurer or plan administrator.

(e) In the event the health insurer or health care plan administrator informs the employer that the Notice is not a "qualified medical child support order" (QMCSO), the employer shall notify the agency in writing.

(f) In the event the health insurer or health care plan administrator informs the employer of a waiting period for enrollment, the employer shall inform the insurer or administrator when the employee is eligible to be enrolled in the plan.

(g) An employer obligated to provide health benefit plan coverage pursuant to this section shall inform the IV-D agency upon termination of the noncustodial parent's employment within 10 business days. The notice shall be in writing to the agency and shall include the obligor's last known address and the name and address of the new employer, if known.

(h) In the event the employee contests the withholding order, the employer shall initiate and continue the withholding until the employer receives notice that the contested case is resolved.

(i) An employer shall not discharge from employment, refuse to employ, or otherwise take disciplinary action against any obligor solely because of the withholding.

(j) If a court finds that an employer has failed to comply with this section, the employer is liable as a payor pursuant to G.S. 110-136.8(e). Additionally, an employer who violates this section is liable in a civil action for reasonable damages. (2001-237, s. 10; 2004-203, s. 9.)

§ 110-136.14. Health insurer or health care plan administrator responsibilities.

(a) Upon receipt of the National Medical Support Notice from the employer, and within 40 business days after the date of the Notice, a health care plan administrator shall determine if the Notice is a "qualified medical child support order" (QMCSO), as defined under the Employee Retirement Income Security Act (ERISA) or the Child Support Performance and Incentive Act (CSPIA). If the Notice is not a qualified medical support order, the plan administrator shall inform the employer within the time set forth in this subsection.

(b) Upon receipt of the Notice in a nonqualified ERISA plan, or upon a finding that the Notice constitutes a qualified medical child support order, the health insurer or plan administrator shall enroll the dependent child or children in a health benefit plan, determine the cost of the coverage, and inform the employer of the amount of the employee contribution to be withheld from the obligor's wages, if appropriate. If the child or children are already enrolled in a health benefit plan, the employer shall be so notified. The employer shall also be notified of any applicable enrollment waiting periods.

(c) If there is more than one health benefit plan in which the dependent child or children may be enrolled, the insurer or plan administrator shall so inform the custodian within the time specified in this subsection. If no plan has been selected within 20 days from the date the insurer or administrator informed the agency of the option, the insurer or administrator may enroll the child or children in the insurer's or administrator's default option.

(d) If the obligor is subject to a waiting period for enrollment, the insurer or administrator shall inform the agency, the employer, the obligor, and the custodial parent. Upon the completion of the waiting period, the enrollment shall be instituted.

(e) When a court finds that a health insurer or health care plan administrator has failed to comply with this section, the employer is liable as a payor pursuant to G.S. 110-136.10(e). Additionally, a health insurer or health care plan administrator who violates this section is liable in a civil action for reasonable damages. (2001-237, s. 11.)

§ 110-137. Acceptance of public assistance constitutes assignment of support rights to the State or county.

By accepting public assistance for or on behalf of a dependent child or children, the recipient shall be deemed to have made an assignment to the State or to the county from which such assistance was received of the right to any child support owed for the child or children up to the amount of public assistance paid. The State or county shall be subrogated to the right of the child or children or the person having custody to initiate a support action under this Article and to recover any payments ordered by the court of this or any other state. (1975, c. 827, s. 1; 1977, 2nd Sess., c. 1186, s. 13.)

§ 110-138. Duty of county to obtain support.

Whenever a county department of social services receives an application for public assistance on behalf of a dependent child, and it shall appear to the satisfaction of the county department that the child has been abandoned by one or both responsible parents, or that the responsible parent(s) has failed to provide support for the child, the county department shall without delay notify the designated representative who shall take appropriate action under this Article to provide that the parent(s) responsible supports the child. (1975, c. 827, s. 1; 1977, 2nd Sess., c. 1186, s. 14.)

§ 110-138.1. Duty of judicial officials to assist in obtaining support.

Any party to whom child support has been ordered to be paid, and who has failed to receive the ordered support payments for two consecutive months, may make application to a magistrate for issuance of criminal process against the responsible parent for violation of G.S. 14-322. If the magistrate determines that the applicant has failed to receive the ordered support for two consecutive months, and that the responsible parent has willfully neglected or refused to make such payments, he shall make a finding of probable cause and issue criminal process for violation of G.S. 14-322. It shall be the duty of the District Attorney to prosecute such charges according to law. It shall be the duty of the Clerk of Superior Court to assist the applicant in making such application to the magistrate for the issuance of criminal process, and to supply such necessary child support records as are in his possession to the magistrate, District Attorney, and the Court. (1981, c. 613, s. 4.)

§ 110-139. Location of absent parents.

(a) The Department of Health and Human Services shall attempt to locate absent parents for the purpose of establishing paternity of and/or securing support for dependent children. The Department is to serve as a registry for the receipt of information which directly relates to the identity or location of absent parents, to assist any governmental agency or department in locating an absent parent, to answer interstate inquiries concerning deserting parents, and to develop guidelines for coordinating activities with any governmental department, board, commission, bureau or agency in providing information necessary for the location of absent parents.

(b) In order to carry out the responsibilities imposed under this Article, the Department may request from any governmental department, board, commission, bureau or agency information and assistance. All State, county and city agencies, officers and employees shall cooperate with the Department in the location of parents who have abandoned and deserted children with all pertinent information relative to the location, income and property of such parents, notwithstanding any provision of law making such information confidential. Except as otherwise stated in this subsection, all nonjudicial records maintained by the Department pertaining to child-support enforcement shall be confidential, and only duly authorized representatives of social service agencies, public officials with child-support enforcement and related duties, and members of legislative committees shall have access to these records. The payment history of an obligor pursuant to a support order may be examined by or released to the court, the obligor, or the person on whose behalf enforcement actions are being taken or that person's designee. Income and expense information of either parent may be released to the other parent for the purpose of establishing or modifying a support order.

(c) Notwithstanding any other provision of law making such information confidential, an employer doing business in this State or incorporated under the laws of this State shall provide the Department with the following information upon certification by the Department that the information is needed to locate a parent for the purpose of collecting child support or to enforce an order for child support: full name, social security account number, date of birth, home address, wages, existing or available medical, hospital, and dental insurance coverage, and number of dependents listed for tax purposes.

(c1) Employment verifications. - For the purpose of establishing, enforcing, or modifying a child support order, the amount of the obligor's gross income may be established by a written statement signed by the obligor's employer or the employer's designee or an Employee Verification form produced by the Automated Collections Tracking System that has been completed and signed by the obligor's employer or the employer's designee. A written statement signed by the employer of the obligor or the employer's designee that sets forth an obligor's gross income, as well as an Employee Verification form signed by the obligor's employer or the employer's designee, shall be admissible evidence in any action establishing, enforcing, or modifying a child support order.

(d) Notwithstanding any other provision of law making this information confidential, including Chapter 53B of the General Statutes, any utility company, cable television company, or financial institution, including federal, State, commercial, or savings banks, savings and loan associations and cooperative banks, federal or State chartered credit unions, benefit associations, insurance companies, safe deposit companies, money market mutual funds, and investment companies doing business in this State or incorporated under the laws of this State shall provide the Department of Health and Human Services with the following information upon certification by the Department that the information is needed to locate a parent for the purpose of collecting child support or to establish or enforce an order for child support: full name, social security number, address, telephone number, account numbers, and other identifying data for any person who maintains an account at the utility company, cable television company, or financial institution. A utility company, cable television company, or financial institution that discloses information pursuant to this subsection in good faith reliance upon certification by the Department is not liable for damages resulting from the disclosure.

(e) Subsection (d) of this section shall not apply to telecommunication utilities or providers of electronic communication service to the general public.

(f) There is established the State Child Support Collection and Disbursement Unit. The duties of the Unit shall be the collection and disbursement of payments under support orders for all cases. The Department may administer and operate the Unit or may contract with another State or private entity for the administration and operation of the Unit. (1975, c. 827, s. 1; 1977, 2nd Sess., c. 1186, s. 15; 1987, c. 591; 1991, c. 419, s. 1; 1995, c. 538, s. 4; 1997-433, ss. 8.1, 9.1; 1997-443, s. 11A.118(a); 1998-17, s. 1; 1999-293, s. 22; 2000-140, s. 20(b); 2001-237, ss. 5, 6; 2003-288, s. 3.1.)

§ 110-139.1. Access to federal parent locator service; parental kidnapping and child custody cases.

(a) Except as otherwise provided in this section, the parent locator service of the Department of Health and Human Services shall transmit, upon payment of the fee prescribed by federal law, requests for information as to the whereabouts of any parent or child to the federal parental locator service when such requests are made by judges, clerks of superior court, district attorneys, or United States attorneys, and when the information is to be used to locate the parent or child for the purpose of enforcing State or federal law with respect to:

(1) The unlawful taking or restraint of a child;

(2) Making or enforcing a child custody determination, including visitation orders;

(3) Establishing paternity; or

(4) Establishing, setting or modifying the amount of, or enforcing child support obligations.

The Department shall not disclose any information from or through the parent locator service if there is reasonable evidence of domestic violence or child abuse and the disclosure of the information could be harmful to the custodial parent or the child of the custodial parent.

(b) For the purpose of this section, custody determination means a judgment, decree, or other order of the court providing for the custody or visitation of a child and includes permanent or temporary orders, and initial orders and modifications.

(c) All nonjudicial records maintained by the Department pertaining to the unlawful taking or restraint of a child or child custody determinations shall be confidential, and only individuals directly connected with the administration of the child support enforcement program and those authorized herein shall have access to these records. (1983, c. 15, s. 1; 1997-433, s. 8.2; 1997-443, s. 11A.118(a); 1998-17, s. 1.)

§ 110-139.2. Data match system; agreements with financial institutions.

(a) The Department of Health and Human Services and financial institutions doing business in this State shall enter into mutual agreements for the purpose of facilitating the enforcement of child support obligations. The agreements shall provide for the development and operation of a data match system that will enable the financial institutions to provide to the Department on a quarterly basis the information required under G.S. 110-139(d). Financial institutions shall provide the information upon certification by the Department that the person about whom the information is requested is subject to a child support order and the information is necessary to enforce the order. The Department may pay a reasonable fee to the financial institution for conducting the data match required under this section provided that the fee shall not exceed the actual costs incurred by the financial institution to conduct the match.

(b) A financial institution shall not be liable under any State law, including but not limited to Chapter 53B of the General Statutes, for disclosure of information to the State child support agency under this section, and for any other action taken by the financial institution in good faith to comply with this section or with G.S. 110-139.

(b1) The Department of Health and Human Services Child Support Enforcement Agency may notify any financial institution doing business in this State that an obligor who maintains an identified account with the financial institution has a child support obligation that may be eligible for levy on the account in an amount that satisfies some or all of the amount of unpaid support owed. In order to be able to attach a lien on and levy an obligor's account, the amount of unpaid support owed shall be an amount not less than the amount of support owed for six months or one thousand dollars ($1,000), whichever is less.

Upon certification of the amount of unpaid support owed in accordance with G.S. 44-86(c), the Child Support Agency shall serve or cause to be served upon the obligor, and when the matched account is owned jointly, any other nonliable owner of the account, and the financial institution a notice as provided by this subsection. The notice shall include the name of the obligor, the financial institution where the account is located, the account number of the account to be levied to satisfy the lien, the certified amount of unpaid support, information for the obligor or account owner on how to remove the lien or contest the lien in order to avoid the levy, and a copy of the applicable law, G.S. 110-139.2. The notice shall be served on the obligor, and any nonliable account owner, in any manner provided in Rule 4 of the North Carolina Rules of Civil Procedure. The financial institution shall be served notice in accordance with Rule 5 of the North

Carolina Rules of Civil Procedure. Upon service of the notice, the financial institution shall proceed in the following manner:

(1)   Immediately attach a lien to the identified account.

(2)   Notify the Child Support Agency of the balance of the account and date of the lien or that the account does not meet the requirement for levy under this subsection.

In order for an obligor or account owner to contest the lien, within 10 days after the obligor or account owner is served with the notice, the obligor or account owner shall send written notice of the basis of the contest to the Child Support Agency and shall request a hearing before the district court in the county where the support order was entered. The obligor account holder may contest the lien only on the basis that the amount owed is an amount less than the amount of support owed for six months, or is less than one thousand dollars ($1,000), whichever is less, or the contesting party is not the person subject to the court order of support. The district court may assess court costs against the nonprevailing party. If no response is received from the obligor or account owner within 10 days of the service of the notice, the Child Support Agency shall notify the financial institution to submit payment, up to the total amount of the child support arrears, if available. This amount is to be applied to the debt of the obligor.

A financial institution shall not be liable to any person for complying in good faith with this subsection. The remedy set forth in this section shall be in addition to all other remedies available to the State for the reduction of the obligor's child support arrears. This remedy shall not prevent the State from taking any and all other concurrent measures available by law.

This levy procedure is to be available for direct use by all states' child support programs to financial institutions in this State without involvement of the Department.

(c)   As used in this subdivision, a financial institution includes federal, State, commercial, or savings banks, savings and loan associations and cooperative banks, federal or State chartered credit unions, benefit associations, insurance companies, safe deposit companies, money market mutual funds, and investment companies doing business in this State or incorporated under the laws of this State. (1997-433, s. 9; 1997-443, s. 11A.122; 1998-17, s. 1; 2003-288, s. 4; 2004-203, s. 42; 2005-389, s. 5.)

§ 110-139.3. High-volume, automated administrative enforcement in interstate cases (AEI).

Upon request of another state, the Department of Health and Human Services shall use automated data processing to search State databases and determine if information is available regarding a parent who owes a child support obligation and shall seize identified assets using the same techniques as used in intrastate cases. Any request by another state to enforce support orders shall certify the amount of each obligor's debt and that appropriate due process requirements have been met by the requesting state with respect to each obligor. The Department of Health and Human Services shall likewise transmit to other states requests for assistance in enforcing support orders through high-volume, automated administrative enforcement where appropriate. (1999-293, s. 7.)

§ 110-140. Conformity with federal requirements; restriction on options without federal funding.

(a)   Nothing in this Article is intended to conflict with any provision of federal law or to result in the loss of federal funds.

(b)   Effective July 24, 1997, the Department of Health and Human Services shall not elect any child support distribution option for families receiving cash assistance under the State Plan for the Temporary Assistance for Needy Families (TANF) Block Grant Program for which the federal government does not provide funding to the State to exercise the option. (1975, c. 827, s. 1; 1997-223, s. 1; 1997-443, s. 11A.122.)

§ 110-141. Effectuation of intent of Article.

The North Carolina Department of Health and Human Services shall supervise the administration of the program in accordance with federal law and shall cause the provisions of this Article to be effectuated and to secure child support from absent, deserting, abandoning and nonsupporting parents.

Effective July 1, 2010, each child support enforcement program being administered by the Department of Health and Human Services on behalf of counties shall be administered, or the administration provided for, by the board of county commissioners of those counties. Until July 1, 2010, it shall be the responsibility of the Department of Health and Human Services to administer or provide for the administration of the program in those counties.

A county may negotiate alternative arrangements to the procedure outlined in G.S. 110-130 for designating a local person or agency to administer the provisions of this Article in that county. (1975, c. 827, s. 1; 1977, 2nd Sess., c. 1186, s. 16; 1979, c. 488; 1983 (Reg. Sess., 1984), c. 1034, s. 76; 1985, c. 244; c. 479, s. 103; 1985 (Reg. Sess., 1986), c. 1014, s. 129; 1997-443, s. 11A.118(a); 2009-451, s. 10.46A(a).)

§ 110-142. Definitions; suspension and revocation of occupational, professional, or business licenses of obligors who are delinquent in court-ordered child support, or who are not in compliance with subpoenas issued pursuant to child support or paternity establishment proceedings.

The definitions in G.S. 110-129 and G.S. 147-54.12 apply to this section and G.S. 110-142.1, and G.S. 110-142.2. In addition, to these sections the following definitions apply:

(1) "Applicant" means any person applying for issuance or renewal of a license.

(2) "Board" means any department, division, agency, officer, board, or other unit of State government that issues licenses.

(3) "Certified list" means a list provided by the designated representative to the Department of Health and Human Services that verifies, under penalty of perjury, that the names contained therein are obligors who have been found to be out of compliance with a judgment or order for support in a IV-D case.

(4) "Compliance with an order for support" means that, as set forth in a judgment or order for child support or family support, the obligor is no more than 90 calendar days in arrears in making payments for current support, in making periodic payments on a support arrearage, or in making periodic payments on a reimbursement for public assistance, has obtained a judicial finding that precludes enforcement of the order, or has entered into a payment schedule, including G.S. 110-142.1(h), for the child support arrearage with the approval of the obligee in a IV-D case.

(5) "License" means (i) for the purposes of G.S. 110-142.1, a license, certificate, permit, registration, or any other authorization issued by a board that allows a person to engage in a business, occupation, or profession or (ii) for the purposes of G.S. 110-142.2, a license to operate a regular or commercial motor vehicle, or to participate in hunting, fishing, or trapping.

(6) "Licensee" means any person holding a license.

(7) "Obligor" means the individual who owes a duty to make child support payments under a court order. (1995, c. 538, s. 1.4; 1997-433, s. 5; 1997-443, s. 11A.118(a); 1998-17, s. 1.)

§ 110-142.1. IV-D notified suspension, revocation, and issuance of occupational, professional, or business licenses of obligors who are delinquent in court-ordered child support or who are not in compliance with subpoenas issued pursuant to child support or paternity establishment proceedings.

(a) Effective July 1, 1996, the Department of Health and Human Services may notify any board that a person licensed by that board is not in compliance with an order for child support or has been found by the court not to be in compliance with a subpoena issued pursuant to child support or paternity establishment proceedings.

(b) The designated representative shall submit a certified list with the names, social security numbers, and last known address of individuals who are not in compliance with a child support order or with a subpoena issued pursuant to a child support or paternity establishment proceeding. The designated representative shall verify, under penalty of perjury, that the individuals listed are subject to an order for the payment of support and are not in compliance with the order, or have been found by the court to be not in compliance with a subpoena issued pursuant to a child support or paternity establishment proceeding. The verification shall include the name, address, and telephone number of the designated representative who certified the list. An updated certified list shall be submitted to the Department on a monthly basis.

The Department of Health and Human Services, Division of Social Services, Child Support Enforcement Office, shall consolidate the certified lists received from the designated representatives and, within 30 calendar days of receipt, shall furnish each board with a certified list of the individuals, as specified in this section.

(c)   Each board shall coordinate with the Department of Health and Human Services, Division of Social Services, Child Support Enforcement Office, in the development of forms and procedures to implement this section.

(d)   Promptly after receiving the certified list of individuals from the Department of Health and Human Services, each board shall determine whether its applicant or licensee is an individual on the list. If the applicant or licensee is on the list, the board shall immediately send notice as specified in this subsection to the applicant or licensee of the board's intent to revoke or suspend the licensee's license in 20 days from the date of the notice, or that the board is withholding issuance or renewal of an applicant's license, until the designated representative certifies that the applicant or licensee is entitled to be licensed or reinstated. The notice shall be made personally or by certified mail to the individual's last known mailing address on file with the board.

(e)   Unless notified by the designated representative as provided in subsection (h) of this section, the board shall revoke or suspend the individual's license 20 days from the date of the notice to the individual of the board's intent to revoke or suspend the license. In the event that a license is revoked or application is denied pursuant to this section, the board is not required to refund fees paid by the individual.

(f)   Notices shall be developed by each board in accordance with guidelines provided by the Department of Health and Human Services and shall be subject to the approval of the Department of Health and Human Services. The notice shall include the address and telephone number of the designated representative who submitted the name on the certified list, and shall emphasize the necessity of obtaining a certification of compliance from the designated representative or the child support enforcement agency as a condition of issuance, renewal, or reinstatement of the license. The notice shall inform the individual that if a license is revoked or application is denied pursuant to this subsection, the board is not required to refund fees paid by the individual. The Department of Health and Human Services shall also develop a form that the individual shall use to request a review by the designated representative. A copy of this form shall be included with every notice sent pursuant to subsection (d) of this section.

(g)   The Department of Health and Human Services shall establish review procedures consistent with this section to allow an individual to have the underlying arrearage and any relevant defenses investigated, to provide an individual information on the process of obtaining a modification of a support order, or, if the circumstances so warrant, to provide an individual assistance in the establishment of a payment schedule on arrears.

(h)   If the individual wishes to challenge the submission of the individual's name on the certified list, or if the individual wishes to negotiate a payment schedule, the individual shall within 14 days of the date of notice from the board request a review from the designated representative. The designated representative shall within six days of the date of the request for review notify the appropriate board of the request for review and direct the board to stay any action revoking or suspending the individual's license until further notice from the designated representative. The designated representative shall review the case and inform the individual in writing of the representative's findings and decision upon completion of the review. If the findings so warrant, the designated representative shall immediately send a notice to the appropriate board certifying the individual's compliance with this section. The agreement shall also provide for the maintenance of current support obligations and shall be incorporated into a consent order to be entered by the court. If the individual fails to meet the conditions of this subsection, the designated representative shall notify the appropriate board to immediately revoke or suspend the individual's license. Upon receipt of notice from the designated representative, the board shall immediately revoke or suspend the individual's license.

(i)   The designated representative shall notify the individual in writing that the individual may, by filing a motion, request any or all of the following:

(1)   Judicial review of the designated representative's decision.

(2)   A judicial determination of compliance.

(3)   A modification of the support order.

The notice shall also contain the name and address of the court in which the individual shall file the motion and inform the individual that the individual's name shall remain on the certified list unless the judicial review results in a finding by the court that the individual is in compliance with this section. The notice shall also inform the individual that the individual must comply with all statutes and rules of court regarding motions and notices of hearing and that any motion filed under this section is subject to the limitations of G.S. 50-13.10.

(j) The motion for judicial review of the designated representative's decision shall state the grounds for which review is requested and judicial review shall be limited to those stated grounds. After service of the request for review, the court shall hold an evidentiary hearing at the next regularly scheduled session for the hearing of child support matters in civil district court. The request for judicial review shall be served by the individual upon the designated representative who submitted the individual's name on the certified list within seven calendar days of the filing of the motion.

(k) If the judicial review results in a finding by the court that the individual is no longer in arrears or that the individual's license should be reinstated to allow the individual an opportunity to comply with a payment schedule on arrears or reimbursement and current support obligations, the designated representative shall immediately send a notice to the appropriate board certifying the individual's compliance with this section. If the judicial review results in a finding that the individual has complied with or is no longer subject to the subpoena that was the basis for the revocation, then the designated representative shall immediately send a notice to the appropriate board certifying the individual's compliance with this section. In the event of an appeal from judicial review, the license revocation shall not be stayed unless the court specifically provides otherwise.

(l) The Department of Health and Human Services shall prescribe forms for use by the designated representative. When the individual is no longer in arrears or negotiates an agreement with the designated representative for a payment schedule on arrears or reimbursement, the designated representative shall mail to the individual and the appropriate board a notice certifying that the individual is in compliance. The receipt of certification shall serve to notify the individual and the board that, for the purposes of this section, the individual is in compliance with the order for support. When the individual has complied with or is no longer subject to a subpoena issued pursuant to a child support or paternity establishment proceeding, the designated representative shall mail to the individual and the appropriate board a notice certifying that the individual is in compliance. The receipt of certification shall serve to notify the individual and the board that the individual is in compliance with this section.

(m) The Department of Health and Human Services may enter into interagency agreements with the boards necessary to implement this section.

(n)   The procedures specified in Articles 3 and 3A of Chapter 150B of the General Statutes, the Administrative Procedure Act, shall not apply to the denial or failure to issue or renew a license pursuant to this section.

(o)   Any board receiving an inquiry as to the licensed status of an applicant or licensee who has had a license denied or revoked under this section shall respond only that the license was denied or revoked pursuant to this section. Information collected pursuant to this section shall be confidential and shall not be disclosed except in accordance with the laws of this State.

(p)   If any provision of this section or its application to any person or circumstance is held invalid, that invalidity shall not affect other provisions or applications of this section that can be given effect without the invalid provision or application, and to this end the provisions of this section are severable. (1995, c. 538, s. 1.4; 1997-433, s. 5.1; 1997-443, ss. 11A.118(a), 122; 1998-17, s. 1; 2007-484, ss. 12(a), (b).)

§ 110-142.2. Suspension, revocation, restriction of license to operate a motor vehicle or hunting, fishing, or trapping licenses; refusal of registration of motor vehicle.

(a)   Effective December 1, 1996, notwithstanding any other provision of law, when an individual is at least 90 days in arrears in making child support payments, or has been found by the court to be not in compliance with a subpoena issued pursuant to child support or paternity establishment proceedings, the child support enforcement agency may apply to the court, pursuant to the regular show cause and contempt provisions of G.S. 50-13.9(d), for an order doing any of the following:

(1)   Revoking the individual's regular or commercial license to operate a motor vehicle;

(2)   Revoking the individual's hunting, fishing, or trapping licenses;

(3)   Directing the Department of Transportation, Division of Motor Vehicles, to refuse, pursuant to G.S. 20-50.4, to register the individual's motor vehicle.

(b)   Upon finding that the individual has willfully failed to comply with the child support order or with a subpoena issued pursuant to child support proceedings, and that the obligor is at least 90 days in arrears, or upon a finding that an individual subject to a subpoena issued pursuant to child support or paternity establishment proceedings has failed to comply with the subpoena, the court may enter an order instituting the sanctions as provided in subsection (a) of this section. If an individual is adjudicated to be in civil or criminal contempt for a third or subsequent time for failure to comply with a child support order, the court shall enter an order instituting any one or more of the sanctions, if applicable, as provided in subsection (a) of this section. The court may stay the effectiveness of the sanctions upon conditions requiring the obligor to make full payment of the delinquency over time. Any court-ordered payment plan under this subsection shall require the individual to extinguish the delinquency within a reasonable period of time. In determining the amount to be applied to the delinquency, the court shall consider the amount of the debt and the individual's financial ability to pay. The payment shall not exceed the limits under G.S. 110-136.6(b). The individual shall make an immediate initial payment representing at least five percent (5%) of the total delinquency or five hundred dollars ($500.00), whichever is less. Any stay of an order under this subsection shall also be conditioned upon the obligor's maintenance of current child support. The court may stay the effectiveness of the sanctions against an individual subject to a subpoena issued pursuant to child support or paternity establishment proceedings upon a finding that the individual has complied with or is no longer subject to the subpoena. Upon entry of an order pursuant to this section that is not stayed, the individual shall surrender any licenses revoked by the court's order to the child support enforcement agency and the agency shall forward a report to the appropriate licensing authority within 30 days of the order.

(c)   If the individual's regular or commercial drivers license is revoked under this section and the court, after the hearing, makes a finding that a license to operate a motor vehicle is necessary to the individual's livelihood, the court may issue a limited driving privilege, with those terms and conditions applying as the court shall prescribe. An individual whose license has been revoked for reasons not related to this section and whose license remains revoked at the time of the hearing shall not be eligible and may not be issued a limited driving privilege. The court may modify or revoke the limited driving privilege pursuant to G.S. 20-179.3(i).

(d)   An individual may file a request with the child support enforcement agency for certification that the individual is no longer delinquent in child support payments upon submission of proof satisfactory to the child support enforcement agency that the individual has paid the delinquent amount in full. An individual subject to a subpoena issued pursuant to a child support or paternity establishment proceeding may file a request with the child support enforcement agency for certification that the individual has complied with or is no longer subject to the subpoena. The child support enforcement agency shall provide a form to be used by the individual for a request for certification. If the child support enforcement agency finds that the individual has met the requirements for reinstatement under this subsection, then the child support enforcement agency shall certify that the individual is no longer delinquent or that the individual has complied with or is no longer subject to a subpoena issued pursuant to child support or paternity establishment proceedings and shall provide a copy of the certification to the individual.

(e) If licensing privileges are revoked under this section, the individual may petition the district court for a reinstatement of such privileges. The court may order the privileges reinstated conditioned upon full payment of the delinquency over time, or. as applicable, may order the reinstatement if the court finds that the individual has complied with or is no longer subject to the subpoena issued pursuant to paternity establishment proceedings. Any order allowing license reinstatement shall additionally require the obligor's maintenance of current child support. Upon reinstatement under this subsection, the child support enforcement agency shall certify that the individual is no longer delinquent, or, as applicable, that the individual has complied with or is no longer subject to the subpoena issued pursuant to child support or paternity establishment proceedings and shall provide a copy of the certification to the individual, as applicable.

(f) Upon receipt of certification under subsection (d) or (e) of this section, the Division of Motor Vehicles shall reinstate the license to operate a motor vehicle in accordance with G.S. 20-24.1, and remove any restriction of the individual's motor vehicle registration.

(g) Upon receipt of certification under subsection (d) or (e) of this section, the licensing board having jurisdiction over the individual's hunting, fishing, or trapping license shall reinstate the license.

(h) If the court imposes sanctions under subdivision (3) of subsection (a) of this section and the sanctions are stayed upon conditions as provided in subsection (b) of this section, the child support enforcement agency may, without any further application to the court, notify the Division of Motor Vehicles if the individual violates the terms and conditions of the stay. The Division shall then take such action as provided in subdivision (3) of subsection (a) of this section. The Division shall not remove any restriction of the individual's motor vehicle registration, until receipt of certification pursuant to subsection (d) or (e) of this section.

(i)   The Department of Health and Human Services, the Administrative Office of the Courts, the Division of Motor Vehicles, and the Department of Environment and Natural Resources shall work together to develop the forms and procedures necessary for the implementation of this process. (1995, c. 538, s. 1.4; 1997-433, s. 5.2; 1997-443, ss. 11A.118(a), 11A.119(a); 1998-17, s. 1; 1999-293, s. 2.)

§§ 110-143 through 110-146. Reserved for future codification purposes.

Article 10.

Prevention of Child Abuse and Neglect.

§§ 110-147 through 110-150. Repealed by Session Laws 1998, c. 202, s. 5, effective July 1, 1999.

Chapter 111.

Aid to the Blind.

Article 1.

General Duties of Department of Health and Human Services.

§§ 111-1 through 111-3: Repealed by Session Laws 1973, c. 476, s. 143.

§ 111-4. Register of State's blind.

(a)   The Department of Health and Human Services shall cause to be maintained a complete register of the blind in the State that shall describe the condition and cause of blindness of each and any other facts that may seem to the Department of Health and Human Services to be of value.

(b) When, upon examination by a physician or optometrist, any person is found to be blind, the examiner shall report the results of the examination to the Department of Health and Human Services within 30 days after the examination is conducted. (1935, c. 53, s. 3; 1973, c. 476, s. 143; 1975, c. 19, s. 35; 1997-443, s. 11A.118(a); 2000-121, s. 1.)

§ 111-5: Repealed by Session Laws 2000-121, s. 2.

§ 111-6. Training schools and workshops; training outside State; sale of products; direct relief; matching of federal funds.

The Department of Health and Human Services may establish one or more training schools and workshops for employment of suitable blind and visually impaired persons, equip and maintain these schools and workshops, pay employees suitable wages, devise means for the sale and distribution of the products of these schools and workshops, and cooperate with shops already established. The Department of Health and Human Services may also pay for lodging, tuition, support and all necessary expenses for blind and visually impaired persons during their training or instruction in any suitable occupation, whether it be in industrial, commercial, professional, or any other establishments, schools or institutions, or through private instruction when in the judgment of the Department of Health and Human Services this instruction or training can be obtained and will contribute to the efficiency or self-support of the blind and visually impaired persons. When special educational opportunities cannot be had within the State, they may be arranged for, at the discretion of the Department of Health and Human Services, outside of the State. The Department of Health and Human Services may also aid individual blind and visually impaired persons or groups of blind and visually impaired persons to become self-supporting by furnishing material or equipment to them and by assisting them in the sale and distribution of their products. Any portion of the funds appropriated to the Department of Health and Human Services under the provisions of this Chapter providing for the rehabilitation of the blind and visually impaired and the prevention of blindness may, when the Commission for the Blind deems wise, be given in direct money payments to the needy blind in accordance with the provisions of G.S. 111-13 through G.S. 111-26. Whenever possible such funds may be matched by funds provided by the federal Social Security Act, 42 U.S.C. § 301, et seq., as amended. (1935, c. 53, s. 5; 1937, c. 124, s. 16; 1973, c. 476, s. 143; 1997-443, s. 11A.118(a); 2000-121, s. 3.)

§ 111-6.1. Rehabilitation center for the blind and visually impaired.

The Department of Health and Human Services shall establish and operate a rehabilitation center for the blind and visually impaired for the purpose of evaluating and providing instruction in specialized independent living, prevocational, and vocational skills to blind and visually impaired persons to prepare them for obtaining and maintaining employment.

The Commission shall make all rules necessary for this purpose and the Department of Health and Human Services may enter into any agreement or contract; to purchase or lease property, both real and personal, to accept grants and gifts of whatever nature, and to do all other things necessary to carry out the intent and purposes of this rehabilitation center.

The Department of Health and Human Services may receive grants-in-aid from the federal government for carrying out the provisions of this section, as well as for other related rehabilitation programs for blind and visually impaired persons under the provisions of the Rehabilitation Act of 1973, Pub. L. No. 93-112, 87 Stat. 355, 29 U.S.C. § 701, et seq., as amended. Blind and visually impaired persons as defined in G.S. 111-11, who are physically present in North Carolina may enjoy the benefits of this section or any other related rehabilitation benefits under the Rehabilitation Act of 1973, as amended. (1945, c. 698; 1951, c. 319, s. 4; 1971, c. 1215, s. 2; 1973, c. 476, s. 143; 1997-443, s. 11A.118(a); 2000-121, s. 4.)

§ 111-7. In-home services.

The Department of Health and Human Services may foster maximum independence of blind and visually impaired persons through the provision of in-home independent living, development of community-based support groups, and related services as it deems advisable. (1935, c. 53, s. 6; 1973, c. 476, s. 143; 1997-443, s. 11A.118(a); 2000-121, s. 5.)

§ 111-8. Investigations; eye examination and treatment.

The Department of Health and Human Services shall continue to make inquiries concerning the cause of blindness, to learn what proportion of these cases are preventable, and to inaugurate and cooperate in any measure for the State it deems advisable. The Department of Health and Human Services may arrange for the examination of the eyes of blind and visually impaired persons and may secure and pay for medical and surgical treatment for these persons whenever in the judgment of a qualified ophthalmologist or optometrist the eyes of this person may be benefited by the treatment. (1935, c. 53, s. 7; 1973, c. 476, s. 143; 1997-443, s. 11A.118(a); 2000-121, s. 6.)

§ 111-8.1: Repealed by Session Laws 2000-121, s. 7.

§§ 111-9 through 111-10. Repealed by Session Laws 1973, c. 476, s. 143.

§ 111-11. Definitions.

For the purposes of this Chapter, the following definitions apply:

(1)   "Blind person" means a person who meets any of the following criteria:

a.   Is totally blind.

b.   Has central visual acuity that does not exceed 20/200 in the better eye with correcting lenses.

c.   Has a visual field that subtends an angle no greater than 20 degrees at its widest diameter.

(2)   "Visually impaired person" means a person whose vision with glasses is so limited as to prevent the performance of ordinary activity for which eyesight is essential. (1935, c. 53, s. 10; 1939, c. 124; 1971, c. 1215, s. 3; 2000-121, s. 8.)

§ 111-11.1. Jurisdiction of certain Divisions within the Department of Health and Human Services.

For the purpose of providing rehabilitative services to people who are visually impaired, the Division of Services for the Blind and the Division of Vocational Rehabilitation Services shall develop and enter into an agreement specifying which agency can most appropriately meet the specific needs of this client population. If the Divisions cannot reach an agreement, the Secretary of Health and Human Services shall determine which Division can most appropriately meet the specific needs of this client population. (2000-121, s. 9.)

§ 111-12. Repealed by Session Laws 1973, c. 476, s. 143.

§ 111-12.1. Acceptance of private contributions for particular facilities authorized.

In addition to other powers and duties granted it by law, the Department of Health and Human Services is hereby authorized to accept contributions of funds made by any private individual, agency or organization even though a condition of the contribution may be that the funds be utilized for the establishment of a particular public or private nonprofit workshop, rehabilitation center or other facility established for the purpose of providing training or employment for eligible blind persons. (1965, c. 906, s. 1; 1973, c. 476, s. 143; 1997-443, s. 11A.118(a).)

§ 111-12.2. Contributions treated as State funds to match federal funds.

The Department of Health and Human Services is further authorized to treat any funds received in accordance with G.S. 111-12.1 as State funds for the purpose of accepting any funds made available under federal law on a matching basis for the establishment of such facilities. (1965, c. 906, s. 2; 1973, c. 476, s. 143; 1997-443, s. 11A.118(a).)

§ 111-12.3. Rules and regulations as to receiving and expending contributions.

The Department of Health and Human Services shall make all rules and regulations necessary for the purpose of receiving and expending any funds mentioned in G.S. 111-12.1 to 111-12.3 which are consistent with the principle of obtaining maximum federal participation and in accordance with established budget procedures of the North Carolina Department of Administration. (1965, c. 906, s. 3; 1973, c. 476, s. 143; 1997-443, s. 11A.118(a).)

§ 111-12.4. Repealed by Session Laws 1973, c. 476, s. 143.

§ 111-12.5. Reserve and operating capital fund.

Funds now held by the Bureau of Employment of the North Carolina State Commission for the Blind or its successor organization not exceeding one hundred thousand dollars ($100,000) shall be retained by the Department of Health and Human Services as a reserve and operating capital fund to be expended by the Department of Health and Human Services for its lawful purposes and objectives in accordance with this Chapter. (1967, c. 1214; 1973, c. 476, s. 143; 1997-443, s. 11A.118(a).)

§ 111-12.6. Disposition of funds deposited with or transferred to State Treasurer.

All funds required under this Article to be deposited with or which have been transferred to the State Treasurer by the Bureau of Employment of the Department of Health and Human Services, and all future net earnings and accumulations of the Bureau or its successor, other than the one hundred thousand dollars ($100,000) reserve fund provided for in G.S. 111-12.5, from whatever source shall be periodically, but not less frequently than annually, paid over to and retained by the State Treasurer as a separate fund or account. The funds deposited with the State Treasurer shall be invested and the income from the corpus shall inure to the sole benefit of the Department of Health and Human Services. The income and corpus shall be expended for services to and for the benefit of blind and visually impaired persons in North Carolina upon recommendation of the Commission for the Blind, by and with the approval of the Governor as the Director of the Budget. (1967, c. 1214; 1973, c. 476, s. 143; 1997-443, s. 11A.118(a); 2000-121, s. 10.)

Article 2.

Aid to the Blind.

§ 111-13. Administration of assistance; objective standards for personnel; rules and regulations.

The Department of Health and Human Services shall be charged with the supervision of the administration of assistance to the needy blind under this Article, and said Department shall establish objective standards for personnel to be qualified for employment in the administration of this Article, and said Commission for the Blind shall make all rules and regulations as may be necessary for carrying out the provisions of this Article, which rules and regulations shall be binding on the boards of county commissioners and all agencies charged with the duties of administering this Article. (1937, c. 124, s. 2; 1973, c. 476, s. 143; 1997-443, s. 11A.118(a).)

§ 111-14. Application for benefits under Article; investigation and award by county commissioners.

Any person claiming benefits under this Article shall file with the commissioners of the county in which he or she is residing an application in writing, in duplicate, upon forms prescribed by the Department of Health and Human Services. This application shall be accompanied by a certificate signed by a reputable physician licensed to practice medicine in the State who is actively engaged in the treatment of diseases of the human eye or by an optometrist, whichever the individual may select, stating that the applicant is blind. This application may be made on the behalf of any blind person by the Department of Health and Human Services or by any other person. The board of county commissioners shall cause an investigation to be made by a qualified person designated as its agent for this purpose and shall pass upon the application without delay, determine the eligibility of the applicant, and allow or disallow the relief sought. In passing upon the application, the board of county commissioners may take into consideration the facts set forth in the application and any other facts that are deemed necessary, and may at any time require an additional examination of the applicant's eyes by an ophthalmologist designated by the Department of Health and Human Services. When satisfied with the merits of the application, the board of county commissioners shall allow the application and grant to the applicant any proper relief according to the rules established by the Commission for the Blind. (1937, c. 124, s. 3; 1939, c. 124; 1951, c. 319, s. 1; 1957, c. 674; 1973, c. 476, s. 143; 1997-443, s. 11A.118(a); 2000-121, s. 12.)

§ 111-15. Eligibility for relief.

Blind persons having the following qualifications shall be eligible for relief under the provisions of this Article:

(1)   Repealed by Session Laws 2000-121, s. 13.

(2)   Who are unable to provide for themselves the necessities of life and who have insufficient means for their own support and who have no relative or relatives or other persons in this State able to provide for them who are legally responsible for their maintenance; and

(3)   Who, at the time his application is filed, is living in the State of North Carolina voluntarily with the intention of making his home in the State and not for a temporary purpose. [and]

(4)   Who are not inmates of any charitable or correctional institution of this State or of any county or city thereof: Provided, that an inmate of such charitable institution may be granted a benefit in order to enable such person to maintain himself or herself outside of an institution; and

(5)   Who are not, because of physical or mental condition, in need of continuing institutional care. Provided, that the State agency shall, in determining need, take into consideration any other income and resources of the individual claiming aid to the blind; except that, in making such determination, the State agency shall disregard such earned income as will enable said agency to receive the maximum grants from the federal government for such purpose. (1937, c. 124, s. 4; 1951, c. 319, s. 3; 1961, c. 666, s. 1; 1971, c. 1215, s. 1; 1981, c. 131; 2000-121, s. 13.)

§ 111-16. Application for aid; notice of award; review.

Promptly after an application for aid is made to the board of county commissioners under this Article, the Department of Health and Human Services shall be notified of the application by mail by the county commissioners. One of the duplicate applications for aid made before the board of county commissioners shall be transmitted with this notice.

As soon as any award has been made or any application declined by the board of county commissioners, prompt notice in writing of the award or the declined application shall be forwarded by mail to the Department of Health and Human Services and to the applicant. This notice shall fully state the particulars of the award or the facts of denial. An applicant may appeal an award or denial pursuant to Article 3 of Chapter 150B of the General Statutes. (1937, c. 124, s. 5; 1971, c. 603, s. 1; 1973, c. 476, s. 143; 1997-443, s. 11A.118(a); 2000-121, s. 14.)

§ 111-17. Amount and payment of assistance; source of funds.

When the board of county commissioners is satisfied that the applicant is entitled to relief under the provisions of this Article, as provided in G.S. 111-14, they shall order necessary relief to be granted under the rules and regulations prescribed by the Commission for the Blind, to be paid from county, State and federal funds available, said relief to be paid in monthly payments from funds hereinafter mentioned.

At the time of fixing the annual budget for the fiscal year beginning July 1, 1937, and annually thereafter, the board of county commissioners in each county shall, based upon such information as they are able to secure and with such information as may be furnished to them by the Department of Health and Human Services, estimate the number of needy blind persons in such county who shall be entitled to aid under the provisions of this Article and the total amount of such county's part thereof required to be paid by such county. Each county shall make appropriations for the purposes of this Article in an amount sufficient to cover its share of aid to the blind and may fund them by levy of property taxes pursuant to G.S. 153A-149 and by the allocation of other revenues whose use is not otherwise restricted by law. This provision is mandatory on each county in the State. Any court of competent jurisdiction is authorized by mandamus to enforce the foregoing provisions. No funds shall be allocated to any county by the Department of Health and Human Services until the provisions hereof have been fully complied with by such county.

In case such appropriation is exhausted within the year and is found to be insufficient to meet the county's part of the amount required for aid to the needy blind, such deficiency may be borrowed, if within constitutional limitations, at the lowest rate of interest obtainable, not exceeding six percent (6%), and provision for payment thereof shall be made in the next annual budget and tax levy.

The board of county commissioners in the several counties of the State shall cause to be transmitted to the State Treasurer their share of the total amount of relief granted to the blind applicants. Such remittances shall be made by the several counties in equal monthly installments on the first day of each month, beginning July 1, 1937. The State Treasurer shall deposit said funds and credit same to the account of the Department of Health and Human Services to be employed in carrying out the provisions of this Article.

Within the limitations of the State appropriation, the maximum payment for aid to the blind is to be such as will make possible maximum matching funds by the federal government. (1937, c. 124, s. 6; 1961, c. 666, s. 3; 1973, c. 476, s. 143; c. 803, s. 11; 1997-443, s. 11A.118(a).)

§ 111-18. Payment of awards.

After an award to a blind person has been made by the board of county commissioners, and approved by the Department of Health and Human Services the Department of Health and Human Services shall thereafter pay to such person to whom such award is made the amount of said award in monthly payments, or in such manner and under such terms as the Department of Health and Human Services shall determine. Such payment shall be drawn upon such funds in the hands of the State Treasurer, at the instance and request and upon a proper voucher signed by the Secretary of Health and Human Services, and shall not be subject to the provisions of the Executive Budget Act as to approval of said expenditure.

It is intended that awards paid to recipients under this Article be for the purpose of assisting in defraying the recipient's day-to-day living expenses. To better achieve this purpose it is hereby provided that no moneys belonging to a recipient of aid to the blind under this Article identifiable as moneys paid pursuant to an aid to the blind award shall be subject to levy under execution, attachment or garnishment. (1937, c. 124, s. 7; 1971, c. 177; c. 603, s. 2; 1973, c. 476, s. 143; 1993, c. 257, s. 8; 1997-443, s. 11A.118(a).)

§ 111-18.1. Award and assistance checks payable to decedents.

(a)   In the event of the death of a recipient of an award made pursuant to G.S. 111-18 during or after the first day of the month for which the award was authorized to be paid, any check or checks in payment of such award made payable to the deceased recipient and not endorsed prior to the payee's death shall be delivered to the clerk of the superior court and be by him administered under the provisions of G.S. 28A-25-6.

(b)   In the event of the death of a recipient of a cash payment service that was rendered as part of a program of public assistance for the blind or visually impaired, any check issued for the payment of that service made payable to that recipient, but not endorsed prior to the recipient's death, shall be returned to the issuing agency and made void. The issuing agency shall then issue a check payable to the provider of the service for the sum remaining due for this service, not to exceed the amount of the returned and voided check. (1979, c. 762, s. 2; 2000-121, s. 15.)

§ 111-19. Intercounty transfer of recipients.

Any recipient of aid to the blind under this Article who moves to another county of this State shall be entitled to receive aid to the blind in the county to which he has moved and the board of county commissioners of such county, or its authorized agent, is hereby directed to make the appropriate aid to the blind grant to such recipient subject to the rules and regulations of the Commission for the Blind, beginning with the next payment period after such recipient has established settlement in the county to which he has moved by continuously maintaining a residence therein for a period of 90 days. The county from which a recipient moves shall continue to pay aid to such recipient until such time as the recipient becomes qualified to receive aid from the county to which he has moved. The county from which a recipient has moved shall forthwith transfer all necessary records relating to the recipient to the appropriate board of county commissioners, or its authorized agent, of the county to which the recipient has moved immediately upon the recipient becoming qualified to receive aid from such county. (1937, c. 124, s. 8; 1947, c. 374; 1965, c. 905; 1971, c. 190, ss. 1, 2; 1973, c. 476, s. 143.)

§ 111-20. Awards subject to reopening upon change in condition.

All awards to needy blind persons made under the provisions of this Article shall be made subject to reopening and reconsideration at any time when there has been any change in the circumstances of any needy blind person or for any other reason. The Department of Health and Human Services and the board of county commissioners of each of the counties in which awards have been made shall at all times keep properly informed as to the circumstances and conditions of the persons to whom the awards are made, making reinvestigations annually, or more often, as may be found necessary. The Department of Health and Human Services may at any time present to the proper board of county commissioners any case in which, in their opinion, the changed circumstances of the case should be reconsidered. The board of county commissioners shall reconsider such cases and any and all other cases which, in the opinion of the board of county commissioners, deserve reconsideration. In all such cases notice of the hearing thereon shall be given to the person to whom the award has been made. Any person to whom an award has been made may apply for a reopening and reconsideration thereof. Upon such hearing, the board of county commissioners may make a new award increasing or decreasing the former award or leaving the same unchanged, or discontinuing the same, as it may find the circumstances of the case to warrant, such changes always to be within the limitations provided by this Article and in accordance with the terms hereof.

Any changes made in such award shall be reported to the Department of Health and Human Services, and shall be subject to the right of appeal and review, as provided in G.S. 111-16. (1937, c. 124, s. 9; 1971, c. 160; 1973, c. 476, s. 143; 1997-443, s. 11A.118(a).)

§ 111-21. Disqualifications for relief.

No aid to needy blind persons shall be given under the provisions of this Article to any individual for any period with respect to which he is receiving aid under the laws of North Carolina providing Work First Family Assistance and/or relief for the aged, and/or aid for the permanently and totally disabled. (1937, c. 124, s. 10; 1951, c. 319, s. 2; 1997-443, s. 12.29.)

§ 111-22. Beneficiaries not deemed paupers.

No blind person shall be deemed a pauper by reason of receiving relief under this Article. (1937, c. 124, s. 11.)

§ 111-23. Misrepresentation or fraud in obtaining assistance.

Any person who shall obtain, or attempt to obtain, by means of a willful, false statement, or representation, or impersonation, or other fraudulent devices, assistance to which he is not entitled shall be guilty of a Class 2 misdemeanor. The superior court and the recorders' courts shall have concurrent jurisdiction in all prosecutions arising under this Article. (1937, c. 124, s. 12; 1993, c. 539, s. 825; 1994, Ex. Sess., c. 24, s. 14(c).)

§ 111-24. Cooperation with federal departments or agencies; grants from federal government.

The Department of Health and Human Services is hereby empowered, authorized and directed to cooperate with the appropriate federal department or agency charged with the administration of the Social Security Act in any reasonable manner as may be necessary to qualify for federal aid for assistance to the needy blind and in conformity with the provisions of this Article, including the making of such reports in such form and containing such information as the appropriate federal department or agency may from time to time require, and the compliance with such regulations as the appropriate federal department or agency may from time to time find necessary to assure the correctness and verification of such reports.

The Department of Health and Human Services is hereby further empowered and authorized to receive grants-in-aid from the United States government for assistance to the blind and grants made for payment of costs of administering the State plan for aid to the blind, and all such grants so received hereunder shall be paid into the State treasury and credited to the account of the Department of Health and Human Services in carrying out the provisions of the

Article. (1937, c. 124, s. 13; 1971, c. 349, s. 1; 1973, c. 476, s. 143; 1997-443, s. 11A.118(a).)

§ 111-25. Acceptance and use of federal aid.

The Department of Health and Human Services may expend under the provisions of the Executive Budget Act, such grants as shall be made to it for paying the cost of administering this Chapter by the appropriate federal department or agency under the Social Security Act. (1937, c. 124, s. 14; 1971, c. 349, s. 2; 1973, c. 476, s. 143; 1997-443, s. 11A.118(a).)

§ 111-26. Termination of federal aid.

If for any reason there should be a termination of federal aid as anticipated in this Article, then and in that event this Article shall be ipso facto repealed and rendered null and void: Provided, however, such repeal shall not become effective or be in force unless and until the Governor of the State of North Carolina has issued a proclamation duly attested by the Secretary of the State of North Carolina to the effect that there has been a termination of such federal aid. In the event that this Article should be ipso facto repealed as herein provided, the State funds on hand shall be converted into the general fund of the State for such use as may be authorized by the Director of the Budget, and the county funds accumulated by the provisions of this Article in the respective counties of the State shall be converted into the general fund of such counties for such use as may be authorized by the county commissioners. (1937, c. 124, s. 15 1/2.)

§ 111-27. Department of Health and Human Services to promote employment of blind persons; vending stands on public property.

For the purpose of assisting blind persons to become self-supporting, the Department of Health and Human Services may carry on activities to promote the employment of blind persons, including the licensing and establishment of blind persons as operators of vending stands in public buildings. The Department of Health and Human Services may cooperate with the federal government in the furtherance of the Randolph-Sheppard Vending Stand Act, 20 U.S.C. §§ 107-107f, as amended, providing for the licensing of blind persons to operate vending stands in federal buildings, or any other act of Congress that may be enacted.

The board of county commissioners of each county and the commissioners or officials in charge of various State and municipal buildings may permit the operation of vending stands by blind persons on the premises of any State, county or municipal property under their respective jurisdictions. These operators shall be first licensed by the Department of Health and Human Services. Additionally, no vending stands may be operated unless, in the opinion of the commissions or officials having control and custody of the property, the vending stands may be properly and satisfactorily operated on the premises without undue interference with the use and needs of the premises or property for public purposes. (1939, c. 123; 1973, c. 476, s. 143; 1997-443, s. 11A.118(a); 2000-121, s. 16.)

§ 111-27.1. Department of Health and Human Services authorized to conduct certain business operations.

For the purpose of assisting blind and visually impaired persons to become self-supporting the Department of Health and Human Services may carry on activities to promote the rehabilitation and employment of the blind and visually impaired, including employment in or the operation of various business enterprises suitable for the blind and visually impaired. The Executive Budget Act applies to the operation of these enterprises as to all appropriations made by the State to aid in the organization and the establishment of these businesses. Purchases and sales of merchandise or equipment, the payment of rents and wages to blind and visually impaired persons operating these businesses, and other expenses of these businesses from funds derived from local subscriptions and from the day-by-day operations are not subject to the provisions of law regulating purchases and contracts, or to the deposit and disbursement that apply to State funds but shall be supervised by the Department of Health and Human Services. All of the business operations under this law are subject to the oversight of the State Auditor pursuant to Article 5A of Chapter 147 of the General Statutes.

Randolph-Sheppard vendors are not State employees. Blind licensees operating vending facilities under contract with the Department of Health and

Human Services, Division of Services for the Blind, are independent contractors. (1945, c. 72, s. 2; 1971, c. 1025, s. 1; 1973, c. 476, s. 143; 1983, c. 867, s. 1; 1993, c. 257, s. 9; 1997-443, s. 11A.118(a); 2000-121, s. 17.)

§ 111-27.2. Blind vending-stand operators; retirement benefits.

The Department of Health and Human Services is authorized and empowered to continue and maintain, in its discretion, any existing retirement system providing retirement benefits for blind vending-stand operators and to expend funds to provide necessary contributions to any existing retirement system for blind vending-stand operators to the extent that the Department determines such retirement system to be in the best interest of the blind vending-stand operators. (1969, c. 1255, s. 4; 1973, c. 476, s. 143; 1997-443, s. 11A.118(a).)

§ 111-28. Department of Health and Human Services authorized to receive grants for benefit of blind and visually impaired; use of information concerning blind persons.

The Department of Health and Human Services may receive grants-in-aid from the federal government or any State or federal agency for the purpose of rendering other services to the blind, visually impaired, and those in danger of becoming blind. All of these grants shall be paid into the State treasury and credited to the account of the Department of Health and Human Services, to be used in carrying out the provisions of this law.

The Commission for the Blind may adopt rules as may be required by the federal government or State or federal agency as a condition for receiving these federal funds, not inconsistent with the laws of this State.

The Department of Health and Human Services may enter into reciprocal agreements with public welfare agencies in other states regarding assistance and services to residents, nonresidents, or transients, and cooperate with other agencies of the State and federal governments in the provisions of assistance and services and in the study of the problems involved.

The Department of Health and Human Services may establish and enforce reasonable rules governing the custody, use and preservation of the records, papers, files, and communications of the Department.

It is unlawful, except for purposes directly connected with the administration of aid to the blind and visually impaired and in accordance with the rules of the Department of Health and Human Services, for any person to solicit, disclose, receive, make use of, or to authorize, knowingly permit, participate in, or acquiesce in the use of, any list of or name of, or any information concerning, persons applying for or receiving aid to the blind and visually impaired, directly or indirectly derived from the records, papers, files, or communications of the Department of Health and Human Services, the board of county commissioners, or the county social services department, or acquired in the course of the performance of official duties.

The Department of Health and Human Services may release to the Division of Motor Vehicles in the Department of Transportation and to the North Carolina Department of Revenue the name and medical records of any person listed in the register of the blind in this State maintained under the provisions of G.S. 111-4. All information and documents released to the Division of Motor Vehicles and the Department of Revenue shall be treated by them as confidential for their use only and shall not be released by them to any person for commercial or political purposes or for any purpose not directly connected with the administration of Chapters 20 and 105 of the General Statutes. The Department of Health and Human Services may also release to the North Carolina Library for the Blind and Physically Handicapped of the Department of Cultural Resources, the name and address of any person listed in the register of the blind in this State maintained under the provisions of G.S. 111-4. All information released to the North Carolina Library for the Blind and Physically Handicapped shall be treated as confidential for its use only and shall not be released to any person for commercial or political purposes or for any purpose not directly connected with providing information concerning services offered by the North Carolina Library for the Blind and Physically Handicapped. (1939, c. 124; 1941, c. 186; 1969, cc. 871, 982; 1973, c. 476, s. 143; 1989, c. 752, s. 141; 1997-443, s. 11A.118(a); 2000-121, s. 18.)

§ 111-28.1. Department of Health and Human Services authorized to cooperate with federal government in rehabilitation of blind and visually impaired.

The Department of Health and Human Services may adopt the necessary rules to cooperate with the federal government in the furtherance of the Rehabilitation Act of 1973, Pub. L. No. 93-112, 87 Stat. 355, 29 U.S.C. § 701, et seq., as amended, providing for the rehabilitation of the blind and visually impaired. (1945, c. 72, s. 1; 1973, c. 476, s. 143; 1997-443, s. 11A.118(a); 2000-121, s. 19.)

§ 111-29. Expenditure of equalizing funds; grants affording maximum federal aid; lending North Carolina reports.

In addition to the powers and duties imposed upon the Department of Health and Human Services, the said Department shall be and hereby is charged with the powers and duties hereinafter enumerated; that is to say:

(1)   The Department of Health and Human Services is hereby authorized to expend such funds as are appropriated to it as an equalizing fund for aid to the needy blind for the purpose of equalizing the financial burden of providing relief to the needy blind in the several counties of the State, and equalizing the grants received by the needy blind recipients. Such amount shall be expended and disbursed solely for the use of the needy blind coming within the eligibility provisions outlined in Chapter 124 of the Public Laws of 1937. Said amount shall be distributed to the counties according to the needs therein in conformity with the rules and regulations adopted by the Commission for the Blind, producing as far as possible a just and fair distribution thereof.

(2)   The Department of Health and Human Services is hereby authorized to make such grants to the needy blind of the State as will enable said Department to receive the maximum grants from the federal government for such purpose.

(3)   The Department of Health and Human Services is hereby authorized to work out plans with the Secretary of State for lending to needy blind lawyers volumes of the North Carolina reports in his custody that are unused or have become damaged. The Secretary of State is hereby authorized to lend such reports to the Department of Health and Human Services for relending to needy blind lawyers. Such reports may be recalled at any time by the Secretary of State upon giving 15 days' written notice to the Department of Health and Human Services which shall remain responsible for said reports until they are returned. The Department shall relend such reports only to blind lawyers, who, after an investigation by the Department, are determined to have no income, or

an income insufficient to purchase such reports. (1943, c. 600; 1973, c. 476, s. 143; 1997-443, s. 11A.118(a).)

§ 111-30. Personal representatives for certain recipients of aid to the blind.

If any otherwise qualified applicant for or recipient of aid to the blind is or shall become unable to manage the assistance payments, or otherwise fails so to manage, to the extent that deprivation or hazard to himself or others results, a petition may be filed by a relative of said blind person, or other interested person, or by the Secretary of Health and Human Services before the appropriate court under G.S. 111-31, in the form of a verified written application for the appointment of a personal representative for the purpose of receiving and managing public assistance payments for any such recipient, which application shall allege one or more of the above grounds for the legal appointment of such personal representative.

The court shall summarily order a hearing on the petition and shall cause the applicant or recipient to be notified at least five days in advance of the time and place for the hearing. Findings of fact shall be made by the court without a jury, and if the court shall find that the applicant for or recipient of aid to the blind is unable to manage the assistance payments, or otherwise fails so to manage, to the extent that deprivation or hazard to himself or others results, the court may thereupon enter an order embracing said findings and appointing some responsible person as personal representative of the applicant or recipient for the purposes set forth herein. The personal representative so appointed shall serve with or without bond, in the discretion of the court, and without compensation. He will be responsible for receiving the monthly assistance payment and using the proceeds of such payment for the benefit of the recipient of aid to the blind. Such personal representative shall be responsible to the court for the faithful discharge of the duties of his trust. The court may consider the recommendation of the Secretary of Health and Human Services in the selection of a suitable person for appointment as personal representative for the limited purposes of G.S. 111-30 to 111-33. The personal representative so appointed may be removed by the court, and the proceeding dismissed, or another suitable personal representative appointed. All costs of court with respect to any such proceedings shall be waived.

From the order of the court appointing or removing such personal representative, an appeal may be had to the judge of superior court who shall hear the matter de novo without a jury. (1945, c. 72, s. 4; 1953, c. 1000; 1961, c. 666, s. 2; 1971, c. 603, s. 3; 1973, c. 476, s. 138; 1997-443, s. 11A.118(a).)

§ 111-31. Courts for purposes of §§ 111-30 to 111-33; records.

For the purposes of G.S. 111-30 to 111-33 the court may be either a domestic relations court established pursuant to Article 13, Chapter 7, General Statutes, or the clerk of the superior court in the county having responsibility for the administration of the particular aid to the blind payments. The court may, for the purposes of G.S. 111-30 to 111-33, direct the Secretary of Health and Human Services to maintain records pertaining to all aspects of any personal representative proceeding, which the court may adopt as the court's record and in lieu of the maintenance of separate records by the court. (1961, c. 666, s. 2; 1971, c. 603, s. 4; 1973, c. 476, s. 138; 1997-443, s. 11A.118(a).)

§ 111-32. Findings under § 111-30 not competent as evidence in other proceedings.

The findings of fact under the provisions of G.S. 111-30 shall not be competent as evidence in any case or proceeding dealing with any subject matter other than provided in G.S. 111-30 to 111-33. (1961, c. 666, s. 2.)

§ 111-33. Sections 111-30 to 111-33 are not to affect provisions for payments for minors.

Nothing in G.S. 111-30 to 111-33 is to be construed as affecting that portion of the State plan for aid to the blind which provides that payments for eligible blind minors should be made to the parent, legal guardian, relatives or other persons "in loco parentis" of the blind minor, and that payments may be made to the minor if he is emancipated. (1961, c. 666, s. 2.)

§ 111-34. Repealed by Session Laws 1973, c. 476, s. 143.

§ 111-35. Authority of director of social services.

The respective boards of county commissioners of each county are hereby authorized to empower and confer upon the county director of social services for their respective counties the authority to perform any or all acts or functions which the previous sections of this Article direct or authorize the county boards of commissioners to perform. Any act or function performed by a county director of social services under the authority of this section shall be reported by him to the respective county board of commissioners for its review, and for alternative action or disposition where deemed appropriate by such board. Provided that the respective boards of county commissioners shall make no alternative or different disposition of a matter which the county director of social services is empowered to act upon which would prejudicially affect the status of any aid to the blind recipient without first affording such recipient reasonable notice and opportunity to be heard. (1971, c. 348, s. 1.)

§§ 111-36 through 111-40. Reserved for future codification purposes.

Article 3.

Operation of Vending Facilities on State Property.

§ 111-41. Preference to blind persons in operation of vending facilities; responsibility of Department of Health and Human Services.

In order to promote the employment and the self-sufficiency of blind persons in North Carolina, State agencies shall upon the request of the Department of Health and Human Services give preference to blind persons in the operation of vending facilities on State property. The Department of Health and Human Services shall encourage and assist the operation of vending facilities by blind persons. (1973, c. 1280, s. 1; 1997-443, s. 11A.118(a); 2000-121, s. 20.)

§ 111-42. Definitions as used in this Article.

(a) "Regular vending facility" means a vending facility where food preparation or cooking is not done on the State property.

(b) "State agency" means department, commission, agency or instrumentality of the State.

(c) "State property or State building" means building and land owned, leased, or otherwise controlled by the State, exclusive of schools, colleges and universities, the North Carolina State Fair, farmers markets and agricultural centers, the Legislative Office Building, and the State Legislative Building.

(d) "Vending facility" includes a snack bar, cafeteria, restaurant, cafe, concession stand, vending stand, cart service, or other facilities at which food, drinks, novelties, newspapers, periodicals, confections, souvenirs, tobacco products or related items are regularly sold.

(e) Repealed by Session Laws 2000-121, s. 21. (1973, c. 1280, s. 1; 2000-121, s. 21; 2001-41, s. 1; 2001-424, s. 17.4.)

§ 111-43. Installation of coin-operated vending machines.

In locations where the Department of Health and Human Services determines that a vending facility may not be operated or should not continue to operate due to insufficient revenues to support a blind vendor or due to the lack of qualified blind applicants, the Department shall have the first opportunity to secure, by negotiation of a contract with one or more licensed commercial vendors, coin-operated vending machines for the location. Profits from coin-operated vending machines secured by the Department of Health and Human Services shall be used by the Department for the support of programs that enable blind and visually impaired people to live more independently, including medical, rehabilitation, independent living, and educational services offered by the Division of Services for the Blind. (1973, c. 1280, s. 1; 1991, c. 689, s. 221.4(a); 1991 (Reg. Sess., 1992), c. 984, s. 1; 2000-121, s. 22.)

§ 111-44. Location and services provided by State agency.

If the Department of Health and Human Services determines that a location is suitable for the operation of a vending facility by a blind person, the State agency with authority over the location shall provide proper space, plumbing, lighting, and electrical outlets for the vending facility in the original planning and construction, or in the alteration and renovation of the present location. The State agency shall provide necessary utilities, janitorial service, and garbage disposal for the operation of the vending facility. Space and services for the vending facilities shall be provided without charge. (1973, c. 1280, s. 1; 1997-443, s. 11A.118(a); 2000-121, s. 23.)

§ 111-45. Duty of State agency to inform the Department of Health and Human Services.

It shall be the duty of the State agencies to inform the Department of Health and Human Services of existing and prospective locations for vending facilities and coin-operated vending machines and to adopt rules, upon request of the Department, to promote the successful operation of the vending facilities of the blind. (1973, c. 1280, s. 1; 2000-121, s. 24.)

§ 111-46. Vending facilities operated by those other than blind persons.

Where vending facilities on State property are operated by those other than blind persons on the date of enactment of this Article, the contract of these vending facilities shall not be renewed or extended unless the Secretary of the Department of Health and Human Services is notified of the proposed renewal or extension and the Secretary determines within 30 days of this notification that the vending facilities are not, or cannot become, suited for operation by the blind. If the Secretary of the Department of Health and Human Services within 30 days of the date of this notification fails to provide for the operation of the vending facilities by the blind, the existing contract may be renewed or extended. (1973, c. 1280, s. 1; 1997-443, s. 11A.118(a); 2000-121, s. 25.)

§ 111-47. Exclusions.

(a) This Article is not intended to cover food services provided by hospitals or residential institutions as a direct service to patients, inmates, trainees, or otherwise institutionalized persons, nor to cover coin-operated vending machines located in State facilities operated under the authority of G.S. 122C.

(b) This Article shall not prohibit the continued use of coin-operated vending machines currently the property of the Division of Services for the Blind of the Department of Health and Human Services and now part of the vending-stand program. (1973, c. 1280, s. 1; 1991 (Reg. Sess., 1992), c. 984, s. 2; 1997-443, s. 11A.118(a).)

§ 111-47.1. Food service at North Carolina aquariums.

(a) Notwithstanding Article 3 of Chapter 111 of the General Statutes, the North Carolina Aquariums may operate or contract for the operation of food or vending services at the North Carolina Aquariums. Notwithstanding G.S. 111-43, the net proceeds of revenue generated by food and vending services that are provided at the North Carolina Aquariums and are operated by or whose operation is contracted for by the Division of North Carolina Aquariums shall be credited to the North Carolina Aquariums Fund.

(b) This section shall not be construed to alter any contract for food or vending services at the North Carolina Aquariums that is in force at the time this section becomes law [effective July 1, 1999]. (1999-237, s. 15.17(a), (b).)

§ 111-47.2. Food service at museums and historic sites operated by the Department of Cultural Resources.

Notwithstanding Article 3 of Chapter 111 of the General Statutes, the North Carolina Department of Cultural Resources may operate or contract for the operation of food or vending services at museums and historic sites operated by the Department. Notwithstanding G.S. 111-43, the net proceeds of revenue generated by food and vending services provided at museums and historic sites operated by the Department or a vendor with whom the Department has contracted shall be credited to the appropriate fund of the museum or historic site where the funds were generated and shall be used for the operation of that museum or historic site. (2013-360, s. 19.3(a).)

Article 4.

Operation of Highway Vending Facilities on North Carolina Highways.

§ 111-48. Preference to blind persons in operation of highway vending facilities.

In order to provide support for programs for the blind and to further promote employment opportunities for blind persons, the Department of Health and Human Services may operate automatic vending machines on State property on North Carolina highways and shall give preference to blind persons in the operation of these facilities. (1991 (Reg. Sess., 1992), c. 984, s. 3; 1997-443, s. 11A.118(a).)

§ 111-49. Definitions as used in this Article.

(a) "Automatic vending" means a coin, currency, token, ticket, or credit card operated machine that dispenses food, drinks, or sundries.

(b) "Blind vendor" means a blind person who has been licensed by the Division of Services for the Blind to operate a vending stand in a public building.

(c) "Highway vending facilities" means automatic vending operations located on North Carolina highways in Welcome Centers and rest areas designated by the State. (1991 (Reg. Sess., 1992), c. 984, s. 3; 2000-121, s. 26.)

§ 111-50. Operations of highway vending.

(a) In locations on North Carolina highways where the Department of Health and Human Services determines that automatic vending is suitable, the Department shall authorize the Division of Services for the Blind to contract with blind vendors in the operation of highway vending facilities. The contracts shall be reviewed and renegotiated by the Division every two years and shall be reviewed by the Transfer and Promotion Committee. The Commission for the Blind shall adopt rules necessary to govern the operations. The highway vending program shall be a part of the Business Enterprises Program operated under the Randolph-Sheppard Act, 20 U.S.C. § 107a.

(b) Repealed by Session Laws 2000, c. 121, s. 27.

(c) The Commission for the Blind may adopt rules to establish applicable set-aside rates for the Business Enterprises Program. The Commission shall only develop rules authorized by this subsection with the active participation of the Elected Committee of Vendors. (1991 (Reg. Sess., 1992), c. 984, s. 3; 1997-443, s. 11A.118(a); 2000-121, s. 27.)

§ 111-51. Priority for specific blind vendors.

Blind vendors who were operating highway vending facilities as of July 31, 1991, and who continue to operate those facilities shall be given priority in renegotiating contracts under this Article to continue to operate those same facilities. (1991 (Reg. Sess., 1992), c. 984, s. 3.)

§ 111-52. Profits from Highway Vending Fund.

Profits generated by highway vending locations as of June 30, 1992, and deposited in a special fund in accordance with the policies of the Office of the State Controller shall be reserved for the construction and maintenance of highway vending facility projects. (1991 (Reg. Sess., 1992), c. 984, s. 3; 2004-199, s. 2.)

Chapter 112.

Confederate Homes and Pensions.

§§ 112-1 through 112-37: Repealed.

Chapter 113.

Conservation and Development.

SUBCHAPTER I. GENERAL PROVISIONS.

Article 1.

Powers and Duties of Department of Environment and Natural Resources Generally.

§ 113-1. Meaning of terms.

In this Article, unless the context otherwise requires, the expression "Department" means the Department of Environment and Natural Resources; "Secretary" means the Secretary of Environment and Natural Resources. (1925, c. 122, s. 3; 1973, c. 1262, ss. 28, 86; 1977, c. 771, s. 4; 1989, c. 727, s. 218(47); 1997-443, s. 11A.119(a).)

§ 113-2. Repealed by Session Laws 1973, c. 1262, s. 28.

§ 113-3. Duties of the Department.

(a) It shall be the duty of the Department, by investigation, recommendation and publication, to aid:

(1) In the promotion of the conservation and development of the natural resources of the State;

(2) In promoting a more profitable use of lands and forests;

(3) Repealed by Session Laws 1977, c. 198, s. 15; c. 771, s. 7;

(4) In coordinating existing scientific investigations and other related agencies in formulating and promoting sound policies of conservation and development; and

(5) Repealed by Session Laws 1977, c. 771, s. 7.

(b) Repealed by Session Laws 1959, c. 779, s. 3. (1925, c. 122, s. 4; 1957, c. 753, s. 3; c. 1424, s. 1; 1959, c. 779, s. 3; 1977, c. 198, s. 15; c. 771, s. 7.)

§§ 113-4 through 113-7. Repealed by Session Laws 1973, c. 1262, s. 28.

§ 113-8. Powers and duties of the Department.

The Department shall make investigations of the natural resources of the State, and take such measures as it may deem best suited to promote the conservation and development of such resources.

It shall have the protection of lands and water supplies; it shall also have the care of State parks, and other recreational areas now owned or to be acquired by the State, including the lakes referred to in G.S. 146-7.

It shall make such examination, survey and mapping of the geology, mineralogy and topography of the State, including their industrial and economic utilization, as it may consider necessary; make investigations of water supplies and water powers, prepare and maintain a general inventory of the water resources of the State, and take such measures as it may consider necessary to promote their development.

It shall have the duty of enforcing all laws relating to the conservation of marine and estuarine resources.

The Department may take such other measures as it may deem advisable to obtain and make public a more complete knowledge of the State and its resources, and it is authorized to cooperate with other departments and agencies of the State in obtaining and making public such information.

The Department may acquire such real and personal property as may be found desirable and necessary for the performance of the duties and functions of the Department and pay for same out of any funds appropriated for the Department or available unappropriated revenues of the Department, when such acquisition is approved by the Governor and Council of State. The title to any real estate acquired shall be in the name of the State of North Carolina for the use and benefit of the Department. (1925, c. 122, s. 9; 1927, c. 57; 1947, c. 118; 1957, c. 753, s. 4; c. 1424, s. 2; 1965, c. 957, s. 11; 1973, c. 1262, ss. 28, 86; 1977, c. 198, ss. 16, 17; c. 771, s. 4; 1989, c. 727, s. 33; 2011-145, s. 13.25(j).)

§ 113-8.01. Pollution Prevention Pays Programs.

There is established within the Department a non-regulatory technical assistance program to be known as the Pollution Prevention Pays Program.

The purpose of this program is to encourage voluntary waste and pollution reduction efforts through research and by providing information, technical assistance, and matching grants to businesses and industries interested in establishing or enhancing activities to prevent, reduce, or recycle waste. The Pollution Prevention Pays Program shall coordinate its activities with the appropriate regulatory agencies. (1989, c. 168, s. 7; 1993, c. 501, s. 10.)

§ 113-8.1. Repealed by Session Laws 1959, c. 779, s. 3.

§§ 113-9 through 113-13. Repealed by Session Laws 1973, c. 1262, s. 28.

§ 113-14. Recodified as § 143B-435 by Session Laws 1977, c. 198, s. 26.

§ 113-14.1. Promotion of seashore industry and recreation.

(a)   Repealed by Session Laws 1973, c. 1262, s. 28.

(b)   The following powers are hereby granted to the Secretary and may be delegated to the administrative head of an existing or new division of the Department as herein authorized:

(1)   through (3) Repealed by Session Laws 1977, c. 198, s. 18.

(4)   Study the development of the seacoast areas and implement policies which will promote the development of the coastal area, with particular emphasis upon the development of the scenic and recreational resources of the seacoast;

(5)   Advise and confer with various interested individuals, organizations and State, federal and local agencies which are interested in development of the seacoast area and use its facilities and efforts in planning, developing and carrying out overall programs for the development of the area as a whole;

(6)   Act as liaison between agencies of the State, local government, and agencies of the federal government concerned with development of the seacoast region;

(7)   Repealed by Session Laws 1973, c. 1262, s. 28;

(8) Make such reports to the Governor as he may request;

(9) File such recommendations or suggestions as it may deem proper with other agencies of the State, local or federal governments.

Provided, however, that the provisions of this section and G.S. 113-14.2 shall not be construed as affecting the authority of the Environmental Management Commission concerning shore-erosion control or prevention, beach protection, or hurricane protection under G.S. 143-355 or any other provision of law. (1969, c. 1143, ss. 2, 3; 1973, c. 1262, s. 28; 1977, c. 198, s. 18, c. 771, s. 4; 1989, c. 727, s. 34.)

§ 113-14.2. Repealed by Session Laws 1971, c. 882, s. 8.

§ 113-14.3. Publications.

The Department shall publish, from time to time, reports and statements, with illustrations, maps, and other descriptions, which shall adequately set forth the natural and material resources of the State for the purpose of furnishing information to educate the people about the natural and material resources of the State. (1977, c. 771, s. 5; 1989, c. 727, s. 35.)

§ 113-15. Recodified as § 143B-436 by Session Laws 1977, c. 198, s. 26.

§ 113-15.1. Repealed by Session Laws 1969, c. 1145, s. 4.

§ 113-15.2. Recodified as § 143B-437 by Session Laws 1977, c. 198, s. 26.

§ 113-16. Cooperation with agencies of the federal government.

The Department is authorized to arrange for and accept such aid and cooperation from the several United States government bureaus and other sources as may assist in completing topographic surveys and in carrying out the other objects of the Department.

The Department is further authorized and directed to cooperate with the Federal Power Commission in carrying out the rules adopted by that Commission; and to act in behalf of the State in carrying out any rules that may be adopted relating to water powers in this State other than those related to making and regulating rates. The provisions of this section are extended to apply to cooperation with authorized agencies of other states. (1925, c. 122, s. 18; 1929, c. 297, s. 2; 1973, c. 1262, s. 28; 1977, c. 771, s. 4; 1989, c. 727, s. 36.)

§ 113-17. Agreements, negotiations and conferences with federal government.

The Department is delegated as the State agency to represent North Carolina in any agreements, negotiations, or conferences with authorized agencies of adjoining or other states, or agencies of the federal government, relating to the joint administration or control over the surface or underground waters passing or flowing from one state to another under the provisions of this section. (1929, c. 297, s. 1; 1973, c. 476, s. 128; c. 1262, s. 86; 1977, c. 771, s. 4; 1989, c. 727, s. 37.)

§ 113-18. Department authorized to receive funds from Federal Power Commission.

All sums payable to the State of North Carolina by the Treasurer of the United States of America under the provisions of section 17 and other sections of the Federal Water Power Act shall be paid to the account of the Department as the authorized agent of the State for receipt of said payments. Such sums shall be used by the Department in prosecuting investigations for the utilization and development of the water resources of the State. (1929, c. 288; 1973, c. 1262, s. 86; 1977, c. 771, s. 4; 1989, c. 727, s. 38.)

§ 113-19. Cooperation with other State departments.

The Department is authorized to cooperate with the North Carolina Utilities Commission in investigating the waterpowers in the State, and to furnish the Utilities Commission such information as is possible regarding the location of the waterpower sites, developed waterpowers, and such other information as may be desired in regard to waterpower in the State; the Department shall also cooperate as far as possible with the Department of Labor, the State Department of Agriculture and Consumer Services, and other departments and institutions of the State in collecting information in regard to the resources of the State and in preparing the same for publication in such manner as may best advance the welfare and improvement of the State. (1925, c. 122, s. 16; 1927, c. 57, s. 1; 1931, c. 312; 1933, c. 134, s. 8; 1973, c. 1262, s. 28; 1977, c. 771, s. 4; 1989, c. 727, s. 39; 1997-261, s. 109.)

§ 113-20. Cooperation with counties and municipal corporations.

The Department is authorized to cooperate with the counties of the State in any surveys to ascertain the natural resources of the county; and with the governing bodies of cities and towns, with boards of trade and other like civic organizations, in examining and locating water supplies and in advising and recommending plans for other municipal improvements and enterprises. Such cooperation is to be conducted upon such terms as the Department may direct. (1925, c. 122, s. 17; 1973, c. 1262, s. 28; 1977, c. 771, s. 4; 1989, c. 727, s. 40.)

§ 113-21. Cooperation of counties with State in making water resource survey.

The board of county commissioners of any county of North Carolina is authorized and empowered, in their discretion, to cooperate with the Department or other association, organization, or corporation in making surveys of any of the natural resources of their county, and to appropriate and pay out of the funds under their control such proportional part of the cost of such survey as they may deem proper and just. (1921, c. 208; 1925, c. 122, s. 4; 1973, c. 1262, s. 86; 1977, c. 771, s. 4; 1989, c. 727, s. 41.)

§ 113-22: Repealed by Session Laws 2011-145, s. 13.25(k), effective July 1, 2011.

§ 113-23. Control of Mount Mitchell Park and other parks in the North Carolina State Parks System.

The Department shall have the control and management of Mount Mitchell Park and of any other parks which have been or may be acquired by the State as part of the North Carolina State Parks System. (1925, c. 122, s. 23; 1973, c. 1262, s. 28; 1977, c. 771, s. 4; 1989, c. 727, s. 43.)

§ 113-24. Repealed by Session Laws 1979, c. 830, s. 5.

§ 113-25. Notice to Department before beginning business of manufacturing products from mineral resources of State.

Every person, firm or corporation engaging in the manufacture or production of any product from any natural resources, classified as mineral products, shall before beginning such operation, or if already engaged in such business, within 90 days after March 9, 1927, notify the Department of its intention to begin or continue such business, and also notify said Department of the product or products it intends to produce.

Every person, firm or corporation now engaged or hereafter engaging in the manufacture or production of any product from any natural resources of the State classified as mineral products, shall notify the Department when such person, firm or corporation shall discontinue such manufacture or production.

Any person, firm or corporation failing to comply with the provisions of this section shall be guilty of a Class 3 misdemeanor, and upon conviction shall only be fined not more than twenty-five dollars ($25.00) and not less than five dollars ($5.00), in the discretion of the court. (1927, c. 258; 1993, c. 539, s. 828; 1994, Ex. Sess., c. 24, s. 14(c).)

§ 113-26. Repealed by Session Laws 1959, c. 683, s. 6.

§ 113-26.1. Bureau of Mines; mineral museum.

The Governor and the Council of State are hereby authorized, in their discretion and at such times as the development of the mineral resources and the expansion of mining operations in the State justify and make reasonably necessary, to create and establish as a part of the Department a Bureau of Mines, or a mineral museum in cooperation with the National Park Service, to be located in the western part of the State, with a view to rendering such aid and assistance to mining developments in this State as may be helpful in this expanding industry, and to allocate from the Contingency and Emergency Fund such funds as may reasonably be necessary for the establishment and operation of such Bureau of Mines or mineral museum.

The Department may adopt rules governing the operation of a Bureau of Mines or mineral museum established under this section. (1943, c. 612; 1953, c. 1104, ss. 1-3; 1973, c. 1262, ss. 28, 86; 1977, c. 771, s. 4; 1987, c. 827, s. 89; 1989, c. 727, s. 44.)

§ 113-27. Repealed by Session Laws 1959, c. 779, s. 3.

§ 113-28: Repealed by Session Laws 2010-96, s. 12, effective July 20, 2010.

Article 1A.

Special Peace Officers.

§ 113-28.1. Designated employees commissioned special peace officers by Governor.

Upon application by the Secretary of Environment and Natural Resources, the Governor is hereby authorized and empowered to commission as special peace officers such of the employees of the Department of Environment and Natural Resources as the Secretary may designate for the purpose of enforcing the laws and rules enacted or adopted for the protection, preservation and government of State parks, lakes, reservations and other lands or waters under the control or supervision of the Department of Environment and Natural Resources. (1947, c. 577; 1973, c. 1262, s. 86; 1977, c. 771, s. 4; 1987, c. 783, s. 5; 1989, c. 727, s. 46; 1997-443, s. 11A.119(a).)

§ 113-28.2. Powers of arrest.

Any employee of the Department of Environment and Natural Resources commissioned as a special peace officer shall have the right to arrest with warrant any person violating any law or rule on or relating to the State parks, lakes, reservations and other lands or waters under the control or supervision of the Department of Environment and Natural Resources, and shall have the power to pursue and arrest without warrant any person violating in his presence any law or rule on or relating to said parks, lakes, reservations and other lands or waters under the control or supervision of the Department of Environment and Natural Resources. (1947, c. 577; 1973, c. 1262, s. 86; 1977, c. 771, s. 4; 1989, c. 727, s. 47; 1997-443, s. 11A.119(a).)

§ 113-28.2A. Cooperation between law enforcement agencies.

Special peace officers employed by the Department of Environment and Natural Resources are officers of a "law enforcement agency" for purposes of G.S. 160A-288, and the Department shall have the same authority as a city or county governing body to approve cooperation between law enforcement agencies under that section. (2002-111, s. 1.)

§ 113-28.3: Repealed by Session Laws 1989, c. 485, s. 1.

§ 113-28.4. Oaths required.

Before any employee of the Department of Environment and Natural Resources commissioned as a special peace officer shall exercise any power of arrest under this Article he shall take the oaths required of public officers before an officer authorized to administer oaths. (1947, c. 577; 1973, c. 1262, s. 86; 1977, c. 771, s. 4; 1989, c. 727, s. 218(48); 1997-443, s. 11A.119(a).)

Article 1B.

Aviation.

§§ 113-28.5 through 113-28.12. Recodified as §§ 63-65 to 63-72 by Session Laws 1979, c. 148, s. 5.

Article 1C.

Commission on International Cooperation.

§§ 113-28.13 through 113-28.20: Repealed by Session Laws 1973, c. 1262, s. 86.

Article 1D.

Community Action Partnership Act.

§§ 113-28.21 through 113-28.26: Recodified as §§ 108B-21 through 108B-26 by Session Laws 1989 (Reg. Sess., 1990), c. 1004, s. 34 (c).

SUBCHAPTER II. STATE PARKS.

Article 2.

Acquisition and Control of State Parks.

§ 113-29. Definitions.

(a) In this Article, unless the context requires otherwise, "Department" means the Department of Environment and Natural Resources; and "Secretary" means the Secretary of Environment and Natural Resources.

(b) Repealed by Session Laws 2011-145, s. 13.25(n), effective July 1, 2011. (1939, c. 317, s. 1; 1969, c. 342, s. 1; 1973, c. 1262, ss. 28, 86; 1977, c. 771, s. 4; 1987, c. 827, s. 90; 1989, c. 727, s. 49; 1991 (Reg. Sess., 1992), c. 890, s. 2; 1997-443, s. 11A.119(a); 2011-145, s. 13.25(n).)

§ 113-29.1: Repealed by Session Laws 2011-145, s. 13.25(n), effective July 1, 2011.

§ 113-30: Repealed by Session Laws 2011-145, s. 13.25(n), effective July 1, 2011.

§ 113-31: Repealed by Session Laws 2011-145, s. 13.25(n), effective July 1, 2011.

§ 113-32: Repealed by Session Laws 2011-145, s. 13.25(n), effective July 1, 2011.

§ 113-33: Repealed by Session Laws 2011-145, s. 13.25(n), effective July 1, 2011.

§ 113-34. Power to acquire lands as State parks, and other recreational areas; donations or leases by United States; leases for recreational purposes.

(a)   The Department may acquire by gift, purchase, or condemnation under the provisions of Chapter 40A of the General Statutes, areas of land in different sections of the State that may in the opinion of the Department be necessary for the purpose of establishing or developing State parks, and other areas and developments essential to the effective operation of the State park activities under its charge. Condemnation proceedings shall be instituted and prosecuted in the name of the State, and any property so acquired shall be administered, developed, and used for public recreation and for other purposes authorized or required by law. Before any action or proceeding under this section can be exercised, the approval of the Governor and Council of State shall be obtained and filed with the clerk of the superior court in the county or counties where the property is located. The Attorney General shall ensure that all deeds to the State for land acquired under this section are properly executed before the gift is accepted or payment of the purchase money is made.

(b)   The Department may accept as gifts to the State any submarginal farmland acquired by the federal government that is suitable for the purpose of creating and maintaining game refuges, public shooting grounds, State parks, State lakes, and other recreational areas, or to enter into longtime leases with the federal government for the areas and administer them with funds secured from their administration in the best interest of longtime public use, supplemented by any appropriations made by the General Assembly. The Department may segregate revenue derived from State hunting and fishing licenses, use permits, and concessions and other proper revenue secured through the administration of State game refuges, public shooting grounds, State parks, State lakes, and other recreational areas to be deposited in the State treasury to the credit of the Department to be used for the administration of these areas.

(c) The Department, with the approval of the Governor and Council of State, may enter into leases of lands and waters for State parks, State lakes, and recreational purposes.

(d), (e) Repealed by Session Laws 2003-284, s. 35.1(a), effective July 1, 2003.

(f) The authority granted to the Department under this section is in addition to any authority granted to the Department under any other provision of law. (1915, c. 253, s. 1; C.S., s. 6124; 1925, c. 122, s. 22; 1935, c. 226; 1941, c. 118, s. 1; 1951, c. 443; 1953, c. 1109; 1957, c. 988, s. 2; 1965, c. 1008, s. 1; 1973, c. 1262, ss. 28, 86; 1977, c. 771, s. 4; 1987, c. 827, s. 91; 1989, c. 727, s. 54; 1993, c. 539, s. 829; 1994, Ex. Sess., c. 24, s. 14(c); 2001-487, s. 38(e); 2003-284, s. 35.1(a); 2011-145, s. 13.25(n).)

§ 113-34.1. Power to acquire conservation lands not included in the State Parks System.

The Department of Administration may acquire and allocate to the Department of Environment and Natural Resources for management by the Division of Parks and Recreation lands that the Department of Environment and Natural Resources finds are important for conservation purposes but which are not included in the State Parks System. Lands acquired pursuant to this section are not subject to Article 2C of Chapter 113 of the General Statutes and may be traded or transferred as necessary to protect, develop, and manage the Mountains to Sea State Park Trail, other State parks, or other conservation lands. This section does not expand the power granted to the Department of Environment and Natural Resources under G.S. 113-34(a) to acquire land by condemnation. (2000-157, s. 3.)

§ 113-35. Control over State parks; operation of public service facilities; concessions to private concerns; authority to charge fees and adopt rules.

(a) The Department shall make reasonable rules governing the use by the public of State parks and State lakes under its charge. These rules shall be posted in conspicuous places on and adjacent to the properties of the State and at the courthouse of the county or counties in which the properties are located. A violation of these rules is punishable as a Class 3 misdemeanor.

(a1) The Department may adopt rules under which the Secretary may issue a special-use permit authorizing the use of pyrotechnics in State parks in connection with public exhibitions. The rules shall require that experts supervise the use of pyrotechnics and that written authorization for the use of pyrotechnics be obtained from the board of commissioners of the county in which the pyrotechnics are to be used, as provided in G.S. 14-410. The Secretary may impose any conditions on a permit that the Secretary determines to be necessary to protect public health, safety, and welfare. These conditions shall include a requirement that the permittee execute an indemnification agreement with the Department and obtain general liability insurance covering personal injury and property damage that may result from the use of pyrotechnics with policy limits determined by the Secretary.

(b) The Department may construct, operate, and maintain within the State parks, State lakes, and other areas under its charge suitable public service facilities and conveniences, and may charge and collect reasonable fees for the use of these facilities and conveniences. The Department may also charge and collect reasonable fees for each of the following:

(1) The erection, maintenance, and use of docks, piers, and any other structures permitted in or on State lakes under rules adopted by the Department.

(2) Fishing privileges in State parks and State lakes, provided that these privileges shall be extended only to holders of State hunting and fishing licenses who comply with all State game and fish laws.

(3) Vehicle access for off-road driving at the beach at Fort Fisher State Recreation Area.

(4) The erection, maintenance, and use of a marina at Carolina Beach.

(b1) Members of the public who pay a fee under subsection (b) of this section for access to Fort Fisher State Recreation Area may have 24-hour access to Fort Fisher State Recreation Area from September 15 through March 15 of each year.

(c) The Department may make reasonable rules for the operation and use of boats or other craft on the surface of the waters under its charge. The Department may charge and collect reasonable fees for the use of boats and other watercraft that are purchased and maintained by the Department; however, the Department shall not charge a fee for the use or operation of any other boat or watercraft on these waters.

(d) The Department may grant to private individuals or companies concessions for operation of public service facilities for such periods and upon such conditions as the Department deems to be in the public interest. The Department may adopt reasonable rules for the regulation of the use by the public of the lands and waters under its charge and of the public service facilities and conveniences authorized under this section. A violation of these rules is punishable as a Class 3 misdemeanor.

(d1) The Department shall implement the following recommendations: validate no less frequently than every five years the number of visitors per car used in the calculation of visitor counts at State Parks.

(e) The authority granted to the Department under this section is in addition to any authority granted to the Department under any other provision of law. (1931, c. 111; 1947, c. 697; 1965, c. 1008, s. 2; 1969, c. 343; 1973, c. 547; c. 1262, ss. 28, 86; 1977, c. 771, s. 4; 1987, c. 827, s. 92; 1989, c. 727, s. 55; 1993, c. 539, ss. 830, 831; 1994, Ex. Sess., c. 24, s. 14(c); 1997-258, s. 2; 1997-443, s. 11A.119(a); 2003-284, ss. 35.1(b), 35.1A(a), 35.1A(b); 2004-124, s. 12.3(a); 2011-145, s. 13.25(n); 2012-93, s. 2(3).)

§ 113-35.1: Repealed by Session Laws 2009-484, s. 5, effective August 26, 2009.

§ 113-36: Repealed by Session Laws 2011-145, s. 13.25(n), effective July 1, 2011.

§ 113-37. Legislative authority necessary for payment.

Nothing in this Article shall operate or be construed as authority for the payment of any money out of the State treasury for the purchase of lands or for other purposes unless by appropriation for said purpose by the General Assembly. (1915, c. 253, s. 2 1/2; C.S., s. 6126.)

§ 113-38: Repealed by Session Laws 2011-145, s. 13.25(n), effective July 1, 2011.

§ 113-39. License fees for hunting and fishing on government-owned property unaffected.

No wording in G.S. 113-307.1(a), or any other North Carolina statute or law, or special act, shall be construed to abrogate the vested rights of the State of North Carolina to collect fees for license for hunting and fishing on any government-owned land or in any government-owned stream in North Carolina including the license for county, State or nonresident hunters or fishermen; or upon any lands or in any streams hereafter acquired by the federal government within the boundaries of the State of North Carolina. The lands and streams within the boundaries of the Great Smoky Mountains National Park to be exempt from this section. (1933, c. 537, s. 2; 1979, c. 830, s. 6; 2011-145, s. 13.25(n).)

§ 113-40. Donations of property for park purposes; agreements with federal government or agencies for acquisition.

The Department is hereby authorized and empowered to accept gifts, donations or contributions of land suitable for park purposes and to enter into agreements with the federal government or other agencies for acquiring by lease, purchase or otherwise such lands as in the judgment of the Department are desirable for State parks. (1935, c. 430, s. 1; 1973, c. 1262, s. 86; 1977, c. 771, s. 4; 1989, c. 727, s. 58; 2011-145, s. 13.25(n).)

§ 113-41. Expenditure of funds for development, etc.; disposition of products from lands; rules.

When lands are acquired or leased under G.S. 113-40, the Department is hereby authorized to make expenditures from any funds not otherwise obligated, for the management, development and utilization of such areas; to sell or otherwise dispose of products from such lands, and to make such rules as may be necessary to carry out the purposes of G.S. 113-40 to 113-44. (1935, c. 430, s. 2; 1987, c. 827, s. 93.)

§ 113-42. Disposition of revenues received from lands acquired.

All revenues derived from lands now owned or later acquired under the provisions of G.S. 113-40 to 113-44 shall be set aside for the use of the Department in acquisition, management, development and use of such lands until all obligations incurred have been paid in full. Thereafter, fifty percent (50%) of all net profits accruing from the administration of such lands shall be applicable for such purposes as the General Assembly may prescribe, and fifty percent (50%) shall be paid into the school fund to be used in the county or counties in which lands are located. (1935, c. 430, s. 3.)

§ 113-43. State not obligated for debts created hereunder.

Obligations for the acquisition of land incurred by the Department under the authority of G.S. 113-40 to 113-44 shall be paid solely and exclusively from revenues derived from such lands and shall not impose any liability upon the general credit and taxing power of the State. (1935, c. 430, s. 4.)

§ 113-44. Disposition of lands acquired.

The Department shall have full power and authority to sell, exchange or lease lands under its jurisdiction when in its judgment it is advantageous to the State to do so in the highest orderly development and management of State parks: Provided, however, said sale, lease or exchange shall not be contrary to the terms of any contract which it has entered into. (1935, c. 430, s. 5; 2011-145, s. 13.25(n).)

Article 2A.

Forestry Advisory Committee.

§§ 113-44.1 through 113-44.2. Repealed by Session Laws 1973, c. 1262, s. 28.

Article 2B.

Forestry Study Act.

§§ 113-44.3 through 113-44.6: Repealed by Session Laws 1995 (Reg. Sess., 1996), c. 653, s. 4.

Article 2C.

State Parks Act.

§ 113-44.7. Short title.

This Article shall be known as the State Parks Act. (1987, c. 243.)

§ 113-44.8. Declaration of policy and purpose.

(a) The State of North Carolina offers unique archaeologic, geologic, biological, scenic, and recreational resources. These resources are part of the heritage of the people of this State. The heritage of a people should be preserved and managed by the people for their use and for the use of their visitors and descendants.

(b) The General Assembly finds it appropriate to establish the State Parks System. This system shall consist of parks which include representative examples of the resources sought to be preserved by this Article, together with such surrounding lands as may be appropriate. Park lands are to be used by the people of this State and their visitors in order to promote understanding of and pride in the natural heritage of this State.

(c) The tax dollars of the people of the State should be expended in an efficient and effective manner for the purpose of assuring that the State Parks System is adequate to accomplish the goals as defined in this Article.

(d) The purpose of this Article is to establish methods and principles for the planned acquisition, development, and operation of State parks. (1987, c. 243, s. 1; 2003-340, s. 1.1.)

§ 113-44.9. Definitions.

As used in this Article, unless the context requires otherwise:

(1) "Department" means the Department of Environment and Natural Resources.

(2) "Park" means any tract of land or body of water comprising part of the State Parks System under this Article, including existing State parks, State natural areas, State recreation areas, State trails, State rivers, and State lakes.

(3) "Plan" means State Parks System Plan.

(4) "Secretary" means the Secretary of Environment and Natural Resources.

(5) "State Parks System" or "system" mean all those lands and waters which comprise the parks system of the State as established under this Article. (1987, c. 243, s. 1; 1989, c. 727, s. 218(50); 1989 (Reg. Sess., 1990), c. 1004, s. 19(b); 1997-443, s. 11A.119(a).)

§ 113-44.10. Powers of the Secretary.

The Secretary shall implement the provisions of this Article and shall be responsible for the administration of the State Parks System. (1987, c. 243.)

§ 113-44.11. Preparation of a System Plan.

(a) The Secretary shall prepare and adopt a State Parks System Plan by December 31, 1988. The Plan, at a minimum, shall:

(1) Outline a method whereby the mission and purposes of the State Parks System as defined in G.S. 113-44.8 can be achieved in a reasonable, timely, and cost-effective manner;

(2) Evaluate existing parks against these standards to determine their statewide significance;

(3) Identify duplications and deficiencies in the current State Parks System and make recommendations for correction;

(4) Describe the resources of the existing State Parks System and their current uses, identify conflicts created by those uses, and propose solutions to them; and

(5) Describe anticipated trends in usage of the State Parks System, detail what impacts these trends may have on the State Parks System, and recommend means and methods to accommodate those trends successfully.

(b) The Plan shall be developed with full public participation, including a series of public meetings held on adequate notice under rules which shall be adopted by the Secretary. The purpose of the public meetings and other public participation shall be to obtain from the public:

(1) Views and information on the needs of the public for recreational resources in the State Parks System;

(2) Views and information on the manner in which these needs should be addressed;

(3) Review of the draft plan prepared by the Secretary before he adopts the Plan.

(c) The Secretary shall revise the Plan at intervals not exceeding five years. Revisions to the Plan shall be made consistent with and under the rules providing public participation in adoption of the Plan.

(d) No later than October 1 of each year, the Department shall submit electronically the State Parks System Plan to the Environmental Review Commission, the Senate and the House of Representatives Appropriations Subcommittees on Natural and Economic Resources, and the Fiscal Research Division. Concurrently, the Department shall submit a summary of each change to the Plan that was made during the previous fiscal year. (1987, c. 243, s. 1; 2010-31, s. 13.13.)

§ 113-44.12. Classification of parks resources.

After adopting the Plan, the Secretary shall identify and classify the major resources of each of the parks in the State Parks System, in order to establish the major purpose or purposes of each of the parks, consistent with the Plan and the purposes of this Article. (1987, c. 243.)

§ 113-44.13. General management plans.

Every park classified pursuant to G.S. 113-44.12 shall have a general management plan. The plan shall include a statement of purpose for the park based upon its relationship to the System Plan and its classification. An analysis of the major resources and facilities on hand to achieve those purposes shall be completed along with a statement of management direction. The general management plan shall be revised as necessary to comply with the System Plan and to achieve the purposes of this Article. (1987, c. 243.)

§ 113-44.14. Additions to and deletions from the State Parks System.

(a) If, in the course of implementing G.S. 113-44.12 the Secretary determines that the major purposes of a park are not consistent with the purposes of this Article and the Plan, the Secretary may propose to the General Assembly the deletion of that park from the State Parks System. On a majority vote of each house of the General Assembly, the General Assembly may remove the park from the State Parks System. No other agency or governmental body of the State shall have the power to remove a park or any part from the State Parks System.

(b)   New parks shall be added to the State Parks System by the Department after authorization by the General Assembly. Each additional park shall be authorized only by an act of the General Assembly. Additions shall be consistent with and shall address the needs of the State Parks System as described in the Plan. All additions shall be accompanied by adequate authorization and appropriations for land acquisition, development, and operations. (1987, c. 243, s. 1.)

§ 113-44.15. Parks and Recreation Trust Fund.

(a)   Fund Created. - There is established a Parks and Recreation Trust Fund in the State Treasurer's Office. The Trust Fund shall be a special revenue fund consisting of gifts and grants to the Trust Fund and other monies appropriated to the Trust Fund by the General Assembly. Investment earnings credited to the assets of the Fund shall become part of the Fund.

(b)   Use. - Funds in the Trust Fund are annually appropriated to the North Carolina Parks and Recreation Authority and, unless otherwise specified by the General Assembly or the terms or conditions of a gift or grant, shall be allocated and used as follows:

(1)   Sixty-five percent (65%) for the State Parks System for capital projects, repairs and renovations of park facilities, and land acquisition.

(2)   Thirty percent (30%) to provide matching funds to local governmental units or public authorities as defined in G.S. 159-7 on a dollar-for-dollar basis for local park and recreation purposes. The appraised value of land that is donated to a local government unit or public authority may be applied to the matching requirement of this subdivision. These funds shall be allocated by the North Carolina Parks and Recreation Authority based on criteria patterned after the Open Project Selection Process established for the Land and Water Conservation Fund administered by the National Park Service of the United States Department of the Interior.

(3) Five percent (5%) for the Coastal and Estuarine Water Beach Access Program.

(b1) Geographic Distribution. - In allocating funds in the Trust Fund under this section, the North Carolina Parks and Recreation Authority shall make geographic distribution across the State to the extent practicable.

(b2) Administrative Expenses. - Of the funds appropriated to the North Carolina Parks and Recreation Authority from the Trust Fund each year, no more than three percent (3%) may be used by the Department for operating expenses associated with managing capital improvements projects, acquiring land, and administration of local grants programs.

(b3) Operating Expenses for State Parks System Allocations. - In allocating funds in the Trust Fund under subdivision (1) of subsection (b) of this section, the North Carolina Parks and Recreation Authority shall consider the operating expenses associated with each capital project, repair and renovation project, and each land acquisition. In considering the operating expenses, the North Carolina Parks and Recreation Authority shall determine both:

(1) The minimal anticipated operating expenses, which are determined by the minimum staff and other operating expenses needed to maintain the project.

(2) The optimal anticipated operating budget, which is determined by the level of staff and other operating expenses required to achieve a more satisfactory level of operation under the project.

(c) Reports. - The North Carolina Parks and Recreation Authority shall report no later than October 1 of each year to the Joint Legislative Commission on Governmental Operations, the House and Senate Appropriations Subcommittees on Natural and Economic Resources, the Fiscal Research Division, and the Environmental Review Commission on allocations from the Trust Fund from the prior fiscal year. For funds allocated from the Trust Fund under subdivision (b1) [subsection (b1)] of this section, this report shall include the operating expenses determined under subdivisions (1) and (2) of subsection (b3) of this section.

(d) Debt. - The Authority may allocate up to fifty percent (50%) of the portion of the annual appropriation identified in subdivision (b)(1) of this section to reimburse the General Fund for debt service on special indebtedness to be issued or incurred under Article 9 of Chapter 142 of the General Statutes for the purposes provided in subdivision (b)(1) of this section and for waterfront access. In order to allocate funds for debt service reimbursement, the Authority must identify to the State Treasurer the specific parks projects for which it would like special indebtedness to be issued or incurred and the annual amount it intends to make available, and request the State Treasurer to issue or incur the indebtedness. After special indebtedness has been issued or incurred for a parks project requested by the Authority, the Authority must credit to the General Fund each year the actual aggregate principal and interest payments to be made in that year on the special indebtedness, as identified by the State Treasurer. (1993 (Reg. Sess., 1994), c. 772, s. 1; 1995, c. 456, s. 2; 1995 (Reg. Sess., 1996), c. 646, s. 20; 1998-212, ss. 14.6(a), 14.7; 2001-114, s. 1; 2001-487, s. 73; 2004-179, s. 2.4; 2007-323, ss. 12.8, 29.14(f); 2009-484, s. 13; 2010-31, s. 13.11; 2013-360, s. 14.4(b); 2013-363, s. 5.8.)

Article 3.

Private Lands Designated as State Forests.

§§ 113-45 through 113-50: Repealed by Session Laws 1975, c. 253.

Article 4.

Protection and Development of Forests; Fire Control.

§§ 113-51 through 113-60.3: Recodified as Article 75 of Chapter 106, G.S. 106-895 through G.S. 106-910, by Session Laws 2011-145, s. 13.25(p), effective July 1, 2011.

Article 4A.

Protection of Forest Against Insect Infestation and Disease.

§§ 113-60.4 through 113-60.10: Recodified as Article 76 of Chapter 106, G.S. 106-920 through G.S. 106-926, by Session Laws 2011-145, s. 13.25(r), effective July 1, 2011.

Article 4B.

Southeastern Interstate Forest Fire Protection Compact.

§§ 113-60.11 through 113-60.15: Recodified as Article 77 of Chapter 106, G.S. 106-930 through 106-934, by Session Laws 2011-145, s. 13.25(t), effective July 1, 2011.

§ 113-60.16: Reserved for future codification purposes.

§ 113-60.17: Reserved for future codification purposes.

§ 113-60.18: Reserved for future codification purposes.

§ 113-60.19: Reserved for future codification purposes.

§ 113-60.20: Reserved for future codification purposes.

Article 4C.

Regulation of Open Fires.

§§ 113-60.21 through 113-60.31: Recodified as Article 78 of Chapter 106, G.S. 106-940 through G.S. 106-950, by Session Laws 2011-145, s. 13.25(w), effective July 1, 2011.

Article 4D.

Fire Fighters on Standby Duty.

§§ 113-60.32, 113-60.33: Recodified as Article 79 of Chapter 106, G.S. 106-955 and G.S. 106-956, by Session Laws 2011-145, s. 13.25(y), effective July 1, 2011.

§§ 113-60.34 through 113-60.39. Reserved for future codification purposes.

Article 4E.

North Carolina Prescribed Burning Act.

§§ 113-60.40 through 113-60.45: Recodified as Article 80 of Chapter 106, G.S. 106-965 through G.S. 106-970, by Session Laws 2011-145, s. 13.25(aa), effective July 1, 2011.

Article 5.

Corporations for Protection and Development of Forests.

§§ 113-61 through 113-77: Recodified as Article 81 of Chapter 106, G.S. 106-980 through G.S. 106-996, by Session Laws 2011-145, s. 13.25(cc), effective July 1, 2011.

§ 113-77.1: Reserved for future codification purposes.

§ 113-77.2: Reserved for future codification purposes.

§ 113-77.3: Reserved for future codification purposes.

§ 113-77.4: Reserved for future codification purposes.

§ 113-77.5: Reserved for future codification purposes.

Article 5A.

Natural Heritage Trust Program.

§§ 113-77.6 through 113-77.9: Repealed by Session Laws 2013-360, s. 14.3(b), effective August 1, 2013.

Article 6.

Fishing Generally.

§ 113-78: Repealed by Session Laws 1979, c. 830, s. 1.

§§ 113-79 through 113-81: Repealed by Session Laws 1947, c. 422, ss. 1, 9.

Article 6A.

Forestry Services and Advice for Owners and Operators of Forestland.

§§ 113-81.1 through 113-81.3: Recodified as Article 82 of Chapter 106, G.S. 106-1001 through G.S. 106-1003, by Session Laws 2011-145, s. 13.25(ee), effective July 1, 2011.

SUBCHAPTER IIA. DISTRIBUTION AND SALE OF HUNTING, FISHING AND TRAPPING LICENSES.

Article 6B.

License Agents.

§§ 113-81.4 through 113-81.13: Repealed by Session Laws 1979, c. 830, s. 1.

SUBCHAPTER III. GAME LAWS.

Article 7.

North Carolina Game Law of 1935.

§§ 113-82 through 113-99: Repealed by Session Laws 1979, c. 830, s. 1.

§ 113-99.1. Recodified as § 113-270.2A.

§§ 113-100 through 113-109. Repealed by Session Laws 1979, c. 830, s. 1.

§§ 113-109.1 through 113-109.5. Reserved for future codification purposes.

Article 7A.

Safe Distances for Hunting Migratory Wild Waterfowl.

§§ 113-109.6 through 113-109.8. Repealed by Session Laws 1979, c. 830, s. 1.

Article 8.

Fox-Hunting Regulations.

§ 113-110. Repealed by Session Laws 1945, c. 217.

§§ 113-110.1 through 113-112. Repealed by Session Laws 1979, c. 830, s. 1.

Article 9.

Federal Regulations on Federal Lands.

§§ 113-113 through 113-113.5: Repealed by Session Laws 1979, c. 830, s. 1.

Article 9A.

Regulation of Trapping.

§§ 113-113.6 through 113-113.19: Repealed by Session Laws 1979, c. 830, s. 1.

Article 9B.

Regulation of Beaver Taking.

§§ 113-113.20 through 113-113.23. Repealed by Session Laws 1979, c. 830, s. 1.

Article 10.

Regulation of Fur Dealers; Licenses.

§§ 113-114 through 113-120. Repealed by Session Laws 1979, c. 830, s. 1.

Article 10A.

Trespassing upon "Posted" Property to Hunt, Fish or Trap.

§§ 113-120.1 through 113-120.4. Transferred to §§ 14-159.6 to 14-159.9 by Session Laws 1979, c. 830, s. 11.

Article 10B.

Liability of Landowners to Authorized Users.

§§ 113-120.5 through 113-120.7. Repealed by Session Laws 1980, c. 830, s. 1.

Article 11.

Miscellaneous Provisions.

§§ 113-121 through 113-126.1. Repealed by Session Laws 1979, c. 830, s. 1.

§ 113-126.2: Not set out.

SUBCHAPTER IV. CONSERVATION OF MARINE AND ESTUARINE AND WILDLIFE RESOURCES.

Article 12.

General Definitions.

§ 113-127. Application of Article.

Unless the context clearly requires otherwise, the definitions in this Article apply throughout this Subchapter. (1965, c. 957, s. 2.)

§ 113-128. Definitions relating to agencies and their powers.

The following definitions and their cognates apply to powers and administration of agencies charged with the conservation of marine and estuarine and wildlife resources:

(1), (2) Repealed by Session Laws 1979, c. 830, s. 1.

(3) Department. - The Department of Environment and Natural Resources.

(4) Executive Director. - Executive Director, North Carolina Wildlife Resources Commission.

(4a) Fisheries Director. - Director, North Carolina Division of Marine Fisheries of the Department of Environment and Natural Resources who shall be qualified for the office by education or experience.

(5) Inspector. - Marine fisheries inspector.

(5a) Marine Fisheries Commission. - The Marine Fisheries Commission of the Department as established by Part 5D of Article 7 of Chapter 143B of the General Statutes.

(5b) Marine Fisheries Inspector. - An employee of the Department, other than a wildlife protector, sworn in as an officer and assigned duties which include exercise of law enforcement powers under this Subchapter. All references in statutes, regulations, contracts, and other legal and official documents to commercial fisheries inspectors and to commercial and sports fisheries inspectors apply to marine fisheries inspectors.

(6) Notice; Notify. - Where it is required that notice be given an agency of a situation within a given number of days, this places the burden on the person giving notice to make sure that the information is received in writing by a responsible member of the agency within the time limit.

(7) Protector. - Wildlife protector.

(8) Secretary. - Secretary of Environment and Natural Resources.

(9) Wildlife Protector. - An employee of the North Carolina Wildlife Resources Commission sworn in as an officer and assigned to duties which include exercise of law-enforcement powers.

(10) Wildlife Resources Commission. - The North Carolina Wildlife Resources Commission as established by Article 24 of Chapter 143 of the General Statutes and Part 3 of Article 7 of Chapter 143B of the General Statutes. (1965, c. 957, s. 2; 1973, c. 1262, s. 28; 1977, c. 512, s. 5; c. 771, s. 4; 1979, c. 388, s. 1; c. 830, s. 1; 1987, c. 641, s. 4; 1989, c. 727, s. 218(57); 1997-443, s. 11A.119(a); 1998-225, s. 1.1.)

§ 113-129. Definitions relating to resources.

The following definitions and their cognates apply in the description of the various marine and estuarine and wildlife resources:

(1) Repealed by Session Laws 1979, c. 830, s. 1.

(1a) Animals. - Wild animals, except when the context clearly indicates a contrary interpretation.

(1b) Big Game. - Bear, wild turkey, and white-tailed deer.

(1c) Birds. - Wild birds, except when the context clearly indicates a contrary interpretation.

(1d) Boating and Fishing Access Area. - An area of land providing access to public waters and which is owned, leased, controlled, or managed by the Wildlife Resources Commission.

(1e) Bushel. - A dry measure containing 2,150.42 cubic inches.

(1f) Cervid or Cervidae. - All animals in the Family Cervidae (elk and deer).

(2) Coastal Fisheries. - Any and every aspect of cultivating, taking, possessing, transporting, processing, selling, utilizing, and disposing of fish taken in coastal fishing waters, whatever the manner or purpose of taking, except for the regulation of inland game fish in coastal fishing waters which is vested in the Wildlife Resources Commission; and all such dealings with fish, wherever taken or found, by a person primarily concerned with fish taken in coastal fishing waters so as to be placed under the administrative supervision of the Department. Provided, that the Department is given no authority over the taking of fish in inland fishing waters. Except as provisions in this Subchapter or

in regulations of the Marine Fisheries Commission authorized under this Subchapter may make such reference inapplicable, all references in statutes, regulations, contracts, and other legal or official documents to commercial fisheries apply to coastal fisheries.

(3) Coastal Fishing. - All fishing in coastal fishing waters. Except as provisions in this Subchapter or in regulations of the Marine Fisheries Commission authorized under this Subchapter may make such references inapplicable, all references in statutes, regulations, contracts, and other legal or official documents to commercial fishing apply to coastal fishing.

(4) Coastal Fishing Waters. - The Atlantic Ocean; the various coastal sounds; and estuarine waters up to the dividing line between coastal fishing waters and inland fishing waters agreed upon by the Marine Fisheries Commission and the Wildlife Resources Commission. Except as provisions in this Subchapter or changes in the agreement between the Marine Fisheries Commission and the Wildlife Resources Commission may make such reference inapplicable, all references in statutes, regulations, contracts, and other legal or official documents to commercial fishing waters apply to coastal fishing waters.

(5) Crustaceans. - Crustacea, specifically including crabs, lobster, and shrimp.

(5a) Deer. - White-tailed deer (Odocoileus virginianus), except when otherwise specified in this Chapter.

(5b) Farmed Cervid. - Any member of the Cervidae family, other than white-tailed deer, elk, mule deer, or black-tailed deer, that is bought and sold for commercial purposes.

(5c) Feral Swine. - Free-ranging mammals of the species Sus scrofa.

(6) Fisheries Resources. - Marine and estuarine resources and such wildlife resources as relate to fish.

(7) Fish; Fishes. - All finfish; all shellfish; and all crustaceans.

(7a) Fur-bearing Animals. - Beaver, mink, muskrat, nutria, otter, skunk, and weasel; bobcat, opossum, and raccoon when lawfully taken with traps.

(7b) Game. - Game animals and game birds.

(7c) Game Animals. - Bear, fox, rabbit, squirrel, white-tailed deer, and, except when trapped in accordance with provisions relating to fur-bearing animals, bobcat, opossum, and raccoon.

(7d) Game Birds. - Migratory game birds and upland game birds.

(8) Game Fish. - Inland game fish and such other game fish in coastal fishing waters as may be regulated by the Department.

(8a) Game Lands. - Lands owned, leased, controlled, or cooperatively managed by the Wildlife Resources Commission for public hunting, trapping, or fishing.

(9) Inland Fishing Waters. - All inland waters except private ponds; and all waters connecting with or tributary to coastal sounds or the ocean extending inland or upstream from:

a. The dividing line between coastal fishing waters and inland fishing waters agreed upon by the Marine Fisheries Commission and the Wildlife Resources Commission; or

b. North Carolina's boundary with another state.

(10) Inland Game Fish. - Those species of freshwater fish, wherever found, and migratory saltwater fish, when found in inland fishing waters, as to which there is an important element of sport in taking and which are denominated as game fish in the regulations of the Wildlife Resources Commission. No species of fish of commercial importance not classified as a game fish in commercial fishing waters as of January 1, 1965, may be classified as an inland game fish in coastal fishing waters without the concurrence of the Marine Fisheries Commission.

(10a) Joint Fishing Waters. - Those coastal fishing waters in which are found a significant number of freshwater fish, as agreed upon by the Marine Fisheries Commission and the Wildlife Resources Commission in accordance with G.S. 113-132(e).

(11) Marine and Estuarine Resources. - All fish, except inland game fish, found in the Atlantic Ocean and in coastal fishing waters; all fisheries based upon such fish; all uncultivated or undomesticated plant and animal life, other

than wildlife resources, inhabiting or dependent upon coastal fishing waters; and the entire ecology supporting such fish, fisheries, and plant and animal life.

(11a) Migratory Birds. - All birds, whether or not raised in captivity, included in the terms of conventions between the United States and any foreign country for the protection of migratory birds and the Migratory Bird Treaty Act, as defined and listed in Part 10 of Title 50 of the Code of Federal Regulations.

(11b) Migratory Game Birds. - Those migratory birds for which open seasons are prescribed by the United States Department of the Interior and belonging to the following families:

a. Anatidae (wild ducks, geese, brant, and swans);

b. Columbidae (wild doves and pigeons);

c. Gruidae (little brown cranes);

d. Rallidae (rails, coots, and gallinules); and

e. Scolopacidae (woodcock and snipe).

The Wildlife Resources Commission is authorized to modify this definition from time to time by regulations only as necessary to keep it in conformity with governing federal laws and regulations pertaining to migratory game birds.

(11c) Migratory Waterfowl; Waterfowl. - Those migratory birds for which open seasons are prescribed by the United States Department of the Interior and belonging to the Family Anatidae (wild ducks, geese, brant, and swans).

(11d) Nongame Animals. - All wild animals except game and fur-bearing animals.

(11e) Nongame Birds. - All wild birds except game birds.

(12) Nongame Fish. - All fish found in inland fishing waters other than inland game fish.

(12a) Repealed by Session Laws 2004-160, s. 1, effective August 2, 2004.

(12b) Repealed by Session Laws 2004-160, s. 1, effective August 2, 2004.

(12c)   Overfished. - The condition of a fishery that occurs when the spawning stock biomass of the fishery is below the level that is adequate for the recruitment class of a fishery to replace the spawning class of the fishery.

(12d)   Overfishing. - Fishing that causes a level of mortality that prevents a fishery from producing a sustainable harvest.

(13)   Private Pond. - A body of water arising within and lying wholly upon a single tract of privately owned land, from which fish cannot escape and into which fish cannot enter from public fishing waters at any time, except that all publicly owned ponds and lakes are classified as public fishing waters. In addition, the private owners of abutting tracts of land on which a pond not exceeding 10 acres is or has been established may by written agreement cooperate to maintain that pond as a private pond if it otherwise meets the requirements of this definition. If a copy of the agreement has been filed with the Wildlife Resources Commission and the pond in fact meets the requirements of this definition, it attains the status of private pond either 60 days after the agreement has been filed or upon the Commission's approving it as private, whichever occurs first.

(13a)   Public Fishing Waters; Public Waters. - Coastal fishing waters, inland fishing waters, or both.

(13b)   Public Hunting Grounds. - Privately owned lands open to the public for hunting under the terms of a cooperative agreement between the owner and the Wildlife Resources Commission.

(13c)   Raptor. - A migratory bird of prey authorized under federal law and regulations for the taking of quarry by falconry.

(14)   Shellfish. - Mollusca, specifically including oysters, clams, mussels, and scallops.

(14a)   Sustainable harvest. - The amount of fish that can be taken from a fishery on a continuing basis without reducing the stock biomass of the fishery or causing the fishery to become overfished.

(14b)   Upland Game Birds. - Grouse, pheasant, quail, and wild turkey.

(15)   Wild Animals. - Game animals; fur-bearing animals; feral swine; and all other wild mammals except marine mammals found in coastal fishing waters. In

addition, this definition includes members of the following groups which are on the federal list of endangered or threatened species: wild amphibians, wild reptiles except sea turtles inhabiting and depending upon coastal fishing waters, and wild invertebrates except invertebrates declared to be pests under the Structural Pest Control Act of North Carolina of 1955 or the North Carolina Pesticide Law of 1971. Nothing in this definition is intended to abrogate G.S. 113-132(c), confer jurisdiction upon the Wildlife Resources Commission as to any subject exclusively regulated by any other agency, or to authorize the Wildlife Resources Commission by its regulations to supersede valid provision of law or regulation administered by any other agency.

(15a) Wild Birds. - Migratory game birds; upland game birds; and all undomesticated feathered vertebrates. The Wildlife Resources Commission may by regulation list specific birds or classes of birds excluded from the definition of wild birds based upon the need for protection or regulation in the interests of conservation of wildlife resources.

(15b) Repealed by Session Laws 2011-369, s. 2, effective October 1, 2011.

(16) Wildlife. - Wild animals; wild birds; all fish found in inland fishing waters; and inland game fish. Unless the context clearly requires otherwise, the definitions of wildlife, wildlife resources, wild animals, wild birds, fish, and the like are deemed to include species normally wild, or indistinguishable from wild species, which are raised or kept in captivity. Nothing in this definition is intended to abrogate the exclusive authority given the Department of Agriculture and Consumer Services to regulate the production and sale of pen-raised quail for food purposes.

(16a) Wildlife Refuge. - An area of land or waters owned, leased, controlled, or cooperatively managed by the Wildlife Resources Commission which is closed to the taking of some or all species of wildlife.

(17) Wildlife Resources. - All wild birds; all wild mammals other than marine mammals found in coastal fishing waters; all fish found in inland fishing waters, including migratory saltwater fish; all inland game fish; all uncultivated or undomesticated plant and animal life inhabiting or depending upon inland fishing waters; waterfowl food plants wherever found, except that to the extent such plants in coastal fishing waters affect the conservation of marine and estuarine resources the Department is given concurrent jurisdiction as to such plants; all undomesticated terrestrial creatures; and the entire ecology supporting such birds, mammals, fish, plant and animal life, and creatures. (1965, c. 957, s. 2;

1973, c. 1262, ss. 18, 28; 1977, c. 771, s. 4; 1979, c. 830, s. 1; 1979, 2nd Sess., c. 1285; 1987, c. 641, ss. 5, 6; 1991, c. 317, ss. 2, 3; c. 761, ss. 38, 39; 1993, c. 515, s. 6; 1997-142, ss. 2, 3; 1997-261, s. 80; 1997-400, s. 3.5; 1999-339, ss. 1-3; 2003-344, ss. 1-4; 2004-160, ss. 1, 2; 2009-89, s. 2; 2011-369, s. 2; 2013-413, s. 37(a).)

§ 113-130. Definitions relating to activities of public.

The following definitions and their cognates apply to activities of the public in regard to marine and estuarine and wildlife resources:

(1)   Repealed by Session Laws 1979, c. 830, s. 1.

(1a)   Falconry. - The sport of taking quarry by means of a trained raptor.

(1b)   Individual. - A human being.

(1c)   Landholder. - Any individual, resident or nonresident, owning land in this State or, when he is the one principally engaged in cultivating the land, leasing land in this State for agricultural purposes.

(2)   Owner; Ownership. - As for personal property, refers to persons having beneficial ownership and not to those holding legal title for security; as for real property, refers to persons having the present right of control, possession, and enjoyment, whether as life tenant, fee holder, beneficiary of a trust, or otherwise. Provided, that this definition does not include lessees of property except where the lease arrangement is a security device to facilitate what is in substance a sale of the property to the lessee.

(3)   Person. - Any individual; or any partnership, firm, association, corporation, or other group of individuals capable of suing or being sued as an entity.

(4)   Resident. - In the case of:

a.   Individuals. - One who at the time in question has resided in North Carolina for the preceding six months or has been domiciled in North Carolina for the preceding 60 days. When domicile in the State for a period of 60 days up to six months is the basis for establishing residence, the individual must sign a certificate on a form supplied by the Department or the Wildlife Resources Commission, as the case may be, stating the necessary facts and the intent to establish domicile here.

b. Corporations. - A corporation which is chartered under the laws of North Carolina and has its principal office within the State.

c. Partnerships. - A partnership in which all partners are residents of North Carolina and which has its principal office in the State.

d. Other Associations and Groups Fitting the Definition of Person. - An association or group principally composed of individual residents of North Carolina, with its principal office, if any, in the State, and organized for a purpose that contemplates more involvement or contact with this State than any other state.

e. Military Personnel and Their Dependents. - A member of the Armed Forces of the United States stationed at a military facility in North Carolina, the member's spouse, and any dependent under 18 years of age residing with the member are deemed residents of the State, of the county in which they live, and also, if different, of any county in which the military facility is located. A member of the Armed Forces of the United States on active duty outside the State of North Carolina shall be deemed an individual resident of the State for purposes of all the following licenses:

1. Coastal Recreational Fishing Licenses issued pursuant to G.S. 113-174.2(c)(1) and (c)(4).

2. Combination Hunting and Inland Fishing Licenses issued pursuant to G.S. 113-270.1C(b)(1).

3. Sportsman Licenses issued pursuant to G.S. 113-270.1D(a).

4. Hunting Licenses issued pursuant to G.S. 113-270.2(c)(1) and (c)(5).

5. Special Activity Licenses issued pursuant to G.S. 113-270.3(b)(1).

6. Trapping Licenses issued pursuant to G.S. 113-270.5(b)(1).

7. Hook-and-Line Licenses issued pursuant to G.S. 113-271(d)(1), (d)(2), and (d)(6)a.

8. Unified Hunting and Fishing Licenses issued pursuant to G.S. 113-351(c)(1) and (c)(2).

f. Students. - Nonresident students attending a university, college, or community college in the State.

(4a) To Buy; Purchase. - Includes a purchase or exchange of property, or an offer or attempt to purchase or exchange, for money or any other valuable consideration.

(5) To Fish. - To take fish.

(5a) To Hunt. - To take wild animals or wild birds.

(6) To Sell; Sale. - Includes a sale or exchange of property, or an offer or attempt to sell or exchange - for money or any other valuable consideration.

(7) To Take. - All operations during, immediately preparatory, and immediately subsequent to an attempt, whether successful or not, to capture, kill, pursue, hunt, or otherwise harm or reduce to possession any fisheries resources or wildlife resources.

(7a) To Trap. - To take wild animals or wild birds by trapping.

(8) Vessel. - Every description of watercraft, other than a seaplane on the water, used or capable of being used as a means of transportation on water. (1965, c. 957, s. 2; 1971, c. 705, s. 3; 1973, c. 1262, s. 18; 1979, c. 830, s. 1; 2005-455, s. 1.21; 2011-183, s. 76; 2013-191, s. 1.)

Article 13.

Jurisdiction of Conservation Agencies.

§ 113-131. Resources belong to public; stewardship of conservation agencies; grant and delegation of powers; injunctive relief.

(a) The marine and estuarine and wildlife resources of the State belong to the people of the State as a whole. The Department and the Wildlife Resources Commission are charged with stewardship of these resources.

(b) The following powers are hereby granted to the Department and the Wildlife Resources Commission and may be delegated to the Fisheries Director and the Executive Director:

(1) Comment on and object to permit applications submitted to State agencies which may affect the public trust resources in the land and water areas subject to their respective management duties so as to conserve and protect the public trust rights in such land and water areas;

(2) Investigate alleged encroachments upon, usurpations of, or other actions in violation of the public trust rights of the people of the State; and

(3) Initiate contested case proceedings under Chapter 150B for review of permit decisions by State agencies which will adversely affect the public trust rights of the people of the State or initiate civil actions to remove or restrain any unlawful or unauthorized encroachment upon, usurpation of, or any other violation of the public trust rights of the people of the State or legal rights of access to such public trust areas.

(c) Whenever there exists reasonable cause to believe that any person or other legal entity has unlawfully encroached upon, usurped, or otherwise violated the public trust rights of the people of the State or legal rights of access to such public trust areas, a civil action may be instituted by the responsible agency for injunctive relief to restrain the violation and for a mandatory preliminary injunction to restore the resources to an undisturbed condition. The action shall be brought in the superior court of the county in which the violation occurred. The institution of an action for injunctive relief under this section shall not relieve any party to such proceeding from any civil or criminal penalty otherwise prescribed for the violation.

(d) The Attorney General shall act as the attorney for the agencies and shall initiate actions in the name of and at the request of the Department or the Wildlife Resources Commission.

(e) In this section, the term "public trust resources" means land and water areas, both public and private, subject to public trust rights as that term is defined in G.S. 1-45.1.

(f) Notwithstanding the provisions of this section, a city may adopt and enforce ordinances as provided in G.S. 160A-203. (1965, c. 957, s. 2; 1973, c. 1262, s. 18; 1987, c. 641, s. 14; 2013-384, s. 4(b).)

§ 113-132. Jurisdiction of fisheries agencies.

(a) The Marine Fisheries Commission has jurisdiction over the conservation of marine and estuarine resources. Except as may be otherwise provided by law, it has jurisdiction over all activities connected with the conservation and regulation of marine and estuarine resources, including the regulation of aquaculture facilities as defined in G.S. 106-758 which cultivate or rear marine and estuarine resources.

(b) The Wildlife Resources Commission has jurisdiction over the conservation of wildlife resources. Except as may be otherwise provided by law, it has jurisdiction over all activities connected with the conservation and regulation of wildlife resources.

(c) Notwithstanding the provisions of this Article, this Subchapter does not give the Marine Fisheries Commission or the Wildlife Resources Commission jurisdiction over matters clearly within the jurisdiction vested in the Department of Agriculture and Consumer Services, the North Carolina Pesticide Board, the Commission for Public Health, the Environmental Management Commission, or other division of the Department regulating air or water pollution.

(d) To the extent that the grant of jurisdiction to the Marine Fisheries Commission and the Wildlife Resources Commission may overlap, the Marine Fisheries Commission and the Wildlife Resources Commission are granted concurrent jurisdiction. In cases of conflict between actions taken or regulations promulgated by either agency, as respects the activities of the other, pursuant to the dominant purpose of such jurisdiction, the Marine Fisheries Commission and the Wildlife Resources Commission are empowered to make agreements concerning the harmonious settlement of such conflict in the best interests of the conservation of the marine and estuarine and wildlife resources of the State. In the event the Marine Fisheries Commission and the Wildlife Resources Commission cannot agree, the Governor is empowered to resolve the differences.

(e) Those coastal fishing waters in which are found a significant number of freshwater fish, as agreed upon by the Marine Fisheries Commission and the Wildlife Resources Commission, may be denominated joint fishing waters. These waters are deemed coastal fishing waters from the standpoint of laws and regulations administered by the Department and are deemed inland fishing waters from the standpoint of laws and regulations administered by the Wildlife Resources Commission. The Marine Fisheries Commission and the Wildlife Resources Commission may make joint regulations governing the responsibilities of each agency and modifying the applicability of licensing and other regulatory provisions as may be necessary for rational and compatible management of the marine and estuarine and wildlife resources in joint fishing waters.

(f) The granting of jurisdiction in this section pertains to the power of agencies to enact regulations and ordinances. Nothing in this section or in G.S. 113-138 is designed to prohibit law-enforcement officers who would otherwise have jurisdiction from making arrests or in any manner enforcing the provisions of this Subchapter. (1965, c. 957, s. 2; 1973, c. 476, s. 128; c. 1262, ss. 18, 28, 38; 1977, c. 771, s. 4; 1979, c. 830, s. 1; 1987, c. 641, s. 5; 1989, c. 281, s. 3; 1997-261, s. 109; 2007-182, s. 2.)

§ 113-133. Abolition of local coastal fishing laws.

The enjoyment of the marine and estuarine resources of the State belongs to the people of the State as a whole and is not properly the subject of local regulation. As the Department is charged with administering the governing statutes and adopting rules in a manner to reconcile as equitably as may be the various competing interests of the people as regards these resources, considering the interests of those whose livelihood depends upon full and wise use of renewable and nonrenewable resources and also the interests of the many whose approach is recreational, all special, local, and private acts and ordinances regulating the conservation of marine and estuarine resources are repealed. Nothing in this section is intended to invalidate local legislation or local ordinances which exercise valid powers over subjects other than the conservation of marine and estuarine resources, even though an incidental effect may consist of an overlapping or conflict of jurisdiction as to some particular provision not essential to the conservation objectives set out in this Subchapter. (1965, c. 957, s. 2; 1987, c. 827, s. 96.)

§ 113-133.1. Limitations upon local regulation of wildlife resources; certain local acts retained.

(a) The enjoyment of the wildlife resources of the State belongs to all of the people of the State.

(b) The Wildlife Resources Commission is charged with administering the governing statutes in a manner to serve as equitably as may be the various competing interests of the people regarding wildlife resources, considering the interests of those whose livelihood depends upon full and wise use of renewable resources and the interests of the many whose approach is recreational. Thus, except as provided in subsection (e), all special, local, and private acts and ordinances enacted prior to the ratification date of the act creating this section regulating the conservation of wildlife resources are repealed. Nothing in this section is intended to invalidate local legislation or local ordinances which exercise valid powers over subjects other than the conservation of wildlife resources, even though an incidental effect may consist of an overlapping or conflict of jurisdiction as to some particular provision not essential to the conservation objectives set out in this Subchapter. In particular, this section does not repeal local acts which restrict hunting primarily for the purpose of protecting travelers on the highway, landowners, or other persons who may be endangered or affected by hunters' weapons or ammunition or whose property may be damaged.

(c) This Subchapter is intended to express State policy relating to the conservation of wildlife resources. Nothing in this section is intended to repeal or prevent the enactment of any city or county ordinance otherwise validly authorized which has only a minor and incidental impact on the conservation of marine and estuarine and wildlife resources. This section does not repeal G.S. 153A-127, G.S. 153A-131, G.S. 160A-182, G.S. 160A-187, and G.S. 160A-188, nor any local act establishing bird sanctuaries, except that local authorities operating bird sanctuaries may not regulate the taking of game or otherwise abrogate valid laws and regulations pertaining to the conservation of wildlife resources.

(d) Nothing in this Subchapter is intended to repeal or abridge the regulatory authority of the Game Commission of Currituck County or the Dare County Game and Wildlife Commission.

(e) Because of strong community interest expressed in their retention, the local acts or portions of local acts listed in this section are not repealed. The following local acts are retained to the extent they apply to the county for which listed:

Alleghany: Session Laws 1951, Chapter 665; Session Laws 1977, Chapter 526; Session Laws 1979, Chapter 556.

Anson: Former G.S. 113-111, as amended by Session Laws 1955, Chapter 286.

Ashe: Former G.S. 113-111; Session Laws 1951, Chapter 665.

Avery: Former G.S. 113-122.

Beaufort: Session Laws 1947, Chapter 466, as amended by Session Laws 1979, Chapter 219; Session Laws 1957, Chapter 1364; Session Laws 1971, Chapter 173.

Bertie: Session Laws 1955, Chapter 1376; Session Laws 1975, Chapter 287.

Bladen: Public-Local Laws 1933, Chapter 550, Section 2 (as it pertains to fox season); Session Laws 1961, Chapter 348 (as it applies to Bladen residents fishing in Robeson County); Session Laws 1961, Chapter 1023; Session Laws 1971, Chapter 384.

Brunswick: Session Laws 1975, Chapter 218.

Buncombe: Public-Local Laws 1933, Chapter 308.

Burke: Public-Local Laws 1921, Chapter 454; Public-Local Laws 1921 (Extra Session), Chapter 213, Section 3 (with respect to fox seasons); Public-Local Laws 1933, Chapter 422, Section 3; Session Laws 1977, Chapter 636.

Caldwell: Former G.S. 113-122; Session Laws 1977, Chapter 636; Session Laws 1979, Chapter 507.

Camden: Session Laws 1955, Chapter 362 (to the extent it applies to inland fishing waters); Session Laws 1967, Chapter 441.

Carteret: Session Laws 1955, Chapter 1036; Session Laws 1977, Chapter 695.

Caswell: Public-Local Laws 1933, Chapter 311; Public-Local Laws 1937, Chapter 411.

Catawba: Former G.S. 113-111, as amended by Session Laws 1955, Chapter 1037.

Chatham: Public-Local Laws 1937 Chapter 236; Session Laws 1963, Chapter 271.

Chowan: Session Laws 1979, Chapter 184; Session Laws 1979, Chapter 582.

Cleveland: Public Laws 1907, Chapter 388; Session Laws 1951, Chapter 1101; Session Laws 1979, Chapter 587.

Columbus: Session Laws 1951, Chapter 492, as amended by Session Laws 1955, Chapter 506.

Craven: Session Laws 1971, Chapter 273, as amended by Session Laws 1971, Chapter 629.

Cumberland: Session Laws 1975, Chapter 748; Session Laws 1977, Chapter 471.

Dare: Session Laws 1973, Chapter 259.

Davie: Former G.S. 113-111, as amended by Session Laws 1947, Chapter 333.

Duplin: Session Laws 1965, Chapter 774; Session Laws 1973 (Second Session 1974), Chapter 1266; Session Laws 1979, Chapter 466.

Edgecombe: Session Laws 1961, Chapter 408.

Gates: Session Laws 1959, Chapter 298; Session Laws 1975, Chapter 269; Session Laws 1975, Chapter 748.

Granville: Session Laws 1963, Chapter 670.

Greene: Session Laws 1975, Chapter 219; Session Laws 1979, Chapter 360.

Halifax: Public-Local Laws 1925, Chapter 571, Section 3 (with respect to fox-hunting seasons); Session Laws 1947, Chapter 954; Session Laws 1955, Chapter 1376.

Haywood: Former G.S. 113-111, as modified by Session Laws 1963, Chapter 322.

Henderson: Former G.S. 113-111.

Hertford: Session Laws 1959, Chapter 298; Session Laws 1975, Chapter 269; Session Laws 1975, Chapter 748; Session Laws 1977, Chapter 67.

Hoke: Session Laws 1963, Chapter 267.

Hyde: Public-Local Laws 1929, Chapter 354, Section 1 (as it relates to foxes); Session Laws 1951, Chapter 932.

Iredell: Session Laws 1979, Chapter 577.

Jackson: Session Laws 1965, Chapter 765.

Johnston: Session Laws 1975, Chapter 342.

Jones: Session Laws 1979, Chapter 441.

Lee: Session Laws 1963, Chapter 271; Session Laws 1977, Chapter 636.

Lenoir: Session Laws 1979, Chapter 441.

Lincoln: Public-Local Laws 1925, Chapter 449, Sections 1 and 2; Session Laws 1955, Chapter 878.

Madison: Public-Local Laws 1925, Chapter 418, Section 4; Session Laws 1951, Chapter 1040.

Martin: Session Laws 1955, Chapter 1376; Session Laws 1977, Chapter 636.

Montgomery: Session Laws 1977 (Second Session 1978), Chapter 1142.

Nash: Session Laws 1961, Chapter 408.

New Hanover: Session Laws 1971, Chapter 559; Session Laws 1975, Chapter 95.

Northampton: Session Laws 1955, Chapter 1376; Session Laws 1975, Chapter 269; Session Laws 1975, Chapter 748; Session Laws 1977, Chapter 67; Session Laws 1979, Chapter 548.

Orange: Public-Local Laws 1913, Chapter 547.

Pamlico: Session Laws 1977, Chapter 636.

Pender: Session Laws 1961, Chapter 333; Session Laws 1967, Chapter 229; Session Laws 1969, Chapter 258, as amended by Session Laws 1973, Chapter 420; Session Laws 1977, Chapter 585, as amended by Session Laws 1985, Chapter 421; Session Laws 1977, Chapter 805; Session Laws 1979, Chapter 546.

Perquimans: Former G.S. 113-111; Session Laws 1973, Chapter 160; Session Laws 1973, Chapter 264.

Polk: Session Laws 1975, Chapter 397; Session Laws 1975, Chapter 269, as amended by Session Laws 1977, Chapter 167.

Randolph: Public-Local Laws 1941, Chapter 246; Session Laws 1947, Chapter 920.

Robeson: Public-Local Laws 1924 (Extra Session), Chapter 92; Session Laws 1961, Chapter 348.

Rockingham: Former G.S. 113-111; Public-Local Laws 1933, Chapter 310.

Rowan: Session Laws 1975, Chapter 269, as amended by Session Laws 1977, Chapter 106, and Session Laws 1977, Chapter 500; Session Laws 1979, Chapter 556.

Rutherford: Session Laws 1973, Chapter 114; Session Laws 1975, Chapter 397.

Sampson: Session Laws 1979, Chapter 373.

Scotland: Session Laws 1959, Chapter 1143; Session Laws 1977, Chapter 436.

Stokes: Former G.S. 113-111; Public-Local Laws 1933, Chapter 310; Session Laws 1979, Chapter 556.

Surry: Public-Local Laws 1925, Chapter 474, Section 6 (as it pertains to fox seasons); Session Laws 1975, Chapter 269, as amended by Session Laws 1977, Chapter 167.

Swain: Public-Local Laws 1935, Chapter 52; Session Laws 1953, Chapter 270; Session Laws 1965, Chapter 765.

Transylvania: Public Laws 1935, Chapter 107, Section 2, as amended by Public Laws 1935, Chapter 238.

Tyrrell: Former G.S. 113-111; Session Laws 1953, Chapter 685.

Wake: Session Laws 1973 (Second Session 1974), Chapter 1382.

Washington: Session Laws 1947, Chapter 620.

Wayne: Session Laws 1975, Chapter 269; Session Laws 1975, Chapter 342, as amended by Session Laws 1977, Chapter 43; Session Laws 1975, Chapter 343, as amended by Session Laws 1977, Chapter 45; Session Laws 1977, Chapter 695.

Wilkes: Former G.S. 113-111, as amended by Session Laws 1971, Chapter 385; Session Laws 1951, Chapter 665; Session Laws 1973, Chapter 106; Session Laws 1979, Chapter 507.

Yadkin: Former G.S. 113-111, as amended by Session Laws 1953, Chapter 199; Session Laws 1979, Chapter 507.

Yancey: Session Laws 1965, Chapter 522.

(f) The Wildlife Resources Commission is directed to review periodically all local acts affecting conservation of wildlife resources and notify local authorities and the General Assembly as to those that:

(1) Substantially duplicate provisions of this Subchapter.

(2) Seriously conflict with conservation policies set out in this Subchapter.

(3) Seriously conflict with conservation policies developed for the people of this State as a whole by the Wildlife Resources Commission.

(g)   Notwithstanding G.S. 113-133.1(b), Chapter 565 of the Session Laws of 1977 is retained in effect. The following local conservation acts which specify that they must be specifically repealed are so repealed: Chapters 434 and 441 of the Session Laws of 1977. To provide for their retention or repeal in accordance with provisions applying to all other local wildlife acts, the following acts are amended to repeal the cited sections: Section 11, Chapter 258, Session Laws of 1969; and Section 4, Chapter 585, Session Laws of 1977. (1979, c. 830, ss. 1, 14; 1979, 2nd Sess., c. 1285, ss. 2, 11; c. 1324, s. 2; 1981, c. 249, s. 2; c. 250, s. 2; 1983, c. 109, s. 2; c. 487, s. 2; 1985, c. 112, s. 1; c. 302, s. 1; c. 689, s. 27; 1986, c. 893, s. 4; 1987, c. 33, s. 4; c. 131, ss. 4, 5; c. 245, s. 2; c. 282, s. 16; 1987 (Reg. Sess., 1988), c. 955, s. 4; 1989, c. 80, s. 2; 1989 (Reg. Sess., 1990), c. 837, s. 2; 1993, c. 65, s. 1; c. 221, s. 3; 1995, c. 509, s. 55; 1997-456, s. 26; 1997-496, s. 18; 2006-21, s. 2; 2006-226, s. 20; 2009-89, s. 1.)

§ 113-134. Rules.

The Marine Fisheries Commission and the Wildlife Resources Commission may, within their jurisdictional limitations imposed by this Article, adopt rules implementing this Subchapter. (1915, c. 84, s. 21; 1917, c. 290, s. 7; C.S., 1878; 1925, c. 168, s. 2; 1935, c. 35; 1945, c. 776; 1953, cc. 774, 1251; 1963, c. 1097, s. 1; 1965, c. 957, s. 2; 1973, c. 1262, s. 28; 1987, c. 827, s. 97.)

§ 113-134.1. Jurisdiction over marine fisheries resources in Atlantic Ocean.

The Marine Fisheries Commission is directed to exercise all regulatory authority over the conservation of marine fisheries resources in the Atlantic Ocean to the seaward extent of the State jurisdiction over the resources as now or hereafter defined. Marine fisheries inspectors may enforce these regulations and all other provisions of law applicable under the authority granted in this section in the same manner and with the same powers elsewhere granted them as enforcement officers. (1973, c. 1315; 1977, c. 771, s. 4; 1979, c. 830, s. 1; 1987, c. 641, ss. 5, 8.)

§ 113-135. General penalties for violating Subchapter or rules; increased penalty for prior convictions; interpretive provisions.

(a) Any person who violates any provision of this Subchapter or any rule adopted by the Marine Fisheries Commission or the Wildlife Resources Commission, as appropriate, pursuant to the authority of this Subchapter, is guilty of a misdemeanor except that punishment for violation of the rules of the Wildlife Resources Commission is limited as set forth in G.S. 113-135.1. Fishing without a license in violation of G.S. 113-174.1(a) or G.S. 113-270.1B(a) is punishable as an infraction. Otherwise, unless a different level of punishment is elsewhere set out, anyone convicted of a misdemeanor under this section is punishable as follows:

(1) For a first conviction, as a Class 3 misdemeanor.

(2) For a second or subsequent conviction within three years, as a Class 2 misdemeanor.

(b) In interpreting this section, provisions elsewhere in this Subchapter making an offense a misdemeanor "punishable in the discretion of the court" must be considered to set a different level of punishment, to be interpreted in the light of G.S. 14-3 or any equivalent or successor statute. Noncriminal sanctions, however, such as license revocation or suspension, and exercise of powers auxiliary to criminal prosecution, such as seizure of property involved in the commission of an offense, do not constitute different levels of punishment so as to oust criminal liability. Any previous conviction of an offense under this Subchapter, or under rules authorized by it, serves to increase the punishment under subsection (a) even though for a different offense than the second or subsequent one.

(c) For the purposes of this Subchapter, violations of laws or rules administered by the Wildlife Resources Commission under any former general or local law replaced by the present provisions of this Subchapter are deemed to be violations of laws or rules under this Subchapter. (1965, c. 957, s. 2; 1973, c. 1262, s. 28; 1979, c. 830, s. 1; 1987, c. 827, s. 98; 1991, c. 176, s. 1; c. 761, s. 50.5; 1993, c. 539, s. 836; 1994, Ex. Sess., c. 24, s. 14(c); 1995, c. 209, s. 3; 2013-360, s. 18B.14(m); 2013-385, s. 6.)

§ 113-135.1. Limitation upon penalty for offense created by rules of Wildlife Resources Commission in certain instances.

(a) To prevent unsuspecting members of the public from being subject to harsh criminal penalties for offenses created by rules of the Wildlife Resources Commission, the penalty for an offense that is solely a violation of rules of the Wildlife Resources Commission is limited to a fine of twenty-five dollars ($25.00) except as follows:

(1) Offenses set out in subsection (b) of this section are punishable as set forth in G.S. 113-135 or other sections of the General Statutes.

(2) A person who parks a vehicle in violation of a rule regulating the parking of vehicles at boating access or boating launch areas is responsible for an infraction and shall pay a fine of fifty dollars ($50.00).

(b) The limitation upon penalty does not apply to any rule violation:

(1) Punishable under G.S. 113-294 or otherwise involving aggravating elements that result in a greater punishment than provided by G.S. 113-135;

(2) That involves a defendant subject to the collection-license provisions of G.S. 113-272.4 or who is a dealer as defined in G.S. 113-273; or

(3) Relating to seasons, bag limits, creel limits, taking fish other than with hook and line, buying or selling wildlife, possessing or transporting live wildlife, taking wildlife at night or with the aid of a conveyance, or falconry. (1979, c. 830, s. 1; 1987, c. 827, s. 98; 2005-164, s. 1; 2012-200, s. 19.)

§ 113-136. Enforcement authority of inspectors and protectors; refusal to obey or allow inspection by inspectors and protectors.

(a) Inspectors and protectors are granted the powers of peace officers anywhere in this State, and beyond its boundaries to the extent provided by law, in enforcing all matters within their respective subject-matter jurisdiction as set out in this section.

(b) The jurisdiction of inspectors extends to all matters within the jurisdiction of the Department set out in this Subchapter, Part 5D of Article 7 of Chapter

143B of the General Statutes, Article 5 of Chapter 76 of the General Statutes, and Article 2 of Chapter 77 of the General Statutes, and to all other matters within the jurisdiction of the Department which it directs inspectors to enforce. In addition, inspectors have jurisdiction over all offenses involving property of or leased to or managed by the Department in connection with the conservation of marine and estuarine resources.

(c)   The jurisdiction of protectors extends to all matters within the jurisdiction of the Wildlife Resources Commission, whether set out in this Chapter, Chapter 75A, Chapter 143, Chapter 143B, or elsewhere. The Wildlife Resources Commission is specifically granted jurisdiction over all aspects of:

(1)   Boating and water safety;

(2)   Hunting and trapping;

(3)   Fishing, exclusive of fishing under the jurisdiction of the Marine Fisheries Commission; and

(4)   Activities in woodlands and on inland waters governed by G.S. 106-908 to G.S. 106-910.

In addition, protectors have jurisdiction over all offenses involving property of or leased by the Wildlife Resources Commission or occurring on wildlife refuges, game lands, or boating and fishing access areas managed by the Wildlife Resources Commission. The authority of protectors over offenses on public hunting grounds is governed by the jurisdiction granted the Commission in G.S. 113-264(c).

(d)   Inspectors and protectors are additionally authorized to arrest without warrant under the terms of G.S. 15A-401(b) for felonies, for breaches of the peace, for assaults upon them or in their presence, and for other offenses evincing a flouting of their authority as enforcement officers or constituting a threat to public peace and order which would tend to subvert the authority of the State if ignored. In particular, they are authorized, subject to the direction of the administrative superiors, to arrest for violations of G.S. 14-223, 14-225, 14-269, and 14-277.

(d1)   In addition to law enforcement authority granted elsewhere, a protector has the authority to enforce criminal laws under the following circumstances:

(1) When the protector has probable cause to believe that a person committed a criminal offense in his presence and at the time of the violation the protector is engaged in the enforcement of laws otherwise within his jurisdiction; or

(2) When the protector is asked to provide temporary assistance by the head of a State or local law enforcement agency or his designee and the request is within the scope of the agency's subject matter jurisdiction.

While acting pursuant to this subsection, a protector shall have the same powers invested in law enforcement officers by statute or common law. When acting pursuant to (2) of this subsection a protector shall not be considered an officer, employee, or agent for the state or local law enforcement agency or designee asking for temporary assistance. Nothing in this subsection shall be construed to expand the authority of protectors to initiate or conduct an independent investigation into violations of criminal laws outside the scope of their subject matter or territorial jurisdiction.

(e) Inspectors and protectors may serve arrest warrants, search warrants, orders for arrest, criminal summonses, subpoenas, and all other process connected with any cases within their subject-matter jurisdiction. In the exercise of their law enforcement powers, inspectors are subject to provisions relating to police officers in general set out in Chapter 15, Chapter 15A, and elsewhere.

(f) Inspectors and protectors are authorized to stop temporarily any persons they reasonably believe to be engaging in activity regulated by their respective agencies to determine whether such activity is being conducted within the requirements of the law, including license requirements. If the person stopped is in a motor vehicle being driven at the time and the inspector or protector in question is also in a motor vehicle, the inspector or protector is required to sound a siren or activate a special light, bell, horn, or exhaust whistle approved for law-enforcement vehicles under the provisions of G.S. 20-125(b) or 20-125(c).

(g) Protectors may not temporarily stop or inspect vehicles proceeding along primary highways of the State without clear evidence that someone within the vehicle is or has recently been engaged in an activity regulated by the Wildlife Resources Commission. Inspectors may temporarily stop vehicles, boats, airplanes, and other conveyances upon reasonable grounds to believe that they are transporting seafood products; they are authorized to inspect any seafood products being transported to determine whether they were taken in accordance with law and to require exhibition of any applicable license, receipts, permits, bills of lading, or other identification required to accompany such seafood products.

(h),   (i) Repealed by Session Laws 1979, c. 830, s. 1.

(j)   The refusal of any person to stop in obedience to the directions of an inspector or protector acting under the authority of this section is unlawful. A violation of this subsection is a Class 3 misdemeanor and may include a fine of not less than fifty dollars ($50.00).

(k)   It is unlawful to refuse to exhibit upon request by any inspector, protector, or other law enforcement officer any item required to be carried by any law or rule as to which inspectors or protectors have enforcement jurisdiction. The items that must be exhibited include boating safety or other equipment or any license, permit, tax receipt, certificate, or identification. It is unlawful to refuse to allow inspectors, protectors, or other law enforcement officers to inspect weapons, equipment, fish, or wildlife that the officer reasonably believes to be possessed incident to an activity regulated by any law or rule as to which inspectors and protectors have enforcement jurisdiction.

(l)   Nothing in this section authorizes searches within the curtilage of a dwelling or of the living quarters of a vessel in contravention of constitutional prohibitions against unreasonable searches and seizures. (1915, c. 84, s. 6; 1917, c. 290, s. 2; C.S., s. 1885; 1935, c. 118; 1957, c. 1423, s. 2; 1965, c. 957, s. 2; 1973, c. 1262, ss. 18, 28, 86; c. 1286, s. 17; c. 1297; 1977, c. 771, s. 4; 1979, c. 830, s. 1; 1987, c. 641, ss. 20, 22; c. 827, s. 98; 1991, c. 730, s. 1; 1997-80, s. 5; 1998-225, ss. 3.1, 3.2; 2011-145, s. 13.25(xx).)

§ 113-137. Search on arrest; seizure and confiscation of property; disposition of confiscated property.

(a)   Every inspector or protector who arrests a person for an offense as to which he has enforcement jurisdiction is authorized to search the person arrested and the surrounding area for weapons and for fruits, instrumentalities, and evidence of any crime for which the person arrested is or might have been arrested.

(b) Every inspector or protector who issues a citation instead of arresting a person, in cases in which the inspector or protector is authorized to arrest, may seize all lawfully discovered evidence, fruits, and instrumentalities of any crime as to which he has arrest jurisdiction and probable cause. When live fish are returned to public fishing bottoms or public waters, the inspector or protector shall state on the citation the quantity returned.

(c) Every inspector or protector who in the lawful pursuit of his duties has probable cause for believing he has discovered a violation of the law over which he has jurisdiction may seize in connection therewith any fish, wildlife, weapons, equipment, vessels, or other evidence, fruits, or instrumentalities of the crime, notwithstanding the absence of any person in the immediate area subject to arrest or the failure or inability of the inspector or protector to capture or otherwise take custody of the person guilty of the violation in question. Where the owner of such property satisfies the Secretary or the Executive Director, as the case may be, of his ownership and that he had no knowledge or culpability in regard to the offense involving the use of his property, such property must be returned to the owner. If after due diligence on the part of employees of the Department or the Wildlife Resources Commission, as the case may be, the identity or whereabouts of the violator or of the owner of the property seized cannot be determined, such property may be sold by the Department or the Wildlife Resources Commission in accordance with the provisions of this section.

(d) The Marine Fisheries Commission and the Wildlife Resources Commission may provide by rule for summary disposition of live or perishable fish or wildlife seized by an inspector or protector. If the property seized consists of live fish which may again be placed to the benefit of the public on public fishing bottoms or in public waters, the inspector or protector may require the person in possession of the seized live fish to transport it the distance necessary to effect placement on appropriate bottoms or waters. In the event of refusal by the person in question to transport the fish, the inspector or protector must take appropriate steps to effect the transportation. The steps may include seizure of any conveyance or vessel of the person refusing to transport the fish if the conveyance or vessel was one on which the fish were located or was used to take or transport the fish. When a conveyance or vessel is seized, it is to be safeguarded by the inspector or protector seizing it pending trial and it becomes subject to the orders of the court. Transportation costs borne by the Department or by the Wildlife Resources Commission, as the case may be, may be collected by the agency from the proceeds of the sale of any other property of the defendant seized and sold in accordance with the provisions of this section.

Except as provided in subsection (g), when the seizure consists of edible fish or wildlife which is not alive, may not live, or may not otherwise benefit conservation objectives if again placed on open lands, on public fishing bottoms, or in public fishing waters, the inspector or protector must dispose of the property in a charitable or noncommercial manner in accordance with the directions of his administrative superiors.

(e)   Except as otherwise specifically provided in this section, all property seized must be safeguarded pending trial by the inspector or protector initiating the prosecution. Upon a conviction the property seized in connection with the offense in question is subject to the disposition ordered by the court. Upon an acquittal, property seized must be returned to the defendant or established owner, except:

(1)   Where the property was summarily disposed of in accordance with subsection (d);

(2)   Where possession of the property by the person to whom it otherwise would be returned would constitute a crime; and

(3)   Where the property seized has been sold in accordance with subsection (g). In this event the net proceeds of the sale must be returned to the defendant or established owner, as the case may be.

Where property seized summarily under subsection (d) is not available for return, an acquitted defendant or established owner is entitled to no compensation where there was probable cause for the action taken. Within 20 days of the final court adjudication of a citation, the Department or the Wildlife Resources Commission shall notify any acquitted defendant or established owner of its duly established procedures whereby reimbursement may be sought for live fish seized summarily under subsection (d) that is not available for return. Any action or proceeding to recover compensation must be begun within 30 days after receipt of the notice of applicable procedures. After the expiration of this period of limitation, no right or action or claim for compensation shall be asserted.

In safeguarding property seized pending trial, an inspector or protector is authorized in his discretion, subject to orders of his administrative superiors, to make his own provisions for storage or safekeeping or to deposit the property with the sheriff of the county in which the trial is to be held for custody pending trial. In the event the mode of safekeeping reasonably selected by the inspector or protector entails a storage or handling charge, such charge is to be paid as follows:

(1)   By the defendant if he is convicted but the court nevertheless orders the return of the property to the defendant;

(2)   From the proceeds of the sale of the property if the property is sold under court order or in accordance with the provisions of this section; or

(3)   By the Department or by the Wildlife Resources Commission, as the case may be, if no other provision for payment exists.

(f)   Subject to orders of his administrative superiors, an inspector or protector in his discretion may leave property which he is authorized to seize in the possession of the defendant with the understanding that such property will be subject to the orders of the court upon disposition of the case. Willful failure or inexcusable neglect of the defendant to keep such property subject to the orders of the court is a Class 1 misdemeanor. In exercising his discretion, the inspector or protector should not permit property to be retained by the defendant if there is any substantial risk of its being used by the defendant in further unlawful activity.

(g)   Where a prosecution involving seized saleable fish is pending and such fish are perishable or seasonal, the inspector or protector may apply to the court in which the trial is pending for an order permitting sale prior to trial. As used in this subsection, seasonal fish are those which command a higher price at one season than at another so that economic loss may occur if there is a delay in the time of sale. When ordered by the court, such sale prior to trial must be conducted in accordance with the order of the court or in accordance with the provisions of this section. The net proceeds of such sale are to be deposited with the court and are subject to the same disposition as would have been applicable to other types of property seized. Where sale is not lawful for public health reasons or otherwise not practicable or where prosecution is not pending, disposal of the fish is in accordance with subsection (d).

(h)   Pending trial, the defendant or the established owner of any nonperishable and nonconsumable property seized may apply to the court designated to try the offense for return of the property. The property must be returned pending trial if:

(1) The court is satisfied that return of the property will not facilitate further violations of the law; and

(2) The claimant posts a bond for return of the property at trial in an amount double the value of the property as assessed by the court.

(i) Upon conviction of any defendant for a violation of the laws or rules administered by the Department or the Wildlife Resources Commission under the authority of this Subchapter, the court in its discretion may order the confiscation of all weapons, equipment, vessels, conveyances, fish, wildlife, and other evidence, fruits, and instrumentalities of the offense in question, whether or not seized or made subject to the orders of the court pending trial. If the confiscated property is lawfully saleable, it must be sold; otherwise it must be disposed of in a manner authorized in this section. Unless otherwise specified in the order of the court, sales are to be held by the Department or the Wildlife Resources Commission, as the case may be.

The Department and the Wildlife Resources Commission may administratively provide for an orderly public sale procedure of property which it may sell under this section. The procedure may include turning the property to be sold over to some other agency for sale, provided that the provisions of subsection (j) are complied with and there is proper accounting for the net proceeds of the sale. In the case of property that cannot lawfully be sold or is unlikely to sell for a sufficient amount to offset the costs of sale, the Department and the Wildlife Resources Commission may provide either for destruction of the property or legitimate utilization of the property by some public agency.

(j) Except as provided in subsection (d), if property is seized under subsection (c) or it appears that a person not a defendant has an interest in any property to be sold, destroyed, or otherwise disposed of, the Department and the Wildlife Resources Commission must provide for public notice of the description of the property and the circumstances of its seizure for a sufficient period prior to the time set for sale or other disposition to allow innocent owners or lienholders to assert their claims. The validity of claims are to be determined by the trial court in the event there is or has been a prosecution in connection with the seizure of the property. If there has been no prosecution and none is pending, the validity of claims must be determined by the Secretary or by the Executive Director, as the case may be. When there has been a sale under subsection (g), the provisions of this subsection apply to the net proceeds of the sale.

(k) Except as provided in subsection (j) and in subdivision (3) of the first paragraph of subsection (e), the net proceeds of all sales made pursuant to this section must be deposited in the school fund of the county in which the property was seized. (1915, c. 84, s. 6; 1917, c. 290, s. 2; C.S., s. 1885; 1935, c. 118; 1953, c. 1134; 1957, c. 1423, s. 2; 1961, c. 1189, s. 4; 1965, c. 957, s. 2; 1973, c. 1262, ss. 18, 28; 1979, c. 830, s. 1; 1983 (Reg. Sess., 1984), c. 1083, ss. 1-3; 1987, c. 827, s. 98; 1993, c. 539, s. 837; 1994, Ex. Sess., c. 24, s. 14(c).)

§ 113-138. Enforcement jurisdiction of special conservation officers.

(a) The Wildlife Resources Commission by rule may confer law-enforcement powers over matters within its jurisdiction with respect to wildlife resources conservation laws and rules within its jurisdiction upon the employees of the United States Fish and Wildlife Service, and the Marine Fisheries Commission may confer law-enforcement powers over matters within its jurisdiction with respect to marine and estuarine resources conservation laws and rules upon the employees of the National Marine Fisheries Service, who:

(1) Possess special law-enforcement jurisdiction that would not otherwise extend to the subject matter of this Subchapter;

(2) Are assigned during the duration of such appointment to duty stations within North Carolina; and

(3) Take the oath required of public officers before an officer authorized to administer oaths.

These conferred powers do not constitute an appointment of any officer to an additional office.

(b) The Marine Fisheries Commission and Wildlife Resources Commission shall limit the exercise of this authority to situations when:

(1) The best interests of the conservation of marine and estuarine and wildlife resources managed by the respective State and federal agencies are

being adversely affected by restrictions upon jurisdictional subject matter that limit law-enforcement authority; and

(2) The best interests of the conservation of marine and estuarine and wildlife resources managed by the adopting Commission will benefit by conferring law-enforcement authority on the employees of the United States Fish and Wildlife Service or the National Marine Fisheries Service.

(c) The enabling rule shall specify the particular officers or class of officers upon whom the law-enforcement powers are conferred and the geographic areas within which the special enforcement officers can exercise the law-enforcement powers over matters within the jurisdiction of the adopting Commission. The conferred powers may be used only during the scope of employment of the special conservation officers.

(d) Unless otherwise provided by the enabling rule, such special enforcement officers shall have the same jurisdiction and powers with respect to resource conservation and the same rights, privileges and immunities (including those relating to the defense of civil actions and payment of judgments) as the State officers in addition to those the federal officer normally possesses. (1965, c. 957, s. 2; 1973, c. 1262, ss. 18, 28; 1977, c. 771, s. 4; 1983, c. 484; 1987, c. 827, s. 98; 1991 (Reg. Sess., 1992), c. 890, s. 5.)

§ 113-139. Repealed by Session Laws 1979, c. 830, s. 1.

§ 113-140. Warning tickets.

(a) In enforcing the laws and rules within their subject matter jurisdiction, wildlife protectors and marine fisheries inspectors may, in accordance with the criteria of this section, issue warning tickets to offenders instead of initiating criminal prosecutions.

(b) To secure uniformity of enforcement, the Executive Director and the Director of the Division of Marine Fisheries may administratively promulgate standards consistent with subsection (c) providing that warning tickets may or may not be issued with respect to particular offenses, classes of offenses, or ways of committing offenses.

(c) A protector or inspector may issue a warning ticket only if all of the following conditions are met:

(1) The protector or inspector is convinced that the offense was not intentional.

(2) The offense is not of a kind or committed in a manner as to which warning tickets have been prohibited by the Executive Director or the Director of the Division of Marine Fisheries.

(3) The conduct of the offender was not calculated to result in any significant destruction of wildlife or fisheries resources.

(4) The conduct of the offender did not constitute a hazard to the public.

A warning ticket may not be issued if the offender has previously been charged with or issued a warning ticket for a similar offense.

(d) If any law-enforcement officer with jurisdiction over the offense or if any employee of the Wildlife Resources Commission or the Department learns that under the criteria of this section a warning ticket was inappropriately issued to an offender, he must take action to secure initiation of prosecution for the appropriate charge or charges unless barred by the statute of limitations or unless prosecution is not otherwise feasible because of unavailability of evidence or necessary witnesses.

(e) Before any warning tickets are issued, the Executive Director or the Director of the Division of Marine Fisheries must institute a procedure to ensure an accurate accounting for and recording of all warning tickets issued. This procedure may include use of prenumbered tickets and immediate notation of issuance of the warning ticket on each appropriate license or permit issued by the Wildlife Resources Commission or Department held by the offender. The Executive Director or the Director of the Division of Marine Fisheries may also provide for issuance of new, replacement, or renewal licenses and permits bearing the notation. The licenses covered by this subsection include certificates of number for motorboats.

(f) This section does not entitle any person who has committed an offense with the right to be issued a warning ticket. That issuance of a warning ticket may be appropriate under the criteria of this section does not restrict in any manner the powers of a wildlife protector or marine fisheries inspector or any other law-enforcement officer under G.S. 113-136, 113-137, and other provisions of law in dealing with hunters, fishermen, operators of vessels, and other offenders and suspected offenders.

(g) Issuance of a warning ticket does not constitute evidence of the commission of an offense, but may be used to prevent issuance of a subsequent warning ticket to the same person for a similar offense. (1981, c. 252, s. 1; 1987, c. 827, s. 98; 1989, c. 308.)

§§ 113-141 through 113-145. Reserved for future codification purposes.

Article 13A.

Clean Water Management Trust Fund.

§§ 113-145.1 through 113-145.8: Recodified as §§ 113A-251 through 113A-259 by Session Laws 2003-340, s. 1.3, effective July 27, 2003.

§§ 113-145.9 through 113-150. Reserved for future codification purposes.

Article 14.

Commercial and Sports Fisheries Licenses.

§§ 113-151 through 113-167. Repealed by Session Laws 1997-400, s. 5.4, effective July 1, 1999.

Article 14A.

Coastal and Estuarine Commercial Fishing Licenses.

§ 113-168. Definitions.

As used in this Article:

(1)   "Commercial fishing operation" means any activity preparatory to, during, or subsequent to the taking of any fish, the taking of which is subject to regulation by the Commission, either with the use of commercial fishing equipment or gear, or by any means if the purpose of the taking is to obtain fish for sale. Commercial fishing operation does not include (i) the taking of fish as part of a recreational fishing tournament, unless commercial fishing equipment or gear is used, (ii) the taking of fish under a RCGL, or (iii) the taking of fish as provided in G.S. 113-261.

(2)   "Commission" means the Marine Fisheries Commission.

(3)   "Division" means the Division of Marine Fisheries in the Department of Environment and Natural Resources.

(3a)   "Immediate family" means the mother, father, brothers, sisters, spouse, children, stepparents, stepbrothers, stepsisters, and stepchildren of a person.

(4)   "License year" means the period beginning 1 July of a year and ending on 30 June of the following year.

(5)   "North Carolina resident" means a person who is a resident within the meaning of G.S. 113-130(4).

(6)   "RCGL" means Recreational Commercial Gear License.

(7)   "RSCFL" means Retired Standard Commercial Fishing License.

(8)   "SCFL" means Standard Commercial Fishing License. (1997-400, s. 5.1; 1997-443, s. 11A.119(b); 1998-225, s. 4.9; 2001-213, s. 2; 2004-187, s. 6.)

§ 113-168.1. General provisions governing licenses and endorsements.

(a) Duration, Fees. - Except as provided in G.S. 113-173(f), all licenses and endorsements issued under this Article expire on the last day of the license year. An applicant for any license or endorsement shall pay the full annual fee at the time the applicant applies for the license or endorsement regardless of when application is made.

(b) Licenses Required to Engage in Commercial Fishing. - It is unlawful for any person to engage in a commercial fishing operation without holding a license and any endorsements required by this Article. It is unlawful for anyone to command a vessel engaged in a commercial fishing operation without complying with the provisions of this Article and rules adopted by the Commission under this Article.

(c) Licenses, Assignments, and Endorsements Available for Inspection. - It is unlawful for any person to engage in a commercial fishing operation in the State without having ready at hand for inspection all valid licenses, assignments, and endorsements required under this Article. To comply with this subsection, a person must have any required endorsements and either a currently valid (i) license issued in the person's true name and bearing the person's current address or (ii) SCFL and an assignment of the SCFL authorized under this Article. It is unlawful for a person to refuse to exhibit any license, assignment, or endorsement required by this Article upon the request of an inspector or other law enforcement officer authorized to enforce federal or State laws, regulations, or rules relating to marine fisheries.

(d) No Dual Residency. - It is unlawful for any person to hold any currently valid license issued under this Article to the person as a North Carolina resident if that person holds any currently valid commercial or recreational fishing license issued by another state to the person as a resident of that state.

(e) License Format. - Licenses issued under this Article shall be issued in the name of the applicant. Each license shall show the type of license and any endorsements; the name, mailing address, physical or residence address, and date of birth of the licensee; the date on which the license is issued; the date on which the license expires; and any other information that the Commission or the Division determines to be necessary to accomplish the purposes of this Subchapter.

(f) License Issuance and Renewal. - Except as provided in G.S. 113-173(d), the Division shall issue licenses and endorsements under this Article to eligible applicants at any office of the Division or by mail from the Morehead City office of the Division. A license or endorsement may be renewed in person at any office of the Division or by mail to the Morehead City office of the Division. Eligibility to renew an expired SCFL shall end one year after the date of expiration of the SCFL.

(g)   Limitations on Eligibility. - A person is not eligible to obtain or renew a license or endorsement under this Article if, at the time the person applies for the license or endorsement, any other license or endorsement issued to the person under this Article is suspended or revoked. A person is not eligible to obtain a license or endorsement under this Article if, within the three years prior to the date of application, the person has been determined to be responsible for four or more violations of state laws, regulations, or rules governing the management of marine and estuarine resources. An applicant shall certify that the applicant has not been determined to be responsible for four or more violations of state laws, regulations, or rules governing the management of marine and estuarine resources during the previous three years. The Division may also consider violations of federal law and regulations governing the management of marine and estuarine resources in determining whether an applicant is eligible for a license.

(h)   Replacement Licenses and Endorsements. - The Division shall issue a replacement license, including any endorsements, to a licensee for a license that has not been suspended or revoked. A licensee may apply for a replacement license for a license that has been lost, stolen, or destroyed and shall apply for a replacement license within 30 days of a change in the licensee's name or address. A licensee may apply for a replacement license in person at any office of the Division or by mail to the Morehead City office of the Division. A licensee may use a copy of the application for a replacement license that has been filed with the Division as a temporary license until the licensee receives the replacement license. The Commission may establish a fee for each type of replacement license, not to exceed twelve dollars and fifty cents ($12.50), that compensates the Division for the administrative costs associated with issuing the replacement license.

(i)   Cancellation. - The Division may cancel a license or endorsement issued on the basis of an application that contains false information supplied by the applicant. A cancelled license or endorsement is void from the date of issuance. A person in possession of a cancelled license or endorsement shall surrender the cancelled license or endorsement to the Division. It is unlawful to refuse to surrender a cancelled license or endorsement upon demand of any authorized agent of the Division.

(j) Advance Sale of Licenses, License Revenue. - To ensure an orderly transition from one license year to the next, the Division may issue a license or endorsement prior to 1 July of the license year for which the license or endorsement is valid. Revenue that the Division receives for the issuance of a license or endorsement prior to the beginning of a license year shall not revert at the end of the fiscal year in which the revenue is received and shall be credited and available to the Division for the license year in which the license or endorsement is valid. (1997-400, s. 5.1; 1998-225, s. 4.10; 1999-209, s. 6; 2001-213, s. 2; 2013-360, s. 14.8(a).)

§ 113-168.2. Standard Commercial Fishing License.

(a) Requirement. - Except as otherwise provided in this Article, it is unlawful for any person to engage in a commercial fishing operation in the coastal fishing waters without holding a SCFL issued by the Division. A person who works as a member of the crew of a vessel engaged in a commercial fishing operation under the direction of a person who holds a valid SCFL is not required to hold a SCFL. A person who holds a SCFL is not authorized to take shellfish unless the SCFL is endorsed as provided in G.S. 113-168.5.

(a1) Use of Vessels. - The holder of a SCFL is authorized to use only one vessel in a commercial fishing operation at any given time. The Commission may adopt a rule to exempt from this requirement a person in command of a vessel that is auxiliary to a vessel engaged in a pound net operation, long-haul operation, or beach seine operation. A person who works as a member of the crew of a vessel engaged in a mechanical shellfish operation under the direction of a person who holds a valid SCFL with a shellfish endorsement is not required to hold a shellfish license.

(b) through (d) Repealed by Session Laws 1998-225, s. 4.11, effective July 1, 1999.

(e) Fees. - The annual SCFL fee for a resident of this State shall be two hundred fifty dollars ($250.00). The annual SCFL fee for a person who is not a resident of this State shall be the amount charged to a resident of this State in the nonresident's state. In no event, however, may the fee be less than two hundred fifty dollars ($250.00). For purposes of this subsection, a "resident of this State" is a person who is a resident within the meaning of:

(1) Sub-subdivisions a. through d. of G.S. 113-130(4) and who filed a State income tax return as a resident of North Carolina for the previous calendar or tax year, or

(2) G.S. 113-130(4)e.

(f) Assignment. - The holder of a SCFL may assign the SCFL to any individual who is eligible to hold a SCFL under this Article. It is unlawful for the holder of an SCFL to assign a shellfish endorsement of an SCFL to any individual who is not a resident of this State. The assignment shall be in writing on a form provided by the Division and shall include the name of the licensee, the license number, any endorsements, the assignee's name, mailing address, physical or residence address, and the duration of the assignment. If a notarized copy of an assignment is not filed with the Morehead City office of the Division within five days of the date of the assignment, the assignment shall expire. It is unlawful for the assignee of a SCFL to assign the SCFL. The assignment shall terminate:

(1) Upon written notification by the assignor to the assignee and the Division that the assignment has been terminated.

(2) Upon written notification by the estate of the assignor to the assignee and the Division that the assignment has been terminated.

(3) If the Division determines that the assignee is operating in violation of the terms and conditions applicable to the assignment.

(4) If the assignee becomes ineligible to hold a license under this Article.

(5) Upon the death of the assignee.

(6) If the Division suspends or revokes the assigned SCFL.

(7) At the end of the license year.

(g) Transfer. - A SCFL may be transferred only by the Division. A SCFL may be transferred pursuant to rules adopted by the Commission or upon the request of:

(1) A licensee, from the licensee to a member of the licensee's immediate family who is eligible to hold a SCFL under this Article.

(2) The administrator or executor of the estate of a deceased licensee, to the administrator or executor of the estate if a surviving member of the deceased licensee's immediate family is eligible to hold a SCFL under this Article. The administrator or executor must request a transfer under this subdivision within six months after the administrator or executor qualifies under Chapter 28A of the General Statutes. An administrator or executor who holds a SCFL under this subdivision may, for the benefit of the estate of the deceased licensee:

a. Engage in a commercial fishing operation under the SCFL if the administrator or executor is eligible to hold a SCFL under this Article.

b. Assign the SCFL as provided in subsection (f) of this section.

c. Renew the SCFL as provided in G.S. 113-168.1.

(3) An administrator or executor to whom a SCFL was transferred pursuant to subdivision (2) of this subsection, to a surviving member of the deceased licensee's immediate family who is eligible to hold a SCFL under this Article.

(4) The surviving member of the deceased licensee's immediate family to whom a SCFL was transferred pursuant to subdivision (3) of this subsection, to a third-party purchaser of the deceased licensee's fishing vessel.

(5) A licensee who is retiring from commercial fishing, to a third-party purchaser of the licensee's fishing vessel.

(h) Identification as Commercial Fisherman. - The receipt of a current and valid SCFL or shellfish license issued by the Division shall serve as proper identification of the licensee as a commercial fisherman.

(i) Record-Keeping Requirements. - The fish dealer shall record each transaction at the time and place of landing on a form provided by the Division. The transaction form shall include the information on the SCFL or shellfish license, the quantity of the fish, the identity of the fish dealer, and other information as the Division deems necessary to accomplish the purposes of this Subchapter. The person who records the transaction shall provide a completed copy of the transaction form to the Division and to the other party of the transaction. The Division's copy of each transaction form shall be transmitted to the Division by the fish dealer on or before the tenth day of the month following the transaction. (1997-400, s. 5.1; 1998-225, s. 4.11; 2001-213, s. 2; 2013-360, s. 14.8(b); 2013-384, s. 2(c).)

§ 113-168.3. Retired Standard Commercial Fishing License.

(a) SCFL Provisions Applicable. - Except as provided in this section, the provisions set forth in this Article concerning the SCFL shall apply to the RSCFL.

(b) Eligibility; Fees. - Any individual who is 65 years of age or older and who is eligible for a SCFL under G.S. 113-168.2 may apply for either a SCFL or RSCFL. An applicant for a RSCFL shall provide proof of age at the time the application is made. The annual fee for a RSCFL for a resident of this State shall be one hundred twenty-five dollars ($125.00). The annual fee for a RSCFL for a person who is not a resident of this State shall be one hundred sixty-two dollars and fifty cents ($162.50). For purposes of this subsection, a "resident of this State" is a person who is a resident within the meaning of:

(1) Sub-subdivisions a. through d. of G.S. 113-130(4) and who filed a State income tax return as a resident of North Carolina for the previous calendar or tax year, or

(2) G.S. 113-130(4)e.

(c) Transfer. - The holder of a RSCFL may transfer the RSCFL as provided in G.S. 113-168.2.

(1) If the transferee is less than 65 years of age, the transferee holds a SCFL. When the transferee renews the SCFL, the transferee shall pay the fee set out in G.S. 113-168.2.

(2) If the transferee is 65 years of age or older, the transferee may elect to hold either a SCFL or RSCFL. If the transferee elects to hold a SCFL, the transferee shall pay the fee set out in G.S. 113-168.2. If the transferee elects to hold a RSCFL, the transferee shall pay the fee set out in this section.

(d) Assignment. - The RSCFL shall not be assignable. (1997-400, s. 5.1; 1998-225, s. 4.12; 2001-213, s. 2; 2013-360, s. 14.8(c).)

§ 113-168.4. Sale of fish.

(a) Except as otherwise provided in this section, it is unlawful for any person who takes or lands any species of fish under the authority of the Commission from coastal fishing waters by any means whatever, including mariculture operations, to sell, offer for sale, barter or exchange these fish for anything of value without holding a license required to sell the type of fish being offered.

(b) Except as otherwise provided in this section, it is unlawful for any person licensed under this Article to sell fish taken outside the territorial waters of the State or to sell fish taken from coastal fishing waters. A person licensed under this Article may sell fish taken outside the territorial waters of the State or sell fish taken from coastal fishing waters under any of the following circumstances:

(1) The sale is to a fish dealer licensed under G.S. 113-169.3.

(2) The sale is to the public and the seller is a licensed fish dealer under G.S. 113-169.3.

(3) The sale is of oysters or clams from a hatchery or aquaculture operation to the holder of an Aquaculture Operation Permit, an Under Dock Culture Permit, or a shellfish cultivation lease for further grow out.

(c) A person who organizes a recreational fishing tournament may sell fish taken in connection with the tournament pursuant to a recreational fishing tournament license to sell fish. A person who organizes a recreational fishing tournament may obtain a recreational fishing tournament license to sell fish upon application to the Division and payment of a fee of one hundred twenty-five dollars ($125.00). It is unlawful for any person licensed under this subsection to sell fish to any person other than a fish dealer licensed under G.S. 113-169.3 unless the seller is also a licensed fish dealer. A recreational fishing tournament is an organized fishing competition occurring within a specified time period not to exceed one week and that is not a commercial fishing operation. Gross proceeds from the sale of fish may be used only for charitable, religious, educational, civic, or conservation purposes and shall not be used to pay tournament expenses. (1997-400, s. 5.1; 1998-225, s. 4.13; 2001-213, s. 2; 2009-433, s. 1; 2013-360, s. 14.8(d).)

§ 113-168.5. License endorsements for Standard Commercial Fishing License.

(a), (b) Repealed by Session Laws 1998-225, s. 4.14, effective July 1, 1999.

(c) Repealed by Session Laws 2013-384, s. 2(a), effective August 23, 2013.

(d) Shellfish Endorsement for North Carolina Residents. - The Division shall issue a shellfish endorsement of a SCFL to a North Carolina resident at no charge. The holder of a SCFL with a shellfish endorsement is authorized to take and sell shellfish. (1997-400, s. 5.1; 1998-225, s. 4.14; 2001-213, s. 2; 2013-384, s. 2(a).)

§ 113-168.6. Commercial fishing vessel registration.

(a) As used in this subsection, a North Carolina vessel is a vessel that has its primary situs in the State. A vessel has its primary situs in the State if:

(1) A certificate of number has been issued for the vessel under Article 1 of Chapter 75A of the General Statutes;

(2) A certificate of title has been issued for the vessel under Article 4 of Chapter 75A of the General Statutes; or

(3) A certification of documentation has been issued for the vessel that lists a home port in the State under 46 U.S.C. § 12101, et seq., as amended.

(b) The owner of a vessel used in a commercial fishing operation in the coastal fishing waters of the State or a North Carolina vessel used to land or sell fish in the State shall register the vessel with the Division. It is unlawful to use a vessel that is not registered with the Division in a commercial fishing operation in the coastal fishing waters of the State. It is unlawful to use a North Carolina vessel that is not registered with the Division to land or sell fish in the State. No registration is required for a vessel of any length that does not have a motor if the vessel is used only in connection with another vessel that is properly registered.

(b1) The vessel owner at the time of application for registration under subsection (b) of this section shall obtain either a commercial vessel endorsement if the vessel is intended to be used primarily for the harvest of fish for sale, a for-hire endorsement if the vessel is intended to be used primarily for for-hire activities, or both endorsements if the vessel is intended to be engaged in both activities. The owner of a vessel applying for a commercial fishing vessel registration with a for-hire endorsement must affirm liability coverage and knowledge of applicable United States Coast Guard safety requirements.

(c) The annual fee for a commercial fishing vessel registration shall be determined by the length of the vessel and shall be in addition to the fee for other licenses issued under this Article. The length of a vessel shall be determined by measuring the distance between the ends of the vessel along the deck and through the cabin, excluding the sheer. The annual fee for a commercial fishing vessel registration is:

(1) One dollar and twenty-five cents ($1.25) per foot for a vessel not over 18 feet in length.

(2) One dollar and ninety cents ($1.90) per foot for a vessel over 18 feet but not over 38 feet in length.

(3) Three dollars and seventy-five cents ($3.75) per foot for a vessel over 38 feet but not over 50 feet in length.

(4) Seven dollars and fifty cents ($7.50) per foot for a vessel over 50 feet in length.

(d) A vessel may be registered at any office of the Division. A commercial fishing vessel registration expires on the last day of the license year.

(e) Within 30 days of the date on which the owner of a registered vessel transfers ownership of the vessel, the new owner of the vessel shall notify the Division of the change in ownership and apply for a replacement commercial fishing vessel registration. An application for a replacement commercial fishing vessel registration shall be accompanied by proof of the transfer of the vessel. The provisions of G.S. 113-168.1(h) apply to a replacement commercial fishing vessel registration. (1998-225, s. 4.15; 2001-213, s. 3; 2013-360, s. 14.8(e).)

§ 113-169: Repealed by Session Laws 2013-384, s. 2(b), effective August 23, 2013.

§ 113-169.1. Permits for gear, equipment, and other specialized activities authorized.

(a) The Commission may adopt rules to establish permits for gear, equipment, and specialized activities, including commercial fishing operations that do not involve the use of a vessel and transplanting oysters or clams. The Commission may establish a fee for each permit established pursuant to this subsection in an amount that compensates the Division for the administrative costs associated with the permit but that does not exceed one hundred dollars ($100.00) per permit.

(b) The Commission may adopt rules to establish gear specific permits to take striped bass from the Atlantic Ocean and to limit the number and type of these permits that may be issued to a person. The Commission may establish a fee for each permit established pursuant to this subsection in an amount that compensates the Division for the administrative costs associated with the permit but that does not exceed thirty dollars ($30.00) per permit.

(c) To ensure an orderly transition from one permit year to the next, the Division may issue a permit prior to July 1 of the permit year for which the permit is valid. Revenue that the Division receives for the issuance of a permit prior to the beginning of a permit year shall not revert at the end of the fiscal year in which the revenue is received and shall be credited and available to the Division for the permit year in which the permit is valid. (1997-400, s. 5.1; 2000-172, s. 6.1; 2001-213, s. 2; 2006-254, s. 1; 2013-360, s. 14.8(f).)

§ 113-169.2. Shellfish license for North Carolina residents without a SCFL.

(a) License or Endorsement Necessary to Take or Sell Shellfish Taken by Hand Methods. - It is unlawful for an individual to take shellfish from the public or private grounds of the State as part of a commercial fishing operation by hand methods without holding either a shellfish license or a shellfish endorsement of a SCFL. A North Carolina resident who seeks only to take shellfish by hand methods and sell such shellfish shall be eligible to obtain a shellfish license without holding a SCFL. The shellfish license authorizes the licensee to sell shellfish.

(a1) License Necessary to Take or Sell Shellfish Taken by Mechanical Means. - Subject to subsection (i) of this section, an individual who takes shellfish from the public or private grounds of the State by mechanical means must obtain an SCFL under the provisions of G.S. 113-168.2.

(b)   Repealed by Session Laws 1998-225, s. 4.17, effective July 1, 1999.

(c)   Fees. - Shellfish licenses issued under this section shall be issued annually upon payment of a fee of thirty-one dollars and twenty-five cents ($31.25) upon proof that the license applicant is a North Carolina resident.

(d)   License Available for Inspection. - It is unlawful for any individual to take shellfish as part of a commercial fishing operation from the public or private grounds of the State without having ready at hand for inspection a current and valid shellfish license issued to the licensee personally and bearing the licensee's correct name and address. It is unlawful for any individual taking or possessing freshly taken shellfish to refuse to exhibit the individual's license upon the request of an officer authorized to enforce the fishing laws.

(e)   Repealed by Session Laws 1998-225, s. 4.17, effective July 1, 1999.

(f)   Name or Address Change. - In the event of a change in name or address or upon receipt of an erroneous shellfish license, the licensee shall, within 30 days, apply for a replacement shellfish license bearing the correct name and address. Upon a showing by the individual that the name or address change occurred within the past 30 days, the trial court or prosecutor shall dismiss any charges brought pursuant to this subsection.

(g)   Transfer Prohibited. - It is unlawful for an individual issued a shellfish license to transfer or offer to transfer the license, either temporarily or permanently, to another. It is unlawful for an individual to secure or attempt to secure a shellfish license from a source not authorized by the Commission.

(h)   Exemption. - Persons under 16 years of age are exempt from the license requirements of this section if accompanied by a parent, grandparent, or guardian who is in compliance with the requirements of this section or if in possession of a parent's, grandparent's or guardian's shellfish license.

(i)   Taking Shellfish Without a License for Personal Use. - Shellfish may be taken without a license for personal use in quantities established by rules of the Marine Fisheries Commission. (1997-400, s. 5.1; 1998-225, s. 4.17; 2001-213, s. 2; 2004-187, s. 3; 2005-455, s. 1.18; 2009-433, s. 2; 2013-360, s. 14.8(g).)

§ 113-169.3. Licenses for fish dealers.

(a)   Eligibility. - A fish dealer license shall be issued to a North Carolina resident upon receipt of a proper application at any office of the Division together with all license fees including the total number of dealer categories set forth in this section. The license shall be issued in the name of the applicant and shall include all dealer categories on the license.

(b)   Application for License. - Applications shall not be accepted from persons ineligible to hold a license issued by the Division, including any applicant whose license is suspended or revoked on the date of the application. The applicant shall be provided with a copy of the application marked received. The copy shall serve as the fish dealer's license until the license issued by the Division is received, or the Division determines that the applicant is ineligible to hold a license. Where an applicant does not have an established location for transacting the fisheries business within the State, the license application shall be denied unless the applicant satisfies the Secretary that his residence, or some other office or address within the State, is a suitable substitute for an established location and that records kept in connection with licensing, sale, and purchase requirements will be available for inspection when necessary. Fish dealers' licenses are issued on a fiscal year basis upon payment of a fee as set forth herein upon proof, satisfactory to the Secretary, that the license applicant is a North Carolina resident.

(c)   License Requirement. - Any person subject to the licensing requirements of this section is a fish dealer. Any person subject to the licensing requirements of this section shall obtain a separate license for each physical location conducting activities required to be licensed under this section. Except as otherwise provided in this section, it is unlawful for any person not licensed pursuant to this Article:

(1)   To buy fish for resale from any person involved in a commercial fishing operation that takes any species of fish from coastal fishing waters. For purposes of this subdivision, a retailer who purchases fish from a fish dealer shall not be liable if the fish dealer has not complied with the licensing requirements of this section;

(2)   To sell fish to the public; or

(3) To sell to the public any species of fish under the authority of the Commission taken from coastal fishing waters.

(d) Exceptions to License Requirements. - The Commission may adopt rules to implement this subsection including rules to clarify the status of the listed classes of exempted persons, require submission of statistical data, and require that records be kept in order to establish compliance with this section. Any person not licensed pursuant to this section is exempt from the licensing requirements of this section if all fish handled within any particular licensing category meet one or more of the following requirements:

(1) The fish are sold by persons whose dealings in fish are primarily educational, scientific, or official, and who have been issued a permit by the Division that authorizes the educational, scientific, or official agency to sell fish taken or processed in connection with research or demonstration projects;

(2) The fish are sold by individual employees of fish dealers when transacting the business of their duly licensed employer;

(3) The fish are shipped to a person by a dealer from without the State;

(4) The fish are of a kind the sale of which is regulated exclusively by the Wildlife Resources Commission; or

(5) The fish are purchased from a licensed dealer.

(e) Application Fee for New Fish Dealers. - An applicant for a new fish dealer license shall pay a nonrefundable application fee of sixty-two dollars and fifty cents ($62.50) in addition to the license category fees set forth in this section.

(f) License Category Fees. - Every fish dealer subject to licensing requirements shall secure an annual license at each established location for each of the following activities transacted there, upon payment of the fee set out:

(1) Dealing in oysters: $62.50.

(2) Dealing in scallops: $62.50.

(3) Dealing in clams: $62.50.

(4) Dealing in hard or soft crabs: $62.50.

(5) Dealing in shrimp, including bait: $62.50.

(6) Dealing in finfish, including bait: $62.50.

(7) Operating menhaden or other fish-dehydrating or oil-extracting processing plants: $62.50.

(8) Consolidated license (all categories): $375.00.

(f1) Other License Categories. - Any person subject to fish dealer licensing requirements who deals in fish not included in the categories listed in subsection (f) of this section shall secure a finfish dealer license. The Commission may adopt rules implementing and clarifying the dealer categories of this section. Bait operations shall be licensed under either the finfish or shrimp dealer license categories.

(g) Repealed by Session Laws 1998-225, s. 4.18, effective July 1, 1999.

(h) Replacement License. - If the licensee fails to comply with the requirements of G.S. 113-168.1(h), the license is revoked.

(i) Unlawful Purchase and Sale of Fish. - It is unlawful for a fish dealer to purchase, possess, or sell fish taken from coastal fishing waters in violation of this Subchapter or the rules adopted by the Commission implementing this Subchapter. It is unlawful for a fish dealer to buy or accept fish unless, at the time of the transaction:

(1) The seller or donor presents a current and valid license to sell the type of fish being offered;

(2) The seller or donor presents the commercial fishing vessel registration of the vessel that was used to take the fish being offered; and

(3) The dealer records the transaction consistent with the record-keeping requirements of G.S. 113-168.2(i).

(j) Transfer Prohibited. - Any fish dealer license issued under this section is nontransferable. It is unlawful to use a fish dealer license issued to another person in the sale or attempted sale of fish or for a licensee to lend or transfer a fish dealer license for the purpose of circumventing the requirements of this section. (1997-400, s. 5.1; 1998-225, s. 4.18; 2001-213, s. 2; 2013-360, s. 14.8(h), (i).)

§ 113-169.4. Licensing of ocean fishing piers; fees.

(a) The owner or operator of an ocean fishing pier within the coastal fishing waters who charges the public a fee to fish in any manner from the pier shall secure a current and valid pier license from the Division. An application for a pier license shall disclose the names of all parties involved in the pier operations, including the owner of the property, owner of the pier if different, and all leasehold or other corporate arrangements, and all persons with a substantial financial interest in the pier.

(b) Within 30 days following a change of ownership of a pier, or a change as to the manager, the manager or new manager shall secure a replacement pier license as provided in G.S. 113-168.1(h).

(c) Pier licenses are issued upon payment of four dollars and fifty cents ($4.50) per linear foot, to the nearest foot, that the pier extends into coastal fishing waters beyond the mean high waterline. The length of the pier shall be measured to include all extensions of the pier.

(d) The manager who secures the pier license shall be the individual with the duty of executive-level supervision of pier operations.

(e) The pier license issued under this section authorizes any individual who does not hold a Coastal Recreational Fishing License under Article 14B or Article 25A of this Chapter to engage in recreational fishing while on the pier. (1997-400, s. 5.1; 1998-225, s. 4.19; 2001-213, s. 2; 2013-360, s. 14.8(j).)

§ 113-169.5. Land or sell license; vessels fishing beyond territorial waters.

(a) Persons aboard vessels not having their primary situs in the State that are carrying a cargo of fish taken outside the waters of the State may land or sell their catch in the State by purchasing a land or sell license as set forth in this section with respect to the vessel in question. The Commission may by rule modify the land or sell licensing procedure in order to devise an efficient and convenient procedure for licensing out-of-state vessels to only land, or after landing to permit sale of cargo.

(b)   The fee for a land or sell license for a vessel not having its primary situs in North Carolina is two hundred fifty dollars ($250.00), or an amount equal to the nonresident fee charged by the nonresident's state, whichever is greater. Persons aboard vessels having a primary situs in a jurisdiction that would allow North Carolina vessels without restriction to land or sell their catch, taken outside the jurisdiction, may land or sell their catch in the State without complying with this section if the persons are in possession of a valid license from their state of residence. (1997-400, s. 5.1; 2001-213, s. 2; 2013-360, s. 14.8(k).)

§ 113-170. Exportation and importation of fish and equipment.

The Commission may adopt rules governing the importation and exportation of fish, and equipment that may be used in taking or processing fish, as necessary to enhance the conservation of marine and estuarine resources of the State. These rules may regulate, license, prohibit, or restrict importation into the State and exportation from the State of any and all species of fish that are native to coastal fishing waters or may thrive if introduced into these waters. (1997-400, s. 5.1; 2001-213, s. 2.)

§ 113-170.1. Nonresidents reciprocal agreements.

Persons who are not North Carolina residents are not eligible to obtain licenses under the provisions of this Article except as provided in this section. Residents of jurisdictions that sell commercial fishing licenses to North Carolina residents are eligible to hold North Carolina commercial fishing licenses under the provisions of G.S. 113-168.2. Licenses may be restricted in terms of area, gear, and fishery by the Commission so that the nonresidents are licensed to engage in North Carolina fisheries on the same or similar terms that North Carolina residents can be licensed to engage in the fisheries of other jurisdictions. The Secretary may enter into reciprocal agreements with other jurisdictions as necessary to allow nonresidents to obtain commercial fishing licenses in the

State subject to the foregoing provisions. (1997-400, s. 5.1; 1998-225, s. 4.20; 2001-213, s. 2.)

§ 113-170.2. Fraud or deception as to licenses, permits, or records.

(a) It is unlawful for any person to give any false information or willfully to omit giving required information to the Division or any license agent when the information is material to the securing of any license or permit under this Article. It is unlawful to falsify, fraudulently alter, or counterfeit any license, permit, identification, or record to which this Article applies or otherwise practice any fraud or deception designed to evade the provisions of this Article or reasonable administrative directives made under the authority of this Article.

(b) A violation of this section is punishable by a fine of not less than one hundred dollars ($100.00) nor more than five hundred dollars ($500.00). (1997-400, s. 5.1; 2001-213, s. 2.)

§ 113-170.3. Record-keeping requirements.

(a) The Commission may require all licensees under this Article to keep and to exhibit upon the request of an authorized agent of the Department records and accounts as may be necessary to the equitable and efficient administration and enforcement of this Article. In addition, licensees may be required to keep additional information of a statistical nature or relating to location of catch as may be needed to determine conservation policy. Records and accounts required to be kept must be preserved for inspection for not less than three years.

(b) It is unlawful for any licensee to refuse or to neglect without justifiable excuse to keep records and accounts as may be reasonably required. The Department may distribute forms to licensees to aid in securing compliance with its requirements, or it may inform licensees of requirements in other effective ways such as distributing memoranda and sending agents of the Department to consult with licensees who have been remiss. Detailed forms or descriptions of records, accounts, collection and inspection procedures, and the like that reasonably implement the objectives of this Article need not be embodied in rules of the Commission in order to be validly required.

(c) The following records collected and compiled by the Department shall not be considered public records within the meaning of Chapter 132 of the General Statutes, but shall be confidential and shall be used only for the equitable and efficient administration and enforcement of this Article or for determining conservation policy, and shall not be disclosed except when required by the order of a court of competent jurisdiction: all records, accounts, and reports that licensees are required by the Commission to make, keep, and exhibit pursuant to the provisions of this section, and all records, accounts, and memoranda compiled by the Department from records, accounts, and reports of licensees and from investigations and inspections, containing data and information concerning the business and operations of licensees reflecting their assets, liabilities, inventories, revenues, and profits; the number, capacity, capability, and type of fishing vessels owned and operated; the type and quantity of fishing gear used; the catch of fish or other seafood by species in numbers, size, weight, quality, and value; the areas in which fishing was engaged in; the location of catch; the time of fishing, number of hauls, and the disposition of the fish and other seafood. The Department may compile statistical information in any aggregate or summary form that does not directly or indirectly disclose the identity of any licensee who is a source of the information, and any compilation of statistical information by the Department shall be a public record open to inspection and examination by any person, and may be disseminated to the public by the Department. (1997-400, s. 5.1; 2001-213, s. 2.)

§ 113-170.4. Rules as to possession, transportation, and disposition of fisheries resources.

The Commission may adopt rules governing possession, transportation, and disposition of fisheries resources by all persons, including those not subject to fish dealer licensing requirements, in order that inspectors may adequately distinguish regulated coastal fisheries resources from those not so regulated and enforce the provisions of this Article equitably and efficiently. These rules may include requirements as to giving notice, filing declarations, securing permits, marking packages, and the like. (1997-400, s. 5.1; 2001-213, s. 2.)

§ 113-170.5. Violations with respect to coastal fisheries resources.

It is unlawful to take, possess, transport, process, sell, buy, or in any way deal in coastal fisheries resources without conforming with the provisions of this Article or of rules adopted under the authority of this Article. (1997-400, s. 5.1; 2001-213, s. 2.)

§ 113-171. Suspension, revocation, and reissuance of licenses.

(a) Upon receipt of reliable notice that a person licensed under this Article, Article 14B, or Article 25A of Chapter 113 of the General Statutes to take resources under the jurisdiction of the Marine Fisheries Commission has had imposed against the person a conviction of a criminal offense within the jurisdiction of the Department under the provisions of this Subchapter or of rules of the Commission adopted under the authority of this Subchapter, the Secretary must suspend, revoke, and reissue all licenses held by the person in accordance with the terms of this section and rules adopted by the Commission. Reliable notice includes information furnished the Secretary in prosecution or other reports from inspectors. As used in this section, a conviction includes a plea of guilty or nolo contendere, any other termination of a criminal prosecution unfavorably to the defendant after jeopardy has attached, or any substitute for criminal prosecution whereby the defendant expressly or impliedly confesses the defendant's guilt. In particular, procedures whereby bond forfeitures are accepted in lieu of proceeding to trial and cases indefinitely continued upon arrest of judgment or prayer for judgment continued are deemed convictions. The Secretary may act to suspend or revoke licenses upon the basis of any conviction in which:

(1) No notice of appeal has been given;

(2) The time for appeal has expired without an appeal having been perfected; or

(3) The conviction is sustained on appeal. Where there is a new trial, finality of any subsequent conviction will be determined in the manner set out above.

(b) The Secretary must initiate an administrative procedure designed to give the Secretary systematic notice of all convictions of criminal offenses by licensees covered by subsection (a) of this section above and keep a file of all convictions reported.

(c), (d) Repealed by Session Laws 2010-145, s. 2, effective October 1, 2012.

(e) A licensee served with a notice of suspension or revocation may obtain an administrative review of the suspension or revocation by filing a petition for a contested case under G.S. 150B-23 within 20 days after receiving the notice. The only issue in the hearing shall be whether the licensee was convicted of a criminal offense for which a license must be suspended or revoked. A license remains suspended or revoked pending the final decision.

(f) If the Secretary refuses to reissue the license of or issue an additional license to an applicant whose license was revoked, the applicant may contest the decision by filing a petition for a contested case under G.S. 150B-23 within 20 days after the Secretary makes the decision. The Commission shall make the final agency decision in a contested case under this subsection. An applicant whose license is denied under this subsection may not reapply for the same license for at least six months.

(g) The Commission may adopt rules to provide for the disclosure of the identity of any individual or individuals in responsible positions of control respecting operations of any licensee that is not an individual. For the purposes of this section, individuals in responsible positions of control are deemed to be individual licensees and subject to suspension and revocation requirements in regard to any applications for license they may make – either as individuals or as persons in responsible positions of control in any corporation, partnership, or association. In the case of individual licensees, the individual applying for a license or licensed under this Article, Article 14B, or Article 25A of Chapter 113 of the General Statutes to take resources under the jurisdiction of the Marine Fisheries Commission must be the real party in interest.

(h) In determining whether a conviction is a second or subsequent offense under the provisions of this section, the Secretary may not consider convictions for:

(1) Offenses that occurred three years prior to the effective date of this Article; or

(2) Offenses that occurred more than three years prior to the time of the latest offense the conviction for which is in issue as a subsequent conviction. (1997-400, s. 5.1; 2001-213, s. 2; 2010-145, s. 2; 2011-398, s. 34.)

§ 113-171.1. Use of spotter planes in commercial fishing operations regulated.

(a)   Spotter Plane Defined. - A "spotter plane" is an aircraft used for aerial identification of the location of fish in coastal fishing waters so that a vessel may be directed to the fish.

(b)   License. - Before an aircraft is used as a spotter plane in a commercial fishing operation, the owner or operator of the aircraft must obtain a license for the aircraft from the Division. The fee for a license for a spotter plane is one hundred twenty-five dollars ($125.00). An applicant for a license for a spotter plane shall include in the application the identity, either by boat or by company, of the specific commercial fishing operations in which the spotter plane will be used during the license year. If, during the course of the license year, the aircraft is used as a spotter plane in a commercial fishing operation that is not identified in the original license application, the owner or operator of the aircraft shall amend the license application to add the identity of the additional commercial fishing operation.

(c)   Unlawful Activity. - It shall be unlawful to:

(1)   Use a spotter plane directed at food fish, except in connection with a purse seine operation authorized by a rule of the Commission.

(2)   Use or permit the use of an unlicensed spotter plane or a licensed spotter plane whose license application does not identify the specific commercial fishing operation involved.

(3)   Participate knowingly in a commercial fishing operation that uses an unlicensed spotter plane or a licensed spotter plane whose license application does not identify the specific commercial fishing operation involved.

(d)   Violation a Misdemeanor. - A violation of subsection (c) of this section is a Class 1 misdemeanor. (1997-400, s. 5.1; 2001-213, s. 2; 2013-360, s. 14.8(l).)

§ 113-172. License agents.

(a)   The Secretary shall designate license agents for the Department. The Division and license agents designated by the Secretary under this section shall issue licenses authorized under this Article in accordance with this Article and the rules of the Commission. The Secretary may require license agents to enter into a contract that provides for their duties and compensation, post a bond, and submit to reasonable inspections and audits. If a license agent violates any provision of this Article, the rules of the Commission, or the terms of the contract, the Secretary may initiate proceedings for the forfeiture of the license agent's bond and may summarily suspend, revoke, or refuse to renew a designation as a license agent and may impound or require the return of all licenses, moneys, record books, reports, license forms and other documents, ledgers, and materials pertinent or apparently pertinent to the license agency. The Secretary shall report evidence or misuse of State property, including license fees, by a license agent to the State Bureau of Investigation as provided by G.S. 114-15.1.

(b)   License agents shall be compensated by adding a surcharge of one dollar ($1.00) to each license sold and retaining the surcharge. If more than one license is listed on a consolidated license form, the license agent shall be compensated as if a single license were sold. It is unlawful for a license agent to add more than the surcharge authorized by this section to the fee for each license sold. (1997-400, s. 5.1; 1999-209, s. 3; 2001-213, s. 2; 2013-384, s. 1.)

§ 113-173. Recreational Commercial Gear License.

(a)   License Required. - Except as provided in subsection (j) of this section, it is unlawful for any person to take or attempt to take fish for recreational purposes by means of commercial fishing equipment or gear in coastal fishing waters without holding a RCGL. As used in this section, fish are taken for recreational purposes if the fish are not taken for the purpose of sale. The RCGL entitles the licensee to use authorized commercial gear to take fish for personal use subject to recreational possession limits. It is unlawful for any person licensed under this section or fishing under a RCGL to possess fish in excess of recreational possession limits.

(b)   Sale of Fish Prohibited. - It is unlawful for the holder of a RCGL or for a person who is exempt under subsection (j) of this section to sell fish taken under the RCGL or pursuant to the exemption.

(c)   Authorized Commercial Gear. -

(1) The Commission shall adopt rules authorizing the use of a limited amount of commercial fishing equipment or gear for recreational fishing under a RCGL. The Commission may authorize the limited use of commercial gear on a uniform basis in all coastal fishing waters or may vary the limited use of commercial gear within specified areas of the coastal fishing waters. The Commission shall periodically evaluate and revise the authorized use of commercial gear for recreational fishing. Authorized commercial gear shall be identified by visible colored tags or other means specified by the Commission in order to distinguish between commercial gear used in a commercial operation and commercial gear used for recreational purposes.

(2) A person who holds a RCGL may use up to 100 yards of gill net to take fish for recreational purposes. Two persons who each hold a RCGL and who are fishing from a single vessel may use up to a combined 200 yards of gill net to take fish for recreational purposes. No more than 200 yards of gill net may be used to take fish for recreational purposes from a single vessel regardless of the number of persons aboard the vessel who hold a RCGL.

(d) Purchase; Renewal. - A RCGL may be purchased at designated offices of the Division and from a license agent authorized under G.S. 113-172. A RCGL may be renewed by mail.

(e) Replacement RCGL. - The provisions of G.S. 113-168.1(h) apply to this section.

(f) Duration; Fees. - The RCGL shall be valid for a one-year period from the date of purchase. The fee for a RCGL for a North Carolina resident shall be forty-three dollars and seventy-five cents ($43.75). The fee for a RCGL for an individual who is not a North Carolina resident shall be three hundred twelve dollars and fifty cents ($312.50).

(g) RCGL Available for Inspection. - It is unlawful for any person to engage in recreational fishing by means of restricted commercial gear in the State without having ready at hand for inspection a valid RCGL. A holder of a RCGL shall not refuse to exhibit the RCGL upon the request of an inspector or any other law enforcement officer authorized to enforce federal or State laws, regulations, or rules relating to marine fisheries.

(h) Assignment and Transfer Prohibited. - A RCGL is not transferable. Except as provided in subsection (j) of this section, it is unlawful to buy, sell, lend, borrow, assign, or otherwise transfer a RCGL, or to attempt to buy, sell, lend, borrow, assign, or otherwise transfer a RCGL.

(i)   Reporting Requirements. - The holder of a RCGL shall comply with the biological data sampling and survey programs of the Commission and the Division.

(j)   Exemptions. -

(1)   A person who is under 16 years of age may take fish for recreational purposes by means of authorized commercial gear without holding a RCGL if the person is accompanied by a parent, grandparent, or guardian who holds a valid RCGL or if the person has in the person's possession a valid RCGL issued to the person's parent, grandparent, or guardian.

(2)   A person may take crabs for recreational purposes by means of one or more crab pots attached to the shore along privately owned land or to a privately owned pier without holding a RCGL provided that the crab pots are attached with the permission of the owner of the land or pier.

(3)   A person who is on a vessel may take fish for recreational purposes by means of authorized commercial gear without holding a RCGL if there is another person on the vessel who holds a valid RCGL. This exemption does not authorize the use of commercial gear in excess of that authorized for use by the person who holds the valid RCGL or, if more than one person on the vessel holds a RCGL, in excess of that authorized for use by those persons.

(4)   A person using nonmechanical means may take shellfish for personal use within the limits specified in G.S. 113-169.2(i) without holding a RCGL.

(5)   A person may take fish for recreational purposes by means of a gig without holding a RCGL. (1997-400, s. 5.1; 1997-456, s. 55.7; 1998-225, s. 4.21; 1999-209, s. 9; 2000-139, s. 1; 2001-213, s. 2; 2003-340, s. 1.2; 2004-187, s. 4; 2005-455, s. 1.18; 2013-360, s. 14.8(m).)

Article 14B.

Coastal Recreational Fishing Licenses.

§ 113-174. Definitions.

As used in this Article:

(1)   Repealed by Session Laws 2005-455, s. 1.2, effective January 1, 2007.

(1a)   "CRFL" means Coastal Recreational Fishing License.

(2)   "Division" means the Division of Marine Fisheries in the Department of Environment and Natural Resources.

(2a)   "For Hire Vessel" means a charter boat, head boat, dive boat, or other vessel hired to allow individuals to engage in recreational fishing.

(3)   "North Carolina resident" means an individual who is a resident within the meaning of G.S. 113-130(4).

(4)   "Recreational fishing" means any activity preparatory to, during, or subsequent to the taking of any finfish, the taking of which is subject to regulation by the Marine Fisheries Commission, by any means if the purpose of the taking is to obtain finfish that are not to be sold. "Recreational fishing" does not include the taking of finfish:

a.   By a commercial fishing operation as defined in G.S. 113-168.

b.   For scientific purposes pursuant to G.S. 113-261.

c.   Under a RCGL issued pursuant to G.S. 113-173.

(5)   Repealed by Session Laws 2005-455, s. 1.2, effective January 1, 2007. (2004-187, s. 2; 2005-455, ss. 1.2, 1.19; 2013-360, s. 14.8(n).)

§ 113-174.1. License required; general provisions governing licenses.

(a)   License Required to Engage in Recreational Fishing. - It is unlawful for any individual to engage in recreational fishing in:

(1) Coastal fishing waters that are not joint fishing waters without holding a current license issued under this Article or under Article 25A of this Chapter that authorizes the individual to engage in recreational fishing in coastal fishing waters.

(2) Joint fishing waters without holding a current license issued under this Article or under Article 21 or Article 25A of this Chapter that authorizes the individual to engage in recreational fishing in joint fishing waters.

(a1) Compliance With Applicable Laws. - It is unlawful for any individual to engage in recreational fishing without complying with applicable requirements of this Article and Articles 21 and 25A of this Chapter and with applicable rules adopted by the Marine Fisheries Commission and the Wildlife Resources Commission.

(a2) Fourth of July Free Fishing Day. - The fourth day of July of each year is declared a free fishing day to promote the sport of fishing, and no license issued under this Article or Article 25A of this Chapter is required to fish in any of the public waters of the State on that day. All other laws and rules pertaining to recreational fishing apply.

(b) Sale of Fish Prohibited. - A license issued under this Article or Article 25A of this Chapter does not authorize an individual who takes or lands any species of fish under the authority of the Marine Fisheries Commission to sell, offer for sale, barter, or exchange the fish for anything of value. Except as provided in G.S. 113-168.4, it is unlawful for any individual who takes or lands any species of fish under the authority of the Marine Fisheries Commission by any means to sell, offer for sale, barter, or exchange these fish for anything of value.

(c) Assignment and Transfer Prohibited. - It is unlawful to buy, sell, lend, borrow, assign, or otherwise transfer a license issued under this Article or Article 25A of this Chapter or to attempt to buy, sell, lend, borrow, assign, or otherwise transfer a license issued under this Article or Article 25A of this Chapter.

(d), (e) Repealed by Session Laws 2005-455, s. 1.3, effective January 1, 2007.

(f) Cancellation of Fraudulent License; Penalties. - The Wildlife Resources Commission may cancel a license issued by the Commission under this Article or Article 25A of this Chapter if the license was issued on the basis of false information supplied by the license applicant. The Division may cancel a For Hire Blanket CRFL issued under G.S. 113-174.3 or an Ocean Fishing Pier Blanket CRFL issued under G.S. 113-174.4 if the license was issued on the basis of false information supplied by the license applicant. A cancelled license is void from the date of issuance. It is a Class 1 misdemeanor for an individual to knowingly do any of the following:

(1) Engage in any activity regulated under this Article with an improper, false, or altered license.

(2) Make any false, fraudulent, or misleading statement in applying for a license issued under this Article or Article 25A of this Chapter.

(3) Counterfeit, alter, or falsify any application or license issued under this Article or Article 25A of this Chapter.

(g) Reporting Requirements. - A person licensed under this Article or Article 25A of this Chapter shall comply with the biological data sampling and survey programs of the Marine Fisheries Commission and the Division.

(h) Replacement Licenses. - Upon receipt of a proper application together with a fee of five dollars ($5.00), the Wildlife Resources Commission or the Division may issue a new license to replace one issued by the respective agency that has been lost or destroyed before its expiration. The application must be on a form of the Wildlife Resources Commission or the Division setting forth information in sufficient detail to allow ready identification of the lost or destroyed license and ascertainment of the applicant's continued entitlement to it. (2004-187, s. 2; 2005-455, ss. 1.3, 1.19.)

§ 113-174.2. Coastal Recreational Fishing License.

(a) Repealed by Session Laws 2005-455, s. 1.4, effective January 1, 2007.

(a1) Authorization to Fish in Coastal and Joint Fishing Waters. - A CRFL issued under this section authorizes the licensee to engage in recreational fishing in coastal fishing waters, including joint fishing waters. A CRFL issued under this section does not authorize the licensee to fish in inland fishing waters.

(b) Repealed by Session Laws 2005-455, s. 1.4, effective January 1, 2007

(c) Types of CRFLs; Fees; Duration. - The Wildlife Resources Commission shall issue the following CRFLs:

(1) Annual Resident CRFL. - $15.00. This license is valid for a period of one year from the date of issuance. This license shall be issued only to an individual who is a resident of the State.

(1a) Annual Nonresident CRFL. - $30.00. This license is valid for a period of one year from the date of issuance. This license shall be issued only to an individual who is not a resident of the State.

(2) Repealed by Session Laws 2005-455, s. 1.4, effective January 1, 2007.

(3) Repealed by Session Laws 2005-455, s. 1.4, effective January 1, 2007.

(4) Ten-Day Resident CRFL. - $5.00. This license is valid for a period of 10 consecutive days, as indicated on the license. This license shall be issued only to an individual who is a resident of the State.

(4a) Ten-Day Nonresident CRFL. - $10.00. This license is valid for a period of 10 consecutive days, as indicated on the license. This license shall be issued only to an individual who is not a resident of the State.

(5) Repealed by Session Laws 2005-455, s. 1.4, effective January 1, 2007.

(6) Lifetime CRFLs. - Except as provided in sub-subdivision j. of this subdivision, CRFLs issued under this subdivision are valid for the lifetime of the licensee.

a. -d. Repealed by Session Laws 2005-455, s. 1.4, effective January 1, 2007.

e. Infant Lifetime CRFL. - $100.00. This license shall be issued only to an individual younger than one year of age.

f. Youth Lifetime CRFL. - $150.00. This license shall be issued only to an individual who is one year of age or older but younger than 12 years of age.

g. (Effective until August 1, 2014) Resident Adult Lifetime CRFL. - $250.00. This license shall be issued only to an individual who is 12 years of age or older but younger than 65 years of age and who is a resident of the State.

g. (Effective August 1, 2014) Resident Adult Lifetime CRFL. - $250.00. This license shall be issued only to an individual who is 12 years of age or older but younger than 70 years of age and who is a resident of the State.

h. Nonresident Adult Lifetime CRFL. - $500.00. This license shall be issued only to an individual who is 12 years of age or older and who is not a resident of the State.

i. (Effective until August 1, 2014) Resident Age 65 Lifetime CRFL. - $15.00. This license shall be issued only to an individual who is 65 years of age or older and who is a resident of the State.

i. (Effective August 1, 2014) Resident Age 70 Lifetime CRFL. - $15.00. This license shall be issued only to an individual who is 70 years of age or older and who is a resident of the State.

j. Resident Disabled Veteran CRFL. - $10.00. This license shall be issued only to an individual who is a resident of the State and who is a fifty percent (50%) or more disabled veteran as determined by the United States Department of Veterans Affairs. This license remains valid for the lifetime of the licensee so long as the licensee remains fifty percent (50%) or more disabled.

k. Resident Totally Disabled CRFL. - $10.00. This license shall be issued only to an individual who is a resident of the State and who is totally and permanently disabled as determined by the Social Security Administration.

(d) Exemptions. - An individual is exempt from the license requirements of G.S. 113-174.1(a) if the individual either:

(1) Is under 16 years of age.

(2) Holds any of the following licenses that were purchased prior to January 1, 2006:

a. Infant Lifetime Sportsman License issued under G.S. 113-270.1D(b)(1).

b. Youth Lifetime Sportsman License issued under G.S. 113-270.1D(b)(2).

c. Adult Resident Lifetime Sportsman License issued under G.S. 113-270.1D(b)(3).

d. Nonresident Lifetime Sportsman License issued under G.S. 113-270.1D(b)(4).

e. Age 70 Resident Lifetime Sportsman License issued under G.S. 113-270.1D(b)(5).

f. Lifetime Resident Comprehensive Fishing License issued under G.S. 113-271(d)(3).

g. Lifetime Combination Hunting and Fishing License for Disabled Residents issued under G.S. 113-270.1C(b)(4).

h. Disabled Resident Sportsman License issued under G.S. 113-270.1D(b)(6).

(3) Holds any of the following licenses:

a. Lifetime Fishing License for the Legally Blind issued under G.S. 113-271(d)(7).

b. Adult Care Home Resident Fishing License issued under G.S. 113-271(d)(8). (2004-187, s. 2; 2005-455, ss. 1.4, 1.19; 2006-79, s. 1; 2013-283, s. 11.)

§ 113-174.3. For-Hire Licenses.

(a), (b) Repealed by Session Laws 2013-360, s. 14.8(o), effective August 1, 2013.

(c) License. - It is unlawful for a person to engage in a for-hire operation without having obtained one of the following licenses issued by the Division:

(1) Blanket For-Hire Captain's CRFL. - This license allows individuals properly licensed by the United States Coast Guard to carry passengers on any vessel with a commercial vessel registration with a for-hire endorsement. A Blanket For-Hire Captain's CRFL authorizes all individuals on the for-hire vessel

who do not hold a license issued under this Article or Article 25A of this Chapter to engage in recreational fishing in coastal fishing waters that are not joint fishing waters. The resident fees for a Blanket For-Hire Captain's CRFL are two hundred fifty dollars ($250.00) for a vessel carrying six or fewer passengers and three hundred fifty dollars ($350.00) for a vessel carrying more than six passengers. The nonresident fees for a Blanket For-Hire Captain's CRFL are three hundred twelve dollars and fifty cents ($312.50) for a vessel carrying six or fewer passengers and four hundred thirty-seven dollars and fifty cents ($437.50) for a vessel carrying more than six passengers. Any vessel whose operator is licensed under this subdivision and that is engaged in for-hire fishing must obtain a Commercial Fishing Vessel Registration with a for-hire endorsement.

(2) Blanket For-Hire Vessel CRFL. - This license allows any United States Coast Guard licensed operator to carry passengers aboard the licensed vessel. A Blanket For-Hire Vessel CRFL authorizes all individuals on the for-hire vessel who do not hold a license issued under this Article or Article 25A of this Chapter to engage in recreational fishing in coastal fishing waters that are not joint fishing waters. The resident fees for a Blanket For-Hire Vessel CRFL are two hundred fifty dollars ($250.00) for a vessel carrying six or fewer passengers and three hundred fifty dollars ($350.00) for a vessel carrying more than six passengers. The nonresident fees for a Blanket For-Hire Vessel CRFL are three hundred twelve dollars and fifty cents ($312.50) for a vessel carrying six or fewer passengers and four hundred thirty-seven dollars and fifty cents ($437.50) for a vessel carrying more than six passengers. Any vessel whose operator is licensed under this subdivision and that is engaged in for-hire fishing is not required to obtain a Commercial Fishing Vessel Registration with a for-hire endorsement.

(3) Non-Blanket For-Hire Vessel License. - This license allows any United States Coast Guard licensed operator to carry passengers aboard the licensed vessel. This license does not authorize individuals aboard the vessel to engage in recreational fishing unless they hold an individual CRFL issued under this Article or Article 25A of this Chapter. The fee for the Non-Blanket For-Hire Vessel License is twenty-five dollars ($25.00) for a vessel operated by a resident operator and thirty-seven dollars and fifty cents ($37.50) for a vessel operated by a nonresident operator. Any vessel whose operator is licensed under this subdivision and that is engaged in for-hire fishing is not required to obtain a Commercial Fishing Vessel Registration with a for-hire endorsement.

(d)   A license issued under this section does not authorize individuals to engage in recreational fishing in joint fishing waters or inland fishing waters. All for-hire licenses expire on the last day of the license year.

(e)   Each individual who obtains a for-hire license shall submit to the Division logbooks summarizing catch and effort statistical data to the Division. The Commission may adopt rules that determine the means and methods to satisfy the requirements of this subsection. (2005-455, s. 1.5; 2006-255, s. 7; 2006-259, s. 20.5; 2013-360, s. 14.8(o).)

§ 113-174.4: Repealed by Session Laws 2013-360, s. 14.8(p), effective August 1, 2013.

§ 113-174.5. Blocks of 10 Ten-Day Coastal Recreational Fishing Licenses.

(a)   The owner of a vessel that is 23 feet or more in length and that is either documented with the United States Coast Guard or registered with the Wildlife Resources Commission pursuant to G.S. 75A-4 may purchase a block of 10 Ten-Day CRFLs issued by the Division. A vessel owner who wishes to obtain a block of 10 Ten-Day CRFLs shall provide the Division with all information required by the Division, including information identifying the vessel on which the Ten-Day CRFLs will be used. Each individual Ten-Day CRFL shall identify the vessel for which the block of 10 Ten-Day CRFLs is issued. An individual Ten-Day CRFL issued as part of a block of 10 Ten-Day CRFLs may only be used on the vessel for which it was issued. An individual Ten-Day CRFL issued as part of a block of 10 Ten-Day CRFLs may not be used on a for hire vessel. A block of 10 Ten-Day CRFLs shall expire two years from the date of purchase.

(b)   The fee for a block of 10 Ten-Day CRFLs is one hundred fifty dollars ($150.00). An individual Ten-Day CRFL issued as part of a block of 10 Ten-Day CRFLs is valid for a period of 10 consecutive days beginning on the date that the license information is recorded as provided by subsection (c) of this section.

(c)   Prior to any recreational fishing occurring under the authority of an individual Ten-Day CRFL issued as part of a block of 10 Ten-Day CRFLs, the vessel owner who purchased the block of 10 Ten-Day CRFLs shall record the date fishing activity will begin and the name, address, telephone number, and date of birth of the individual who will be fishing under the authority of the individual Ten-Day CRFL.

(d)   A vessel owner who purchases a block of 10 Ten-Day CRFLs shall comply with all data and information reporting requirements of the Division.

(e)   A vessel owner who fails to comply with any of the requirements governing the issuance, use, recording, or reporting of blocks of 10 Ten-Day CRFLs will be ineligible to purchase any additional blocks of 10 Ten-Day CRFLs for a period of two years from the date of noncompliance. (2008-141, s. 1; 2013-360, s. 14.8(q).)

Article 14C.

Marine Resources Fund and Marine Resources Endowment Fund.

§ 113-175. Definitions.

As used in this Article:

(1)   Repealed by Session Laws 2005-455, s. 2.2, effective January 1, 2006.

(1a)   "Endowment Fund" means the North Carolina Marine Resources Endowment Fund.

(1b)   "Endowment investment income" means interest and other income earned from the investment of the principal of the Endowment Fund.

(1c)   "Endowment license revenues" means the net proceeds from the sale of licenses issued under G.S. 113-174.2(c)(6) and a portion of the net proceeds from the sale of licenses issued under G.S. 113-351(c)(3) and (4). The apportionment of the net proceeds from the sale of licenses issued under G.S. 113-351(c)(3) and (4) shall be jointly determined by the Division of Marine Fisheries and the Wildlife Resources Commission. In the event that the Division of Marine Fisheries and the Wildlife Resources Commission cannot agree on the apportionment, the Governor is authorized to determine the apportionment.

(2) "Marine Resources Fund" means the North Carolina Marine Resources Fund.

(3) "Marine resources investment income" means interest earned from the investment of the principal of the Marine Resources Fund.

(4) "Marine resources license revenues" means the net proceeds from the sale of licenses issued under Article 14B of this Chapter and a portion of the net proceeds from the sale of licenses issued under Article 25A of this Chapter, excluding endowment license revenues. The apportionment of the net proceeds from the sale of licenses issued under Article 25A of this Chapter shall be jointly determined by the Division of Marine Fisheries and the Wildlife Resources Commission. In the event that the Division of Marine Fisheries and the Wildlife Resources Commission cannot agree on the apportionment, the Governor is authorized to determine the apportionment. (2004-187, s. 1; 2005-455, s. 2.2.)

§ 113-175.1. North Carolina Marine Resources Fund.

(a) There is hereby established the North Carolina Marine Resources Fund as a nonreverting special revenue fund in the office of the State Treasurer. The purpose of the Marine Resources Fund is to enhance the marine resources of the State. The principal of the Marine Resources Fund shall consist of:

(1) Marine resources license revenues.

(2) Proceeds of any gifts, grants, and contributions to the State that are specifically designated for inclusion in the Marine Resources Fund.

(3) Funds realized from the sale, lease, rental, or other grant of rights to real or personal property acquired or produced from funds disbursed from the Marine Resources Fund.

(4) Federal aid project reimbursements to the extent that funds disbursed from the Marine Resources Fund originally funded the project for which the reimbursement is made.

(b) The State Treasurer shall hold the Marine Resources Fund separate and apart from all other moneys, funds, and accounts. The State Treasurer shall invest the assets of the Marine Resources Fund in accordance with the provisions of G.S. 147-69.2 and G.S. 147-69.3, and all marine resources investment income shall be deposited to the credit of the Marine Resources Fund. The State Treasurer shall disburse the principal of the Marine Resources Fund and marine resources investment income only upon the written direction of the Marine Fisheries Commission.

(c) The Marine Fisheries Commission may authorize the disbursement of the principal of the Marine Resources Fund and marine resources investment income only to manage, protect, restore, develop, cultivate, conserve, and enhance the marine resources of the State. The Marine Fisheries Commission is encouraged to consider supporting the Oyster Sanctuary Program managed by the Division of Marine Fisheries. The Marine Fisheries Commission may not authorize the disbursement of the principal of the Marine Resources Fund and marine resources investment income to establish positions without specific authorization from the General Assembly. All proposals to the Marine Fisheries Commission for the disbursement of funds from the Marine Resources Fund shall be made by and through the Fisheries Director. Prior to authorizing disbursements from the Marine Resources Fund, the Marine Fisheries Commission shall consult with the Wildlife Resources Commission about these proposals. Expenditure of the assets of the Marine Resources Fund shall be made through the State budget accounts of the Division of Marine Fisheries in accordance with the provisions of the Executive Budget Act. The Marine Resources Fund is subject to the oversight of the State Auditor pursuant to Article 5A of Chapter 147 of the General Statutes. (2004-187, s. 1; 2005-455, s. 2.3; 2011-145, s. 13.18; 2013-360, s. 14.9(a), (b).)

§§ 113-175.2 through 113-175.4: Repealed by Session Laws 2005-455, ss. 2.4 through 2.6, effective January 1, 2006.

§ 113-175.5. North Carolina Marine Resources Endowment Fund.

(a) There is hereby established the North Carolina Marine Resources Endowment Fund as a nonreverting special revenue fund in the office of the State Treasurer. The purpose of the Endowment Fund is to provide the citizens and residents of the State with the opportunity to invest in the future of the marine resources of the State. The principal of the Endowment Fund shall consist of:

(1) Endowment license revenues.

(2) Proceeds of any gifts, grants, or contributions to the State that are specifically designated for inclusion in the Endowment Fund.

(3) Proceeds of any gifts, grants, or contributions to the Marine Fisheries Commission or the Division of Marine Fisheries that are not specifically designated for another purpose.

(4) Funds realized from the sale, lease, rental, or other grant of rights to real or personal property acquired or produced from endowment investment income.

(5) Federal aid project reimbursements to the extent that endowment investment income originally funded the project for which the reimbursement is made.

(6) Transfers to the Endowment Fund.

(7) Any endowment investment income or marine resources license revenue that is credited to the Endowment Fund for the purpose of increasing the principal of the Endowment Fund.

(b) The State Treasurer shall hold the Endowment Fund separate and apart from all other moneys, funds, and accounts. The State Treasurer shall invest the assets of the Endowment Fund in accordance with the provisions of G.S. 147-69.2 and G.S. 147-69.3. The State Treasurer shall disburse the endowment investment income only upon the written direction of both the Marine Fisheries Commission.

(c) Subject to the limitations set out in subsection (d) of this section, the Marine Fisheries Commission may authorize the disbursement of endowment investment income only to manage, protect, restore, develop, cultivate, conserve, and enhance the marine resources of the State. The Marine Fisheries Commission may not authorize the disbursement of endowment investment income to establish positions without specific authorization from the General Assembly. All proposals to the Marine Fisheries Commission for the disbursement of funds from the Endowment Fund shall be made by and through the Fisheries Director. Prior to authorizing disbursements from the Marine Resources Endowment Fund, the Marine Fisheries Commission shall consult with the Wildlife Resources Commission about these proposals.

(d)   The Endowment Fund is declared to constitute a special trust derived from a contractual relationship between the State and the members of the public whose investments contribute to the Endowment Fund. In recognition of this special trust, all of the following limitations are placed on disbursement of funds held in the Endowment Fund:

(1)   Any restrictions specified by the donors on the uses of income derived from gifts, grants, and voluntary contributions shall be respected but shall not be binding.

(2)   No disbursements of the endowment investment income derived from the endowment license revenues generated by the sale of Infant Lifetime CRFLs under G.S. 113-174.2(c)(6)e., Youth Lifetime CRFLs under G.S. 113-174.2(c)(6)f., Infant Lifetime Unified Sportsman/Coastal Recreational Fishing Licenses under G.S. 113-351(c)(3)a., or Youth Lifetime Unified Sportsman/Coastal Recreational Fishing Licenses under G.S. 113-351(c)(3)b. shall be made for any purpose until the respective licensees attain the age of 16 years. The State Treasurer shall periodically make an actuarial determination as to the amount of endowment investment income within the Endowment Fund that remains encumbered by the restriction of this subdivision and the amount that is free of the restriction. The Executive Director of the Wildlife Resources Commission shall provide the State Treasurer with the information necessary to make this determination.

(3)   No disbursement shall be made from the principal of the Endowment Fund except as otherwise provided by law.

(e)   Expenditure of the endowment investment income shall be made through the State budget accounts of the Division of Marine Fisheries in accordance with the provisions of the Executive Budget Act. The Endowment Fund is subject to the oversight of the State Auditor pursuant to Article 5A of Chapter 147 of the General Statutes. (2005-455, s. 2.7; 2013-360, s. 14.9(c), (d).)

§ 113-175.6. Report.

The Chair of the Marine Fisheries Commission and the Chair of the Wildlife Resources Commission shall jointly submit to the Joint Legislative Commission on Governmental Operations by October 1 of each year a report on the Marine

Resources Fund and the Endowment Fund that shall include the source and amounts of all moneys credited to each fund and the purpose and amount of all disbursements from each fund during the prior fiscal year. (2005-455, s. 2.7; 2011-291, s. 2.26.)

§ 113-176. Reserved for future codification purposes.

§ 113-177. Reserved for future codification purposes.

§ 113-178. Reserved for future codification purposes.

§ 113-179. Reserved for future codification purposes.

§ 113-180. Reserved for future codification purposes.

Article 15.

Regulation of Coastal Fisheries.

§ 113-181. Duties and powers of Department.

(a)   It is the duty of the Department to administer and enforce the provisions of this Subchapter pertaining to the conservation of marine and estuarine resources. In execution of this duty, the Department may collect such statistics, market information, and research data as is necessary or useful to the promotion of sports and commercial fisheries in North Carolina and the conservation of marine and estuarine resources generally; conduct or contract for research programs or research and development programs applicable to resources generally and to methods of cultivating, harvesting, marketing, or processing fish as may be beneficial in achieving the objectives of this Subchapter; enter into reciprocal agreements with other jurisdictions with regard to the conservation of marine and estuarine resources; and regulate placement of nets and other sports or commercial fishing apparatus in coastal fishing waters with regard to navigational and recreational safety as well as from a conservation standpoint.

(b)   The Department is directed to make every reasonable effort to carry out the duties imposed in this Subchapter. (1915, c. 84, s. 5; 1917, c. 290, s. 10;

C.S., s. 1883; 1953, c. 1086; 1965, c. 957, s. 2; 1973, c. 1262, s. 28; 1987, c. 827, s. 101.)

§ 113-182. Regulation of fishing and fisheries.

(a) The Marine Fisheries Commission is authorized to authorize, license, regulate, prohibit, prescribe, or restrict all forms of marine and estuarine resources in coastal fishing waters with respect to:

(1) Time, place, character, or dimensions of any methods or equipment that may be employed in taking fish;

(2) Seasons for taking fish;

(3) Size limits on and maximum quantities of fish that may be taken, possessed, bailed to another, transported, bought, sold, or given away.

(b) The Marine Fisheries Commission is authorized to authorize, regulate, prohibit, prescribe, or restrict and the Department is authorized to license:

(1) The opening and closing of coastal fishing waters, except as to inland game fish, whether entirely or only as to the taking of particular classes of fish, use of particular equipment, or as to other activities within the jurisdiction of the Department; and

(2) The possession, cultivation, transportation, importation, exportation, sale, purchase, acquisition, and disposition of all marine and estuarine resources and all related equipment, implements, vessels, and conveyances as necessary to implement the work of the Department in carrying out its duties.

(3) The possession, transportation, importation, exportation, sale, purchase, acquisition, and disposition of all fish taken in the Atlantic Ocean out to a distance of 200 miles from the State's mean low watermark, consistent with the Magnuson Fishery Conservation and Management Act, 16 U.S.C. § 1801, et seq., as amended. (1915, c. 84, s. 21; 1917, c. 290, s. 7; C.S., s. 1878; 1925, c. 168, s. 2; 1935, c. 35; 1945, c. 776; 1953, cc. 774, 1251; 1961, c. 1189, s. 1; 1963, c. 1097, s. 1; 1965, c. 957, s. 2; 1973, c. 1262, s. 28; 1995, c. 507, s. 26.5(c); 1997-400, s. 6.6.)

§ 113-182.1. Fishery Management Plans.

(a) The Department shall prepare proposed Fishery Management Plans for adoption by the Marine Fisheries Commission for all commercially or recreationally significant species or fisheries that comprise State marine or estuarine resources. Proposed Fishery Management Plans shall be developed in accordance with the Priority List, Schedule, and guidance criteria established by the Marine Fisheries Commission under G.S. 143B-289.52.

(b) The goal of the plans shall be to ensure the long-term viability of the State's commercially and recreationally significant species or fisheries. Each plan shall be designed to reflect fishing practices so that one plan may apply to a specific fishery, while other plans may be based on gear or geographic areas. Each plan shall:

(1) Contain necessary information pertaining to the fishery or fisheries, including management goals and objectives, status of relevant fish stocks, stock assessments for multiyear species, fishery habitat and water quality considerations consistent with Coastal Habitat Protection Plans adopted pursuant to G.S. 143B-279.8, social and economic impact of the fishery to the State, and user conflicts.

(2) Recommend management actions pertaining to the fishery or fisheries.

(3) Include conservation and management measures that will provide the greatest overall benefit to the State, particularly with respect to food production, recreational opportunities, and the protection of marine ecosystems, and that will produce a sustainable harvest.

(4) Repealed by Session Laws 2010-13, s. 1, effective June 23, 2010.

(5) Specify a time period, not to exceed two years from the date of the adoption of the plan, to end overfishing. This subdivision shall not apply if the Fisheries Director determines that the biology of the fish, environmental conditions, or lack of sufficient data make implementing the requirements of this subdivision incompatible with professional standards for fisheries management.

(6) Specify a time period, not to exceed 10 years from the date of the adoption of the plan, for achieving a sustainable harvest. This subdivision shall not apply if the Fisheries Director determines that the biology of the fish, environmental conditions, or lack of sufficient data make implementing the

requirements of this subdivision incompatible with professional standards for fisheries management.

(7) Include a standard of at least fifty percent (50%) probability of achieving sustainable harvest for the fishery or fisheries. This subdivision shall not apply if the Fisheries Director determines that the biology of the fish, environmental conditions, or lack of sufficient data make implementing the requirements of this subdivision incompatible with professional standards for fisheries management.

(c) To assist in the development of each Fishery Management Plan, the Chair of the Marine Fisheries Commission shall appoint a fishery management plan advisory committee. Each fishery management plan advisory committee shall be composed of commercial fishermen, recreational fishermen, and scientists, all with expertise in the fishery for which the Fishery Management Plan is being developed.

(c1) The Department shall consult with the regional advisory committees established pursuant to G.S. 143B-289.57(e) regarding the preparation of each Fishery Management Plan. Before submission of a plan for review by the Joint Legislative Commission on Governmental Operations, the Department shall review any comment or recommendation regarding the plan that a regional advisory committee submits to the Department within the time limits established in the Schedule for the development and adoption of Fishery Management Plans established by G.S. 143B-289.52. Before the Commission adopts a management measure to implement a plan, the Commission shall review any comment or recommendation regarding the management measure that a regional advisory committee submits to the Commission.

(d) Each Fishery Management Plan shall be reviewed at least once every five years. The Marine Fisheries Commission may revise the Priority List and guidance criteria whenever it determines that a revision of the Priority List or guidance criteria will facilitate or improve the development of Fishery Management Plans or is necessary to restore, conserve, or protect the marine and estuarine resources of the State. The Marine Fisheries Commission may not revise the Schedule for the development of a Fishery Management Plan, once adopted, without the approval of the Secretary of Environment and Natural Resources.

(e) The Secretary of Environment and Natural Resources shall monitor progress in the development and adoption of Fishery Management Plans in relation to the Schedule for development and adoption of the plans established by the Marine Fisheries Commission. The Secretary of Environment and Natural Resources shall report to the Joint Legislative Commission on Governmental Operations on progress in developing and implementing the Fishery Management Plans on or before 1 September of each year. The Secretary of Environment and Natural Resources shall report to the Joint Legislative Commission on Governmental Operations within 30 days of the completion or substantial revision of each proposed Fishery Management Plan. The Joint Legislative Commission on Governmental Operations shall review each proposed Fishery Management Plan within 30 days of the date the proposed Plan is submitted by the Secretary. The Joint Legislative Commission on Governmental Operations may submit comments and recommendations on the proposed Plan to the Secretary within 30 days of the date the proposed Plan is submitted by the Secretary.

(e1) If the Secretary determines that it is in the interest of the long-term viability of a fishery, the Secretary may authorize the Commission to develop temporary management measures to supplement an existing Fishery Management Plan pursuant to this subsection. Development of temporary management measures pursuant to this subsection is exempt from subsections (c), (c1), and (e) of this section and the Priority List, Schedule, and guidance criteria established by the Marine Fisheries Commission under G.S. 143B-289.52. During the next review period for a Fishery Management Plan supplemented pursuant to this subsection, the Commission shall either incorporate the temporary management measures into the revised Fishery Management Plan or the temporary management measures shall expire on the date the revised Fishery Management Plan is adopted.

(f) The Marine Fisheries Commission shall adopt rules to implement Fishery Management Plans in accordance with Chapter 150B of the General Statutes.

(g) To achieve sustainable harvest under a Fishery Management Plan, the Marine Fisheries Commission may include in the Plan a recommendation that the General Assembly limit the number of fishermen authorized to participate in the fishery. The Commission may recommend that the General Assembly limit participation in a fishery only if the Commission determines that sustainable harvest cannot otherwise be achieved. In determining whether to recommend that the General Assembly limit participation in a fishery, the Commission shall consider all of the following factors:

(1) Current participation in and dependence on the fishery.

(2) Past fishing practices in the fishery.

(3) Economics of the fishery.

(4) Capability of fishing vessels used in the fishery to engage in other fisheries.

(5) Cultural and social factors relevant to the fishery and any affected fishing communities.

(6) Capacity of the fishery to support biological parameters.

(7) Equitable resolution of competing social and economic interests.

(8) Any other relevant considerations. (1997-400, s. 3.4; 1997-443, s. 11A.119(b); 1998-212, s. 14.3; 1998-225, s. 2.1; 2001-213, s. 1; 2001-452, s. 2.1; 2004-160, ss. 3, 4; 2007-495, ss. 6, 7; 2010-13, s. 1; 2010-15, s. 1; 2011-291, ss. 2.27, 2.28; 2012-201, s. 1; 2013-360, s. 14.8(r).)

§ 113-183. Unlawful possession, transportation and sale of fish.

(a) It is unlawful to possess, transport, offer to transport, sell, offer to sell, receive, buy, or attempt to buy any fish regulated by the Department with knowledge or reason to believe that such fish are illicit.

(b) Fish are illicit when taken, possessed, or dealt with unlawfully, or when there has occurred at any time with respect to such fish a substantial failure of compliance with the applicable provisions of this Subchapter or of rules made under the authority of this Subchapter. (1961, c. 1189, s. 2; 1965, c. 957, s. 2; 1987, c. 827, s. 98.)

§ 113-184. Possession and transportation of prohibited oyster equipment.

(a) It is unlawful to carry aboard any vessel subject to licensing requirements under Article 14A under way or at anchor in coastal fishing waters during the regular closed oyster season any scoops, scrapes, dredges, or winders such as are usually or can be used for taking oysters. Provided that when such vessels are engaged in lawfully permitted oyster harvesting operations on any privately held shellfish bottom lease under G.S. 113-202 or G.S. 113-205, the vessel shall be exempt from this requirement.

(b)   If any vessel has recently been under way or at anchor in coastal fishing waters engaged in activity similar in manner to that in which oysters are taken with scoops, scrapes, or dredges and at a time or place in which the taking of oysters is prohibited, the presence on board of the vessel of wet oysters or scoops, scrapes, dredges, lines, or deck wet, indicating the taking of oysters, constitutes prima facie evidence that the vessel was engaged in taking oysters unlawfully with scoops, scrapes, or dredges at the time or place prohibited.

(c)   Repealed by Session Laws 1991, c. 86, s. 1. (1903, c. 516, ss. 13-15, 28; Rev., ss. 2385, 2397; C.S., s. 1926; 1963, c. 452; 1965, c. 957, s. 2; 1991, c. 86, s. 1; 1991 (Reg. Sess., 1992), c. 788, s. 1; 1998-225, s. 3.3.)

§ 113-185. Fishing near ocean piers; trash or scrap fishing.

(a)   It is unlawful to fish in the ocean from vessels or with a net within 750 feet of an ocean pier licensed in accordance with G.S. 113-169.4. The prohibition shall be effective when:

(1)   Buoys or beach markers, placed at the owner's expense in accordance with the rules adopted by the Marine Fisheries Commission, indicate clearly to fishermen in vessels and on the beach the requisite distance of 750 feet from the pier, and

(2)   The public is allowed to fish from the pier for a reasonable fee.

The prohibition shall not apply to littoral proprietors whose property is within 750 feet of a duly licensed ocean pier.

(b)   It is unlawful to engage in any fishing operations known as trash fishing or scrap fishing. "Trash fishing" or "scrap fishing" consists of taking the young of edible fish before they are of sufficient size to be of value as individual food fish:

(1)   For commercial disposition as bait; or

(2)   For sale to any dehydrating or nonfood processing plant; or

(3) For sale or commercial disposition in any manner.

The Marine Fisheries Commission may by rule authorize the disposition of the young of edible fish taken in connection with the legitimate commercial fishing operations, provided that the quantity of such fish that may be disposed of is sufficiently limited, or the taking and disposition is otherwise so regulated, as to discourage any practice of trash or scrap fishing for its own sake. (1965, c. 957, s. 2; 1973, c. 1262, ss. 28, 86; 1985, c. 452, ss. 1-4; 1987, c. 641, s. 5; c. 827, s. 98; 1991, c. 86, s. 2; 1998-225, s. 3.4.)

§ 113-186. Measures for fish scrap and oil.

All persons buying or selling menhaden for the purpose of manufacturing fish scrap and oil within the State must buy or sell according to the measure prescribed in this section: 22,000 cubic inches for every 1,000 fish. Each day of failure to use the prescribed measure constitutes a separate offense. (1911, c. 101; C.S., s. 1963; 1965, c. 957, s. 2.)

§ 113-187. Penalties for violations of Subchapter and rules.

(a) Any person who participates in a commercial fishing operation conducted in violation of any provision of this Subchapter and its implementing rules or in an operation in connection with which any vessel is used in violation of any provision of this Subchapter and its implementing rules is guilty of a Class A1 misdemeanor.

(b) Any owner of a vessel who knowingly permits it to be used in violation of any provision of this Subchapter and its implementing rules is guilty of a Class A1 misdemeanor.

(c) Any person in charge of a commercial fishing operation conducted in violation of any provision of this Subchapter and its implementing rules or in charge of any vessel used in violation of any provision of this Subchapter and its implementing rules is guilty of a Class A1 misdemeanor.

(d) Any person in charge of a commercial fishing operation conducted in violation of the following provisions of this Subchapter or the following rules of the Marine Fisheries Commission; and any person in charge of any vessel used in violation of the following provisions of the Subchapter or the following rules, shall be guilty of a Class A1 misdemeanor. The violations of the statute or the rules for which the penalty is mandatory are:

(1) Taking or attempting to take, possess, sell, or offer for sale any oysters, mussels, or clams taken from areas closed by statute, rule, or proclamation because of suspected pollution.

(2) Taking or attempting to take or have in possession aboard a vessel, shrimp taken by the use of a trawl net, in areas not opened to shrimping, pulled by a vessel not showing lights required by G.S. 75A-6 after sunset and before sunrise.

(3) Using a trawl net in any coastal fishing waters closed by proclamation or rule to trawl nets.

(4) Violating the provisions of a special permit or gear license issued by the Department.

(5) Using or attempting to use any trawl net, long haul seine, swipe net, mechanical methods for oyster or clam harvest or dredge in designated primary nursery areas.

(e) Any person who takes menhaden or Atlantic thread herring by the use of a purse seine net deployed by a mother ship and one or more runner boats in coastal fishing waters is guilty of a Class A1 misdemeanor. (1965, c. 957, s. 2; 1973, c. 1102; c. 1262, ss. 28, 86; 1977, c. 771, s. 4; 1979, c. 388, s. 5; 1987, c. 641, s. 6; c. 827, s. 98; 1989, c. 275, s. 2; 1993, c. 539, s. 839; 1994, Ex. Sess., c. 24, s. 14(c); 1997-400, s. 4.1; 2012-190, s. 3(a).)

§ 113-188. Additional restrictions authorized.

The setting out of particular offenses or requirements with regard to specific species of fish or with regard to certain types of equipment does not affect the authority of the Marine Fisheries Commission to make similar additional restrictions not in conflict with the provisions of this Article under authority granted in this Chapter. (1965, c. 957, s. 2; 1973, c. 1262, s. 28; 1987, c. 827, s. 102.)

§ 113-189. Protection of sea turtles, marine mammals, migratory birds, and finfish.

(a) It is unlawful to willfully take, harm, disturb or destroy any sea turtles protected under the federal Endangered Species Act of 1973 (Public Law 93-205), as it may be subsequently amended, including green, hawksbill, loggerhead, Kemp's ridley, and leatherback turtles, or their nests or eggs.

(b) It shall be unlawful willfully to take, harm, disturb, or destroy marine mammals protected under the federal Marine Mammal Protection Act of 1972 (Public Law 92-522), as it may be subsequently amended.

(c) It shall be unlawful willfully to take, harm, disturb, or destroy migratory birds protected under the federal Migratory Bird Treaty Act of 1918 (16 U.S.C. §§ 703 through 712), as it may be subsequently amended, unless such action is permitted by regulations.

(d) It shall be unlawful willfully to take, harm, disturb, or destroy finfish protected under the federal Endangered Species Act of 1973 (Public Law 93-205), as it may be subsequently amended. (1967, cc. 198, 1225; 1981, c. 873; 1991, c. 86, s. 3; 2013-413, s. 37(b).)

§ 113-190: Recodified as § 113-200 by Session Laws 1997-400, s. 6.7.

§ 113-191. Unlawful sale or purchase of fish; criminal and civil penalties.

(a) Any person who sells fish in violation of G.S. 113-168.4 or a rule of the Marine Fisheries Commission to implement that section is guilty of a Class A1 misdemeanor.

(b) Any person who purchases fish in violation of G.S. 113-169.3 or a rule of the Marine Fisheries Commission to implement that section is guilty of a Class A1 misdemeanor.

(c) A civil penalty of not more than ten thousand dollars ($10,000) may be assessed by the Secretary against any person who sells fish in violation of G.S. 113-168.4 or purchases fish in violation of G.S. 113-169.3.

(d) In determining the amount of the penalty, the Secretary shall consider the factors set out in G.S. 143B-289.53(b). The procedures set out in G.S. 143B-289.53 shall apply to civil penalty assessments that are presented to the Commission for final agency decision.

(e) The Secretary shall notify any person assessed a civil penalty of the assessment and the specific reasons therefor by registered or certified mail or by any means authorized by G.S. 1A-1, Rule 4. Contested case petitions shall be filed pursuant to G.S. 150B-23 within 30 days of receipt of the notice of assessment.

(f) Requests for remission of civil penalties shall be filed with the Secretary. Remission requests shall not be considered unless filed within 30 days of receipt of the notice of assessment. Remission requests must be accompanied by a waiver of the right to a contested case hearing pursuant to Chapter 150B of the General Statutes and a stipulation of the facts on which the assessment was based. Consistent with the limitations in G.S. 143B-289.53(c), remission requests may be resolved by the Secretary and the violator. If the Secretary and the violator are unable to resolve the request, the Secretary shall deliver remission requests and his recommended action to the Committee on Civil Penalty Remissions of the Marine Fisheries Commission appointed pursuant to G.S. 143B-289.53(c).

(g) If any civil penalty has not been paid within 30 days after notice of assessment has been served on the violator, the Secretary shall request the Attorney General to institute a civil action in the superior court of any county in which the violator resides or has his or its principal place of business to recover the amount of the assessment, unless the violator contests the assessment as provided in subsection (e) of this section, or requests remission of the assessment in whole or in part as provided in subsection (f) of this section. If any civil penalty has not been paid within 30 days after the final agency decision or court order has been served on the violator, the Secretary shall request the Attorney General to institute a civil action in the superior court of any county in which the violator resides or has his or its principal place of business to recover the amount of the assessment. Civil actions must be filed within three years of the date the final agency decision or court order was served on the violator. (1997-400, ss. 4.2, 4.5; 1998-225, ss. 3.5, 3.6.)

§§ 113-192 through 113-199. Reserved for future codification purposes.

§ 113-200: Repealed by Session Laws 2013-360, s. 14.7(a), effective July 1, 2013.

Article 16.

Cultivation of Shellfish.

§ 113-201. Legislative findings and declaration of policy; authority of Marine Fisheries Commission.

(a) The General Assembly finds that shellfish cultivation provides increased seafood production and long-term economic and employment opportunities. The General Assembly also finds that shellfish cultivation provides increased ecological benefits to the estuarine environment by promoting natural water filtration and increased fishery habitats. The General Assembly declares that it is the policy of the State to encourage the development of private, commercial shellfish cultivation in ways that are compatible with other public uses of marine and estuarine resources such as navigation, fishing, and recreation.

(b) The Marine Fisheries Commission is empowered to make rules and take all steps necessary to develop and improve the cultivation, harvesting, and marketing of shellfish in North Carolina both from public grounds and private beds. In order to assure the public that some waters will remain open and free from shellfish cultivation activities, the Marine Fisheries Commission may limit the number of acres in any area that may be granted as shellfish cultivation leases.

(c) The Marine Fisheries Commission shall adopt rules to establish training requirements for persons applying for new shellfish cultivation leases and for persons acquiring shellfish cultivation leases by lawful transfer. These training requirements shall be designed to encourage the productive use of shellfish cultivation leases. Training requirements established pursuant to this subsection shall not apply to either:

(1) An applicant who applies for a new shellfish cultivation lease if, at the time of the application, the applicant holds one or more shellfish cultivation

leases and all of the leases meet the shellfish production requirements established by the Marine Fisheries Commission.

(2) A person who receives a shellfish cultivation lease by lawful transfer if, at the time of the transfer, the person holds one or more shellfish cultivation leases and all of the leases meet the shellfish production requirements established by the Marine Fisheries Commission. (1921, c. 132, s. 1; C.S., s. 1959(a); 1965, c. 957, s. 2; 1973, c. 1262, s. 28; 1983, c. 621, s. 2; 1987, c. 827, s. 98; 2004-150, s. 1; 2009-433, s. 3.)

§ 113-201.1. Definitions.

As used in this Article:

(1) "Natural shellfish bed" means an area of public bottom where oysters, clams, scallops, mussels or other shellfish are found to be growing in sufficient quantities to be valuable to the public.

(2) "Riparian owner" means the holder(s) of the fee title to land that is bordered by waters of an arm of the sea or any other navigable body of water.

(3) "Shellfish" means oysters, clams, scallops, mussels or any other species of mollusks that the Marine Fisheries Commission determines suitable for cultivation, harvesting, and marketing from public grounds and private beds.

(4) "Single family unit" means the husband and wife and any unemancipated children in the household.

(5) "Water column" means the vertical extent of water, including the surface thereof, above a designated area of submerged bottom land. (1983, c. 621, s. 3; 1987, c. 641, s. 15.)

§ 113-202. New and renewal leases for shellfish cultivation; termination of leases issued prior to January 1, 1966.

(a) To increase the use of suitable areas underlying coastal fishing waters for the production of shellfish, the Secretary may grant shellfish cultivation leases to persons who reside in North Carolina under the terms of this section when the Secretary determines, in accordance with his duty to conserve the marine and estuarine resources of the State, that the public interest will benefit from issuance of the lease. Suitable areas for the production of shellfish shall meet the following minimum standards:

(1) The area leased must be suitable for the cultivation and harvesting of shellfish in commercial quantities.

(2) The area leased must not contain a natural shellfish bed.

(3) Cultivation of shellfish in the leased area will be compatible with lawful utilization by the public of other marine and estuarine resources. Other public uses which may be considered include, but are not limited to, navigation, fishing and recreation.

(4) Cultivation of shellfish in the leased area will not impinge upon the rights of riparian owners.

(5) The area leased must not include an area designated for inclusion in the Department's Shellfish Management Program.

(6) The area leased must not include an area which the State Health Director has recommended be closed to shellfish harvest by reason of pollution.

(b) The Secretary may delete any part of an area proposed for lease or may condition a lease to protect the public interest with respect to the factors enumerated in subsection (a) of this section. The Secretary may not grant a new lease in an area heavily used for recreational purposes.

(c) No person, including a corporate entity, or single family unit may acquire and hold by lease, lease renewal, or purchase more than 50 acres of public bottoms under shellfish cultivation leases. For purposes of this subsection, the number of acres of leases held by a person includes acres held by a corporation in which the person holds an interest. The Marine Fisheries Commission may adopt rules to require the submission of information necessary to ensure compliance with this subsection.

(d) Any person desiring to apply for a lease must make written application to the Secretary on forms prepared by the Department containing such information as deemed necessary to determine the desirability of granting or not granting the lease requested. Except in the case of renewal leases, the application must be accompanied by a map or diagram made at the expense of the applicant, showing the area proposed to be leased.

(d1) The map or diagram must conform to standards prescribed by the Secretary concerning accuracy of map or diagram and the amount of detail that must be shown. If on the basis of the application information and map or diagram the Secretary deems that granting the lease would benefit the shellfish culture of North Carolina, the Secretary, in the case of initial lease applications, must order an investigation of the bottom proposed to be leased. The investigation is to be made by the Secretary or his authorized agent to determine whether the area proposed to be leased is consistent with the standards in subsection (a) of this section and any other applicable standards under this Article and the rules of the Marine Fisheries Commission. In the event the Secretary finds the application inconsistent with the applicable standards, the Secretary shall deny the application or propose that a conditional lease be issued that is consistent with the applicable standards. In the event the Secretary authorizes amendment of the application, the applicant must furnish a new map or diagram meeting requisite standards showing the area proposed to be leased under the amended application. At the time of making application for an initial lease, the applicant must pay a filing fee of two hundred dollars ($200.00).

(e) The area of bottom applied for in the case of an initial lease or amended initial lease must be as compact as possible, taking into consideration the shape of the body of water, the consistency of the bottom, and the desirability of separating the boundaries of a leasehold by a sufficient distance from any known natural shellfish bed to prevent the likelihood of disputes arising between the leaseholder and members of the public taking shellfish from the natural bed.

(f) Within a reasonable time after receipt of an application that complies with subsection (d), the Secretary shall notify the applicant of the intended action on the lease application. If the intended action is approval of the application as submitted or approval with a modification to which the applicant agrees, the Secretary shall conduct a public hearing in the county where the proposed leasehold lies. The Secretary must publish at least two notices of the intention to lease in a newspaper of general circulation in the county in which the proposed leasehold lies. The first publication must precede the public hearing by more than 20 days; the second publication must follow the first by seven to 11 days. The notice of intention to lease must contain a sufficient description of the area of the proposed leasehold that its boundaries may be established with reasonable ease and certainty and must also contain the date, hour and place of the hearing.

(g) After consideration of the public comment received and any additional investigations the Secretary orders to evaluate the comments, the Secretary shall notify the applicant in person or by certified or registered mail of the decision on the lease application. The Secretary shall also notify persons who submitted comments at the public hearing and requested notice of the lease decision. An applicant who is dissatisfied with the Secretary's decision or another person aggrieved by the decision may commence a contested case by filing a petition under G.S. 150B-23 within 20 days after receiving notice of the Secretary's decision. In the event the Secretary's decision is a modification to which the applicant agrees, the lease applicant must furnish an amended map or diagram before the lease can be issued by the Secretary.

(h) Repealed by Session Laws 1993, c. 466, s. 1.

(i) After a lease application is approved by the Secretary, the applicant shall submit to the Secretary a survey of the area approved for leasing and define the bounds of the area approved for leasing with markers in accordance with the rules of the Commission. The survey shall conform to standards prescribed by the Secretary concerning accuracy of survey and the amount of detail to be shown. When an acceptable survey is submitted, the boundaries are marked and all fees and rents due in advance are paid, the Secretary shall execute the lease on forms approved by the Attorney General. The Secretary is authorized, with the approval of the lessee, to amend an existing lease by reducing the area under lease or by combining contiguous leases without increasing the total area leased.

(j) Initial leases begin upon the issuance of the lease by the Secretary and expire at noon on the first day of July following the fifth anniversary of the granting of the lease. Renewal leases are issued for a period of five years from the time of expiration of the previous lease. At the time of making application for renewal of a lease, the applicant must pay a filing fee of one hundred dollars ($100.00). The rental for initial leases is one dollar ($1.00) per acre for all leases entered into before July 1, 1965, and for all other leases until noon on the first day of July following the first anniversary of the lease. Thereafter, for initial leases entered into after July 1, 1965, and from the beginning for renewals of leases entered into after that date, the rental is ten dollars ($10.00) per acre per year. Rental must be paid annually in advance prior to the first day of April each year. Upon initial granting of a lease, the pro rata amount for the portion of the year left until the first day of July must be paid in advance at the rate of one dollar ($1.00) per acre per year; then, on or before the first day of April next, the lessee must pay the rental for the next full year.

(k)   Except as restricted by this Subchapter, leaseholds granted under this section are to be treated as if they were real property and are subject to all laws relating to taxation, sale, devise, inheritance, gift, seizure and sale under execution or other legal process, and the like. Leases properly acknowledged and probated are eligible for recordation in the same manner as instruments conveying an estate in real property. Within 30 days after transfer of beneficial ownership of all or any portion of or interest in a leasehold to another, the new owner must notify the Secretary of such fact. Such transfer is not valid until notice is furnished the Secretary. In the event such transferee is a nonresident, the Secretary must initiate proceedings to terminate the lease.

(l)   Upon receipt of notice by the Secretary of any of the following occurrences, he must commence action to terminate the leasehold:

(1)   Failure to pay the annual rent in advance.

(2)   Failure to file information required by the Secretary upon annual remittance of rental or filing false information on the form required to accompany the annual remittance of rental.

(3)   Failure by new owner to report a transfer of beneficial ownership of all or any portion of or interest in the leasehold.

(4)   Failure to mark the boundaries in the leasehold and to keep them marked as required in the rules of the Marine Fisheries Commission.

(5)   Failure to utilize the leasehold on a continuing basis for the commercial production of shellfish.

(6)   Transfer of all or part of the beneficial ownership of a leasehold to a nonresident.

(7)   Substantial breach of compliance with the provisions of this Article or of rules of the Marine Fisheries Commission governing use of the leasehold.

(8)   Failure to comply with the training requirements established by the Marine Fisheries Commission pursuant to G.S. 113-201(c).

(l1) The Marine Fisheries Commission is authorized to make rules defining commercial production of shellfish, based upon the productive potential of particular areas climatic or biological conditions at particular areas or particular times, availability of seed shellfish, availability for purchase by lessees of shells or other material to which oyster spat may attach, and the like. Commercial production may be defined in terms of planting effort made as well as in terms of quantities of shellfish harvested. Provided, however, that if a lessee has made a diligent effort to effectively and efficiently manage his lease according to accepted standards and practices in such management, and because of reasons beyond his control, such as acts of God, such lessee has not and cannot meet the requirements set out by the Marine Fisheries Commission under the provisions of this subsection, his leasehold shall not be terminated under subdivision (5) of subsection (I) of this section.

(m) In the event the leaseholder takes steps within 30 days to remedy the situation upon which the notice of intention to terminate was based and the Secretary is satisfied that continuation of the lease is in the best interests of the shellfish culture of the State, the Secretary may discontinue termination procedures. Where there is no discontinuance of termination procedures, the leaseholder may initiate a contested case by filing a petition under G.S. 150B-23 within 30 days of receipt of notice of intention to terminate. Where the leaseholder does not initiate a contested case, or the final decision upholds termination, the Secretary must send a final letter of termination to the leaseholder. The final letter of termination may not be mailed sooner than 30 days after receipt by the leaseholder of the Secretary's notice of intention to terminate, or of the final agency decision, as appropriate. The lease is terminated effective at midnight on the day the final notice of termination is served on the leaseholder. The final notice of termination may not be issued pending hearing of a contested case initiated by the leaseholder.

Service of any notice required in this subsection may be accomplished by certified mail, return receipt requested; personal service by any law-enforcement officer; or upon the failure of these two methods, publication. Service by publication shall be accomplished by publishing such notices in a newspaper of general circulation within the county where the lease is located for at least once a week for three successive weeks. The format for notice by publication shall be approved by the Attorney General.

(n) Upon final termination of any leasehold, the bottom in question is thrown open to the public for use in accordance with laws and rules governing use of public grounds generally. Within 30 days of final termination of the leasehold, the former leaseholder shall remove all abandoned markers denominating the area of the leasehold as a private bottom. The State may, after 10 days' notice to the owner of the abandoned markers thereof, remove the abandoned structure and have the area cleaned up. The cost of such removal and cleanup shall be payable by the owner of the abandoned markers and the State may bring suit to recover the costs thereof.

(o)   Every year between January 1 and February 15 the Secretary must mail to all leaseholders a notice of the annual rental due and include forms designed by him for determining the amount of shellfish or shells planted on the leasehold during the preceding calendar year, and the amount of harvest gathered. Such forms may contain other pertinent questions relating to the utilization of the leasehold in the best interests of the shellfish culture of the State, and must be executed and returned by the leaseholder with the payment of his rental. Any leaseholder or his agent executing such forms for him who knowingly makes a false statement on such forms is guilty of a Class 1 misdemeanor.

(p)   All leases and renewal leases granted after the effective date of this Article are made subject to this Article and to reasonable amendment of governing statutes, rules of the Marine Fisheries Commission, and requirements imposed by the Secretary or his agents in regulating the use of the leasehold or in processing applications of rentals. This includes such statutory increase in rentals as may be necessitated by changing conditions and refusal to renew lease after expiration, in the discretion of the Secretary. No increase in rentals, however, may be given retroactive effect.

The General Assembly declares it to be contrary to public policy to the oyster and clam bottoms which were leased prior to January 1, 1966, and which are not being used to produce oysters and clams in commercial quantities to continue to be held by private individuals, thus depriving the public of a resource which belongs to all the people of the State. Therefore, when the Secretary determines, after due notice to the lessee, and after opportunity for the lessee to be heard, that oysters or clams are not being produced in commercial quantities, due to the lessee's failure to make diligent effort to produce oysters and clams in commercial quantities, the Secretary may decline to renew, at the end of the current term, any oyster or clam bottom lease which was executed prior to January 1, 1966. The lessee may appeal the denial of the Secretary to renew the lease by initiating a contested case pursuant to G.S. 150B-23. In such contested cases, the burden of proof, by the greater weight of the evidence, shall be on the lessee.

(q) Repealed by Session Laws 1983, c. 621, s. 16. (1893, c. 287, s. 1; Rev., s. 2371; 1909, c. 871, ss. 1-9; 1919, c. 333, s. 6; C.S., ss. 1902-1911; Ex. Sess. 1921, c. 46, s. 1; 1933, c. 346; 1953, cc. 842, 1139; 1963, c. 1260, ss. 1-3; 1965, c. 957, s. 2; 1967, c. 24, s. 16; c. 88; c. 876, s. 1; 1971, c. 447; 1973, c. 476, s. 128; c. 1262, ss. 28, 86; 1983, c. 601, ss. 1-3; c. 621, ss. 4-16; 1985, c. 275, ss. 1-3; 1987, c. 641, s. 16; c. 773, s. 11; c. 827, s. 98; 1989, c. 423, s. 2; c. 727, s. 99; 1991 (Reg. Sess., 1992), c. 788, s. 2; 1993, c. 466, s. 1; c. 539, s. 840; 1994, Ex. Sess., c. 24, s. 14(c); 2004-150, ss. 2, 3, 4; 2009-433, ss. 4, 5; 2011-398, s. 35.)

§ 113-202.1. Water column leases for aquaculture.

(a) To increase the productivity of leases for shellfish culture issued under G.S. 113-202, the Secretary may amend shellfish cultivation leases to authorize use of the water column superjacent to the leased bottom under the terms of this section when he determines the public interest will benefit from amendment of the leases. Leases with water column amendments must produce shellfish in commercial quantities at four times the minimum production rate of leases issued under G.S. 113-202, or any higher quantity required by the Marine Fisheries Commission through duly adopted rules.

(b) Suitable areas for the authorization of water column use shall meet the following minimum standards:

(1) Aquaculture use of the leased area must not significantly impair navigation;

(2) The leased area must not be within a navigation channel marked or maintained by a state or federal agency;

(3) The leased area must not be within an area traditionally used and available for fishing or hunting activities incompatible with the activities proposed by the leaseholder, such as trawling or seining;

(4) Aquaculture use of the leased area must not significantly interfere with the exercise of riparian rights by adjacent property owners including access to navigation channels from piers or other means of access; and

(5) Any additional standards, established by the Commission in duly adopted rules, to protect the public interest in coastal fishing waters.

(c) The Secretary shall not amend shellfish cultivation leases to authorize use of the water column unless:

(1) The leaseholder submits an application, accompanied by a nonrefundable application fee of one hundred dollars ($100.00), which conforms to the standards for lease applications in G.S. 113-202(d) and the duly adopted rules of the Commission;

(2) The proposed amendment has been noticed consistent with G.S. 113-202(f);

(3) Public hearings have been conducted consistent with G.S. 113-202(g);

(4) The aspects of the proposals which require use and dedication of the water column have been documented and are recognized by the Secretary as commercially feasible forms of aquaculture which will enhance shellfish production on the leased area;

(5) It is not feasible to undertake the aquaculture activity outside of coastal fishing waters; and

(6) The authorized water column use has the least disruptive effect on other public trust uses of the waters of any available technology to produce the shellfish identified in the proposal.

(d) Amendments of shellfish cultivation leases to authorize use of the water column are issued for a period of five years or the remainder of the term of the lease, whichever is shorter. The annual rental for a new or renewal water column amendment is one hundred dollars ($100.00) an acre. If a water column amendment is issued for less than a 12-month period, the rental shall be prorated based on the number of months remaining in the year. The annual rental for an amendment is payable at the beginning of the year. The rental is in addition to that required in G.S. 113-202.

(e) Amendments of shellfish cultivation leases to authorize use of the water column are subject to termination in accordance with the procedures established in G.S. 113-202 for the termination of shellfish cultivation leases. Additionally, such amendments may be terminated for unauthorized or unlawful interference with the exercise of public trust rights by the leaseholder, agents and employees of the leaseholder.

(f) Amendments of shellfish cultivation leases to authorize use of the water column are not transferrable except when the Secretary approves the transfer after public notice and hearing consistent with subsection (c) of this section.

(g) After public notice and hearing consistent with subsection (c) of this section, the Secretary may renew an amendment, in whole or in part, when the leaseholder has produced commercial quantities of shellfish and has otherwise complied with the rules of the Commission. Renewals may be denied or reduced in scope when the public interest so requires. Appeal of renewal decisions shall be conducted in accordance with G.S. 113-202(p). Renewals are subject to the lease terms and rates established in subsection (d) of this section.

(h) The procedures and requirements of G.S. 113-202 shall apply to proposed amendments or amendments of shellfish cultivation leases considered under this section except more specific provisions of this section control conflicts between the two sections.

(i) To the extent required by demonstration or research aquaculture development projects, the Secretary may amend existing leases and issue leases that authorize use of the bottom and the water column. Demonstration or research aquaculture development projects may be authorized for two years with no more than one renewal and when the project is proposed or formally sponsored by an educational institution which conducts research or demonstration of aquaculture. Production of shellfish with a sales value in excess of one thousand dollars ($1,000) per acre per year shall constitute commercial production. Demonstration or research aquaculture development projects shall be exempt for the rental rate in subsection (d) of this section unless commercial production occurs as a result of the project. (1989, c. 423, s. 1; 1989 (Reg. Sess., 1990), c. 1004, s. 4; c. 1024, s. 22; 1993, c. 322, s. 1; c. 466, s. 2; 2004-150, s. 5.)

§ 113-202.2. Water column leases for aquaculture for perpetual franchises.

(a) To increase the productivity of shellfish grants and perpetual franchises for shellfish culture recognized under G.S. 113-206, the Secretary may lease the water column superjacent to such grants or perpetual franchises (hereinafter "perpetual franchises") under the terms of this section when it determines the public interest will benefit from the lease. Perpetual franchises with water column leases must produce shellfish in commercial quantities at four times the minimum production rate of leases issued under G.S. 113-202, or any higher quantity required by the Marine Fisheries Commission by rule.

(b) Suitable areas for the authorization of water column use shall meet the following minimum standards:

(1) Aquaculture use of the leased water column area must not significantly impair navigation;

(2) The leased water column area must not be within a navigation channel marked or maintained by a State or federal agency;

(3) The leased water column area must not be within an area traditionally used and available for fishing or hunting activities incompatible with the activities proposed by the perpetual franchise holder, such as trawling or seining;

(4) Aquaculture use of the leased water column area must not significantly interfere with the exercise of riparian rights by adjacent property owners including access to navigation channels from piers or other means of access;

(5) The leased water column area may not exceed 10 acres for grants or perpetual franchises recognized pursuant to G.S. 113-206;

(6) The leased water column area must not extend more than one-third of the distance across any body of water or into the channel third of any body of water for grants or perpetual franchises recognized pursuant to G.S. 113-206; and

(7) Any additional rules to protect the public interest in coastal fishing waters adopted by the Commission.

(c) The Secretary shall not lease the water column superjacent to oyster or other shellfish grants or perpetual franchises unless:

(1) The perpetual franchise holder submits an application, accompanied by a nonrefundable application fee of one hundred dollars ($100.00), which conforms to the standards for lease applications in G.S. 113-202(d) and rules adopted by the Commission;

(2) Notice of the proposed lease has been given consistent with G.S. 113-202(f);

(3) Public hearings have been conducted consistent with G.S. 113-202(g);

(4) The aspects of the proposals which require use and dedication of the water column have been documented and are recognized by the Secretary as commercially feasible forms of aquaculture which will enhance shellfish production;

(5) It is not feasible to undertake the aquaculture activity outside of coastal fishing waters; and

(6) The authorized water column use has the least disruptive effect on other public trust uses of the waters of any available technology to produce the shellfish identified in the proposal.

(d) Water column leases to perpetual franchises shall be issued for a period of five years and may be renewed pursuant to subsection (g) of this section. The rental for an initial water column lease issued under this section is the same as the rental set in G.S. 113-202.1 for an initial water column amendment issued under that section, and the rental for a renewed water column lease issued under this section is the same as the rental set in G.S. 113-202.1 for a renewed water column amendment issued under that section.

(e) Water column leases to perpetual franchises may be terminated for unauthorized or unlawful interference with the exercise of public trust rights by the leaseholder or his agents or employees.

(f) Water column leases to perpetual franchises are not transferrable except when the Secretary approves the transfer after public notice and hearing consistent with G.S. 113-202(f) and (g).

(g) After public notice and hearing consistent with G.S. 113-202(f) and (g), the Secretary may renew a water column lease, in whole or in part, if the leaseholder has produced commercial quantities of shellfish and has otherwise complied with this section and the rules of the Commission. Renewals may be denied or reduced in scope when the public interest so requires. Appeal of renewal decisions shall be conducted in accordance with G.S. 113-202(p). Renewals are subject to the lease terms and rates set out in subsection (d) of this section.

(h) The procedures and requirements of G.S. 113-202 shall apply to proposed water column leases or water column leases to perpetual franchises considered under this section except that more specific provisions of this section control conflicts between the two sections.

(i) Demonstration or research aquaculture development projects may be authorized for two years with no more than one renewal and when the project is proposed or formally sponsored by an educational institution which conducts aquaculture research or demonstration projects. Production of shellfish with a sales value in excess of one thousand dollars ($1,000) per acre per year shall constitute commercial production. Demonstration or research aquaculture development projects shall be exempt from the rental rate in subsection (d) of this section unless commercial production occurs as a result of the project. (1989 (Reg. Sess., 1990), c. 958, s. 1; 1993, c. 322, s. 2, c. 466, s. 3.)

§ 113-203. Transplanting of oysters and clams.

(a) It is unlawful to transplant oysters taken from public grounds to private beds except:

(1) When lawfully taken during open season and transported directly to a private bed in accordance with rules of the Marine Fisheries Commission.

(2) Repealed by Session Laws 2009-433, s. 6, effective August 7, 2009.

(3) When the transplanting is done in accordance with the provisions of this section and implementing rules.

(a1) It is lawful to transplant seed clams less than 12 millimeters in their largest dimension and seed oysters less than 25 millimeters in their largest dimension and when the seed clams and seed oysters originate from an aquaculture operation permitted by the Secretary.

(b) It is lawful to transplant to private beds oysters or clams taken from polluted waters with a permit from the Secretary setting out the waters from which the oysters or clams may be taken, the quantities which may be taken, the times during which the taking is permissible, and other reasonable restrictions imposed by the Secretary for the regulation of transplanting operations. Any transplanting operation which does not substantially comply with the restrictions of the permit issued is unlawful.

(c)   Repealed by Session Laws 2009-433, s. 6, effective August 7, 2009.

(d)   It is lawful to transplant to private beds in North Carolina oysters taken from natural or managed public beds designated by the Marine Fisheries Commission as seed oyster management areas. The Secretary shall issue permits to all qualified individuals who are residents of North Carolina without regard to county of residence to transplant seed oysters from said designated seed oyster management areas, setting out the quantity which may be taken, the times which the taking is permissible and other reasonable restrictions imposed to aid the Secretary in the Secretary's duty of regulating such transplanting operations. Persons taking such seed oysters may, in the discretion of the Marine Fisheries Commission, be required to pay to the Department for oysters taken an amount to reimburse the Department in full or in part for the costs of seed oyster management operations. Any transplanting operation which does not substantially comply with the restrictions of the permit issued is unlawful.

(e)   The Marine Fisheries Commission may implement the provisions of this section by rules governing sale, possession, transportation, storage, handling, planting, and harvesting of oysters and clams and setting out any system of marking oysters and clams or of permits or receipts relating to them generally, from both public and private beds, as necessary to regulate the lawful transplanting of seed oysters and oysters or clams taken from or placed on public or private beds.

(f)   The Commission may establish a fee for each permit established pursuant to this subsection in an amount that compensates the Division for the administrative costs associated with the permit but that does not exceed one hundred dollars ($100.00) per permit.

(g)   Advance Sale of Permits; Permit Revenue. - To ensure an orderly transition from one permit year to the next, the Division may issue a permit prior to July 1 of the permit year for which the permit is valid. Revenue that the Division receives for the issuance of a permit prior to the beginning of a permit year shall not revert at the end of the fiscal year in which the revenue is received and shall be credited and available to the Division for the permit year in which the permit is valid. (1921, c. 132, s. 2; C.S., s. 1959(b); 1961, c. 1189, s. 1; 1965, c. 957, s. 2; 1967, c. 878; 1973, c. 1262, s. 28; 1977, c. 771, s. 4; 1987,

c. 641, s. 6; c. 827, s. 98; 1989, c. 727, s. 100; 1997-400, s. 5.7; 2007-495, s. 3; 2009-433, s. 6; 2013-360, s. 14.8(s).)

§ 113-204. Propagation of shellfish.

The Department is authorized to close areas of public bottoms under coastal fishing waters for such time as may be necessary in any program of propagation of shellfish. The Department is authorized to expend State funds planting such areas and to manage them in ways beneficial to the overall productivity of the shellfish industry in North Carolina. The Department in its discretion in accordance with desirable conservation objectives may make shellfish produced by it available to commercial fishermen generally, to those in possession of private shellfish beds, or to selected individuals cooperating with the Department in demonstration projects concerned with the cultivation, harvesting, or processing of shellfish. (1921, c. 132, s. 1; C.S., s. 1959(a); 1961, c. 1189, s. 1; 1965, c. 957, s. 2; 1973, c. 1262, s. 28; 1977, c. 771, s. 4; 1989, c. 727, s. 101.)

§ 113-205. Registration of grants in navigable waters; exercise of private fishery rights.

(a) Every person claiming to any part of the bed lying under navigable waters of any coastal county of North Carolina or any right of fishery in navigable waters of any coastal county superior to that of the general public must register the grant, charter, or other authorization under which he claims with the Secretary. Such registration must be accompanied by a survey of the claimed area, meeting criteria established by the Secretary for surveys of oyster and clam leases. All rights and titles not registered in accordance with this section on or before January 1, 1970, are hereby declared null and void. The Secretary must give notice of this section at least once each calendar year for three years by publication in a newspaper or newspapers of general circulation throughout all coastal counties of the State. For the purpose of this subsection, "coastal county" shall mean all the following counties: Beaufort, Bertie, Bladen, Brunswick, Camden, Carteret, Chowan, Columbus, Craven, Currituck, Dare, Gates, Halifax, Hertford, Hyde, Martin, New Hanover, Northampton, Onslow, Pamlico, Pasquotank, Pender, Perquimans, Tyrrell, and Washington. The provisions of this section shall not apply to the land lying under any private fish pond or irrigation pond.

(b) The Marine Fisheries Commission may make reasonable rules governing utilization of private fisheries and may require grantees or others with private rights to mark their fishery areas or private beds in navigable waters as a precondition to the right of excluding the public from exercising the private rights claimed to be secured to them. Nothing in this section is to be deemed to confer upon any grantee or other person with private rights the power to impede navigation upon or hinder any other appropriate use of the surface of navigable waters of North Carolina. (1965, c. 957, s. 2; 1971, c. 346, s. 1; 1973, c. 1262, s. 28; 1987, c. 827, s. 98.)

§ 113-206. Chart of grants, leases and fishery rights; overlapping leases and rights; contest or condemnation of claims; damages for taking of property.

(a) The Secretary must commence to prepare as expeditiously as possible charts of the waters of North Carolina containing the locations of all oyster and clam leaseholds made by the Department under the provisions of this Article and of all existing leaseholds as they are renewed under the provisions of this Article, the locations of all claims of grant of title to portions of the bed under navigable waters registered with him, and the locations of all areas in navigable waters to which a right of private fishery is claimed and registered with him. Charting or registering any claim by the Secretary in no way implies recognition by the State of the validity of the claim.

(a1) If a claim is based on an oyster or other shellfish grantor a perpetual franchise for shellfish cultivation, the Secretary may, to resolve the claim, grant a shellfish lease to the claimant for part or all of the area claimed. If a claim of exclusive shellfishing rights was registered based upon a conveyance by the Literary Fund, the North Carolina Literary Board or the State Board of Education, and the claimant shows that the area had been cultivated by the claimant or his predecessor in title for the seven-year period prior to registration of the claim, the Secretary may, to resolve the claim, grant a shellfish lease to the claimant for all or part of the area claimed, not to exceed ten acres. A shellfish lease granted under this subsection is subject to the restrictions imposed on shellfish leases in G.S. 113-202, except the prohibition against leasing an area that contains a natural shellfish bed in G.S. 113-202(a)(2). This restriction is waived because, due to the cultivation efforts of the claimant, the area is likely to contain a natural shellfish bed.

(b) In the event of any overlapping of areas leased by the Department, the Secretary shall recommend modification of the areas leased as he deems equitable to all parties. Appeal from the recommendation of the Secretary lies for either party in the same manner as for a lease applicant as to which there is a recommendation of denial or modification of lease. If there is no appeal, or upon settlement of the issue upon appeal, the modified leases must be approved by the Marine Fisheries Commission and reissued by the Secretary in the same manner as initial or renewal leases. Leaseholders must furnish the Secretary surveys of the modified leasehold areas, meeting the requisite criteria for surveys established by the Secretary.

(c) In the event of any overlapping of areas leased by the Department and of areas in which title or conflicting private right of fishery is claimed and registered under the provisions of this Article, the Secretary must give preference to the leaseholder engaged in the production of oysters or clams in commercial quantities who received the lease with no notice of the existence of any claimed grant or right of fishery. To this end, the Secretary shall cause a modification of the claim registered with him and its accompanying survey to exclude the leasehold area. Such modification effected by the Secretary has the effect of voiding the grant of title or right of fishing to the extent indicated.

(d) In the interest of conservation of the marine and estuarine resources of North Carolina, the Department may institute an action in the superior court to contest the claim of title or claimed right of fishery in any navigable waters of North Carolina registered with the Secretary. In such proceeding, the burden of showing title or right of fishery, by the preponderance of the evidence, shall be upon the claiming title or right holder. In the event the claiming title or right holder prevails, the trier of fact shall fix the monetary worth of the claim. The Department may elect to condemn the claim upon payment of the established owners or right holders their pro rata shares of the amount so fixed. The Department may make such payments from such funds as may be available to it. An appeal lies to the appellate division by either party both as to the validity of the claim and as to the fairness of the amount fixed. The Department in such actions may be represented by the Attorney General. In determining the availability of funds to the Department to underwrite the costs of litigation or make condemnation payments, the use which the Department proposes to make of the area in question may be considered; such payments are to be deemed necessary expenses in the course of operations attending such use or of developing or attempting to develop the area in the proposed manner.

(e) A person who claims that the application of G.S. 113-205 or this section has deprived him of his private property rights in land under navigable waters or his right of fishery in navigable waters without just compensation may file a complaint in the superior court of the county in which the property is located to contest the application of G.S. 113-205 or this section. If the plaintiff prevails, the trier of fact shall fix the monetary worth of the claim, and the Department may condemn the claim upon payment of this amount to him if the Secretary considers condemnation appropriate and necessary to conserve the marine and estuarine resources of the State. The Department may pay for a condemned claim from available funds. An action under this subsection is considered a condemnation action and is therefore subject to G.S. 7A-248.

The limitation period for an action brought under this subsection is three years. This period is tolled during the disability of the plaintiff. No action, however, may be instituted under this subsection after December 31, 2006.

(f) In evaluating claims registered pursuant to G.S. 113-205, the Secretary shall favor public ownership of submerged lands and public trust rights. The Secretary's action does not alter or affect in any way the rights of a claimant or the State. (1965, c. 957, s. 2; 1969, c. 44, s. 69; c. 541, s. 11; 1973, c. 1262, s. 28; 1977, c. 771, s. 4; 1985, c. 279; c. 762; 1989, c. 423, s. 3; c. 727, s. 102; 1989 (Reg. Sess., 1990), c. 869, ss. 1, 2; 1993 (Reg. Sess., 1994), c. 717, ss. 1-3; 1998-179, s. 1; 2006-79, s. 11.)

§ 113-207. Taking shellfish from certain areas forbidden; penalty.

(a), (b) Repealed by Session Laws 2009-433, s. 7, effective August 7, 2009.

(c) It is unlawful for any person to take shellfish within 150 feet of any part of a publicly owned pier beneath which the Division of Marine Fisheries has deposited cultch material.

(d) A person who violates this section is guilty of a Class 3 misdemeanor. (1977, c. 515, s. 1; c. 771, s. 4; 1989, c. 727, s. 103; 1993, c. 539, s. 841; 1994, Ex. Sess., c. 24, s. 14(c); 1999-143, s. 1; 2009-433, s. 7.)

Vision Books Order Form

Fax Orders:	1-980-299-5965
Phone Orders:	1-704-898-0770
E-mail Orders:	www.visionbooks.org
Mail Orders:	Vision Books, LLC P.O. Box 42406 Charlotte, NC 28215

Shipp To:
Name_____
Address_____
City_____State_____Zip_____
Phone_____Fax_____
Email_____@_____

Bill To: We can bill a third party on your behalf.
Name_____
Address_____
City_____State_____Zip_____
Phone___(_____)_____Fax_____
Email_____@_____

Pamphlet Number ($15.00 Each)	Qty	Total Cost
_____	_____	_____
_____	_____	_____
_____	_____	_____
_____	_____	_____
_____	_____	_____
_____	_____	_____
_____	_____	_____
Full Volume Set 1-92	92 Pamphlets	1,380.00

Free Shipping Shipping & Handling on Full Volume Orders
Add $1.00 Shipping & Handling per pamphlet $_____

Total Cost $_____

Thank you for you support. Management!

DID YOU ENJOY THIS BOOK?

Vision Books, LLC would like to hear from you! If you or someone you know has been fasely imprisoned, we would like to hear your story. If the 'North Carolina Criminal Law and Procedure' has had an effect in your life or if you have suggestions, we would like to hear from you. Send your letters to:

Vision Books, LLC
Attn: Staff Writers
P.O. Box 42406
Charlotte, NC 28215
Email: staff@visionbooks.org

Order Additional Copies:

Fax Orders:	1-980-299-5965
Phone Orders:	1-704-898-0770
E-mail Orders:	www.visionbooks.org
Mail Orders:	Vision Books, LLC P.O. Box 42406 Charlotte, NC 28215